HOME
MADE EASY
DECORATING

HOME
MADE EASY
DECORATING

MEREHURST

EDITORIAL
Managing Editor: Judy Poulos
Craft Editor: Tonia Todman
Editorial Assistant: Ella Martin,
Allen Robinson
Editorial Coordinator: Margaret Kelly,
Rachel Blackmore
Consultant Editor: Dieter Mylius,
Susan Tomnay, How-To Publications (UK)

PHOTOGRAPHY
Andrew Elton, Harm Mol, David Young,
Vantuan, Murray Cummings, Andrew Payne

ILLUSTRATIONS
Lesley Griffith, Margie Mulray, Greg Gaul,
Carol Dunn, Rod Westblade

DESIGN AND PRODUCTION
Manager: Sheridan Carter, Anna Maguire
Design: Jenny Pace
Layout: Lulu Dougherty, Margie Mulray,
Tara Barrett, Julia Becker, Gavin Murrell

Published 1994 by Merehurst Limited
Ferry House, 51/57 Lacy Road
Putney, London, SW 15 1PR
By arrangement with
J.B. Fairfax Press Pty Limited
80-82 McLachlan Ave
Rushcutters Bay, NSW 2011
Australia

The contents of this book have been previously
published in other J.B. Fairfax Press
publications.

Formatted by J.B. Fairfax Press Pty Limited
Printed by Toppan Printing Co, Singapore

HOME DECORATING MADE EASY
Includes Index
ISBN 1 86343 172 1

A catalogue record for this book is available
from the British Library.

JBFP 339UK

INTRODUCTION

Regard your home as an artist would a canvas. If you are very lucky and can afford the cost, you may have a blank canvas on which you can paint the picture you have dreamed about.

Most of us are not quite so lucky. Our canvas already has certain outlines and colours marked on it which limit what else we can add. Make these limitations work for you: they can provide a framework and a stimulus for your creativity, while still preventing you from going overboard with your plans.

It is very important to assess your own situation carefully, before you make a start on any work. If you are renting your home, limit expenditure on permanent fixtures and concentrate on those things which you can take with you when you move, such as rugs, lamps, pictures, cushions and so on. It can be heartbreaking to leave behind expensive curtains made to fit an oddly shaped window, when simple rod pocket curtains, without expensive tracks, could happily grace a similar-sized window in a new flat.

If you own the home you are decorating (even if it is in partnership with the bank!), your problems will be different. There may be so much that you want or need to do that you hardly know where to begin. This is the time to make a plan and a list of priorities. In this book, you will find dozens of decorative options. Look them over carefully to give you an idea of where you might begin.

Finally, do not slavishly follow current fashion, but try to establish an atmosphere that you are comfortable with and which works for you and your family. If all the glossy magazines dictate white carpet and a white leather-covered settee, but you have small children and a large dog, clearly this is not the look for you. You might be happier with polished boards and some serviceable loose covers which can be easily cleaned.

CONTENTS

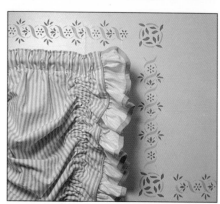

PAGE 68
WHAT'S AFOOT
All about floors and floor coverings, including laying a vinyl floor, stencilling a floor cloth and applying various finishes to floorboards.

PAGE 80
SEATING ARRANGEMENTS
All about furniture and furniture covers, including making slipcovers for a dining chair or a director's chair and making a versatile sofa bed from foam blocks.

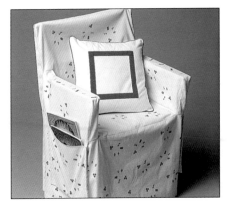

PAGE 94
TABLE TOPS
Clever ways to dress up your home with table linen, using a variety of techniques, such as embroidery, stencilling and appliqué.

PAGE 112
COUNTRY CHARM
How to create a country look with traditional crafts, such as découpage, stencilling, patchwork and folk art; a step-by-step guide to painting a folk art stool.

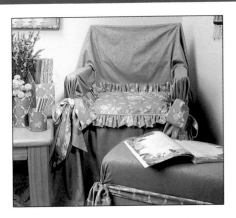

The First Steps

*B*righten a dull room in a flash
with new curtains or practical,
sophisticated fabric blinds. Decide
which look best suits your window,
the rest of your decor and lifestyle.
If you like the softness of gathered
and ruffled material, then curtains are
more your style. If you prefer the clean
lines and monochromatic feel
of the city apartment, then Roman
blinds are just right for you.

Starting Out

*The secret of successful home decorating is to combine careful planning and a sensible budget with your own creative flair and energy. If you research the project thoroughly, you'll wind up having a lot of fun, learn new skills, save money **and** increase the value of your home. On top of all that, there's the satisfaction of knowing you did it yourself!*

What are your needs?

❑ Is this your first nest? Does it look a bit tired and in need of some tender loving care?

❑ Have you lived there for many years? Do you feel it's time for a change now that the children are nearly off your hands and you can indulge your own tastes at long last?

❑ Are you renting an apartment, and limited in the amount of redecoration you can attempt, but want to update with new curtains and bright accessories?

A business couple who spend little time in their tiny city apartment have different needs to young parents with two children and a dog. Students need more bookshelves and study space than a single parent with a couple of active toddlers in tow.

Have a good look at what you can live with for a little bit longer and what just has to go right now. Fake it, if you can, with budget-conscious decorative paint techniques for walls, floors and furniture (see pages 52, 62, 76). 'Faux' decorating is all the rage but it has to look great to avoid ending up with a tawdry result, so prepare the surfaces carefully and read the instructions.

A good scrub with sugar soap works wonders on tired walls and ceilings. It could enable you to postpone a full paint job in the bathroom, allowing you to spend a little more on new curtains or a beautifully framed print for the living room.

Make sure your planned renovations are user-friendly and will actually improve your quality of life. If you want to start a family next year, don't choose a plush upholstery fabric – it simply isn't practical.

If you are an apartment dweller or rent your home, consider the advantages of portable decorating projects, such as cushions, loose covers and accessories. Wonderful effects can be achieved with a little ingenuity – and you can take them with you when you move!

Sit down with the family and discuss everyone's needs. Write them down in a sturdy notebook – used wisely, this will become your 'bible' and you'll carry it everywhere. Add a pen, a good tape measure and a colour card and you are ready to begin exploring the possibilities. A camera for taking pictures from different angles in the home may prove useful.

Laura Ashley (Australia) Pty Limited

Laura Ashley (Australia) Pty Limited

Saving money makes sense. Always ask if you can get a price reduction for cash and shop around for the best price and service. Comparison shopping may take a little time but can save you lots of money. How can you be sure you've really discovered a bargain if you don't know the usual price? Take advantage of genuine sales, always buy the best product and most comprehensive service you can afford and do it right! A good carpet laid over a quality underlay is a better buy than a 'bargain' that doesn't wear well. You may have to wait a little longer for something special or do the work in stages, but it's worth the trouble to get what you really want. In the meantime, we can show you how to make beautiful alternatives that won't break the bank.

Left and below: Remember, always decorate to suit your lifestyle and your budget

What can you afford?

Working to a budget is vital. Obviously you will have certain financial commitments that must take priority over new curtains or a pot of paint, whether you're paying rent or paying off a mortgage. Decide how much cash you can spare now and, say, over the next year...or will you need to borrow money – and from whom? How does borrowing fit into your long term plans for holidays, new clothes, the children's education? Even if your decorating project won't cost much, decide how much you can afford and then stick to your budget! Interest on borrowings can be a trap. That new chair you buy in the sale won't be a bargain if you buy it on credit and pay interest.

Nairn Floors

Make your plans

Having a plan is essential to the success of any home decorating exercise, no matter how big or small. A plan will help you to save money, avoiding those impulse buys (that you regret the next day), and feel satisfied with the end results. After all, you'll have to live with them – perhaps for a long time.

This is when you really need your 'bible'.

❑ Measure everything – walls to estimate paint quantities, wallpaper and friezes; windows for tracks, rods and curtain fabric; floors for carpets and tiles; doors for new handles; furniture and cupboards…the lot!

❑ Take photographs of rooms and features you want to change.

❑ Making a floor plan is essential and it's easy if you use graph paper to scale down room sizes. Don't forget to include windows and doors, steps, built-in cupboards, electrical and plumbing fittings room by room. Now you can cut out paper models of all your existing furniture to move around the paper plan, instead of dragging heavy furniture around the room.

Store the measurements, photographs and room plan in envelopes pasted inside the cover of your 'bible' so that you'll have them with you all the time. If you know the floor size of all your rooms, you'll be able to snap up a bargain when you see a carpet or tile sale.

Calling in a professional

Paying a professional tradesman is unavoidable in some cases. Local regulations may demand that electrical, plumbing or building work is carried out by

accredited tradespeople who have the training, the tools and the authority to tackle some jobs which amateurs should never attempt. Check with your local authority. You may need to consult an expert about the soundness of walls and floors before you start redecorating.

Get it in writing

This is the golden rule whenever you commission work. A written quote should include all costs and details of all materials to be used (quality and quantity); it should stipulate a completion date and must be written in clear language. Don't accept the quote unless you can understand it and

accept everything in it. Ask for proof of the contractor's licence, or other accreditation. Satisfy yourself that you are adequately protected by his or her insurance, covering damage to your property and injury to anyone employed by the contractor to do your job.

Do you need an interior designer?

Paying for advice from an interior designer is a sound investment if you can afford it. It costs nothing to ask for an 'advisory price' and scale of fees. Don't be embarrassed to say you have a budget – reputable designers will be delighted to find a client who

Left: Natural timbers
are the perfect
choice for your
kitchen. Properly
prepared and
sealed, they are
easy to care for and
pleasant to live with
for many years
Below right: Putting
together a new
decorating scheme
can be a great
challenge and lots of
fun! For a bright
contemporary look,
use lots of high tech,
shiny chrome and
strong colours

knows how much he or she
wants to spend. If you're not sure
how to find a designer, refer to
the local telephone directory.
There may be a national association, such as The Interior Decorators' and Designers' Association,
who will supply a list of their
members. Or try chatting to staff
at your favourite soft furnishing
supplier. Some department stores
offer a 'free' decorating service to
their customers. There is no
charge if you subsequently place
an order, otherwise a nominal fee
applies. Ask for details before
committing yourself to avoid
misunderstandings and
unexpected costs.

Plan your schedule

Good timing can help things run
smoothly and can ease the financial burden of the work. Will
redecorating disrupt your household, and how long will your
routine be affected? An asthmatic
child may need to spend a couple of days with friends while old

carpet is ripped up. Before you
commission tradespeople to work
for you, coordinate the job to be
done – each stage has to be
completed in the right sequence
or you may face a lot of extra
costs and many frustrating delays.

It's very important to allow
sufficient time to do a good job –
don't try to rush it. If you can't
quite afford the exact curtains
you want, maybe you could
manage with lining fabric for a
while? Thorough research and
the right tools won't guarantee
satisfactory results but a comprehensive schedule which gives
you plenty of time for preparation, application and finishing
will help a great deal. If you
think the job is too big to tackle
on your own, throw a 'working
party'. You supply the materials
and all the food and drinks (and
the work!) and ask family and
friends to come over and lend a
hand in return for a few laughs
and supper.

Learning can be fun, whether
you're acquiring new skills or

brushing up old ones. We'll help
you with tips on choosing fabric
and displaying your accessories;
we'll show you clever ways with
paint and paper but you can also
take classes in colour, lighting,
painting techniques, tile-laying.
You name it, somebody's teach-
ing it! Adult education groups,
technical schools, manufacturers,
department stores and building
information centres are all
valuable sources of free or
moderately priced tuition. Avoid
expensive correspondence
courses – you really need the
hands-on experience. Take a
course in household repairs and
restoration, a sound investment
which will teach you how to save
money by doing your own
repairs. Remember, knowing the

'nuts and bolts' of a job helps you tell the difference between a fair quote and a rip-off.

It's important to be able to recognise a bargain when you see one. But look carefully – will that old dresser respond to restorative techniques or would you be wasting your money buying a piece of junk?

Decorating with colour

Choosing the right colour is as important when decorating your house as it is when choosing your clothes – you live in both of them! Colour is affected by lighting (particularly artificial lights) and where you use it. You can make rooms seem bigger, smaller, taller, wider or even

create a special mood with the right colours.

Whenever you select furnishings or paint, take a sample home so that you can judge the colour in the place and lighting conditions you have planned for it. Give yourself two or three options to choose from in case your first choice isn't available.

Collecting samples

Collecting samples will become a passion once you start planning. Fabric swatches, scraps of wallpaper and friezes, paint cards, colour wheels and lighting brochures will burst from your 'bible'. Your diary will be filled with appointments to view carpets, curtains, blinds and furnishings at home (check that this service is obligation-free). Seeing them at home is the most efficient way to choose colours and textures for large areas – and cuts your time and fuel costs, too!

Trial and error

Before starting a big project, try out your ideas on a small scale. Buy sample-sized pots of paint and try them on the wall, remembering that colours can change. For instance, pastels paint up three or four times more intensely than they appear on a colour card.

All laminated surfaces can be painted – the trick is to find the right 'key' or surface preparation to accept the paint. Treat a small, unobtrusive section first to test your 'key' before embarking on the entire job.

Don't be deterred by little disappointments and mistakes. They're all learning experiences that can help you avoid costly problems when you tackle the

real thing. Keep a record of tests and results, successes and failures in your 'bible' for future reference. Note what went wrong and if you were able to correct it – a photograph might help, too. Living with your new look is the best part. Looking at a beautiful finish and knowing you did it yourself is a very satisfying experience.

Now you have an endless source of suggestions for fellow do-it-yourself fans and, if you were clever enough to take 'before' and 'after' photos for your 'bible', you will have the best brag book in town!

So off you go – just remember the basic principles of good planning, sensible budgeting and learning from your mistakes. When you've finished the first project, start another one. We have lots of suggestions for you and practical, easy to follow instructions. Good luck!

Clever Ways to Recycle

FEATURE

Old or antique furniture was usually made from quality timber and had a craftsman-like finish. Furniture makers of yesteryear had time to create well-designed pieces that were both functional and very stylish. These qualities alone make furniture recycling worthwhile.

Modern lifestyles and changing needs also demand a practical and often ingenious approach to home furnishing, especially where storage is concerned. When you are on a shoestring budget and have minimal or odd spaces to play with, you need to carefully assess how and where a piece of furniture will fit in. So find yourself some wonderful, old or down-at-heel treasure and start by analysing its potential.

Does it have 'good bones'? Look beyond the shabby outward appearance of an object for fresh new refurbishing ideas – for example, the basic bookcase. It may be covered with peeling paint, look uninteresting and, as it stands, certainly wouldn't fit in with a fresh, bright furnishing look. However, once it has been repaired, stripped and perhaps stained or repainted, there are many decorative and practical ways of using it.

You could fix it to a wall above floor level and make a set of feature shelves; use it as a bedhead or a room divider; fit it into or in front of a no-longer-used doorway to display a treasured collection; place it in the garage for extra tool storage; cut it into two lower units and seal it with paint to make an accessible pot-plant stand; or stand it in a hanging-only cupboard as storage for folded clothes and shoes. Your once-shabby bookcase can be transformed in even more subtle ways by covering it completely with wallpaper or fabric to blend in with the rest of your decor. The list goes on – and this was only a humble bookcase!

Once you enter into the spirit of searching for unwanted treasures, you will begin to see possibilities in just about any piece of furniture. But beware, it's important to recognise the strengths and weaknesses of your 'find'.

Thinking about buying and refurbishing an old cupboard? There are many real advantages in doing-up an old cupboard: good-quality timber and workmanship, spacious deep drawers and generous hanging capacity, for example. There are, alas, some potential drawbacks:

❑ Is the timber used heavily lacquered? This may be a real problem to strip and restain; in this case you may be forced to paint over the lacquer.

❑ Is it solid and free of insect attack? Look for tell-tale small holes and piles of sawdust. Professional fumigation may be required, or treatment with woodworm fluid and polish to restore the surface.

❑ Does it have door hinges and locks? These can be replaced but often not cheaply. Quality brass fittings can be expensive at retail outlets, so shop around. Brass

Left and below: A set of stacked cane suitcases are a great recycling idea. Paint them inside and out with gloss spray paint in a bright colour.

To dress up your suitcases, simply line the inside of the lid and the suitcase with polyester wadding, gluing the edges to secure. Cover the wadding with a pretty print fabric, gluing it in place.

A rummage in the garden shed revealed this well-shaped old tin trunk. It was not rusty and only needed to have the old paint removed to prepare it for its new life. It was painted with undercoat and paint suitable for metal and the design was added using a commercial stencil and spray paints. Take care to screen the area with cardboard to prevent excess paint escaping and drifting where it is not needed.

restoration experts often have oddments available, and are well worth visiting.

❑ Do the drawers run smoothly? You may need to replace the drawer runners or use sandpaper to smooth off damp-swollen timber.

❑ Can you get the cupboard through the door when moving it to its new address? If the tape measure says this is not to be, is it possible to unscrew parts of the cupboard and reassemble it once moved?

Visit auctions, fairs, church bazaars and garage sales. Check the newspaper often for auctions of office furniture (you'll be surprised by the variety and the bargains!). Two second-hand identical filing cabinets, perhaps repainted then set apart by about

1.50 m with a wide softwood table top resting across the tops, makes a fine desk. If no old table top is available, consider buying a new one from contemporary knockdown furniture suppliers.

Remember that opportunities often present themselves in obscure and unpredictable ways. To help you with your treasure hunt, consider how different pieces of furniture can be adapted:

❑ Tables can have legs shortened to become casual occasional tables. They are perfect for stencilling or covering with fabric, and are a natural for a simple paint-over.

❑ Strongly woven baskets provide all sorts of storage possibilities: paint them, line them with fabric, stack lidded baskets, or

use them in rows on open shelves for kitchen storage. Flat baskets with rims can become excellent trays. Old cane laundry baskets make ideal toy storage and can easily become a decorative feature when cleverly coloured. A deep, strongly woven basket with handles can be both stylish and practical when filled with wood ready for an open fire. Leave it outside under shelter for wood storage all year round, and carry it in when the weather sends smoke signals.

❑ Old luggage can provide decorative storage. Paint tin trunks, restain old leather luggage or refurbish a truly authentic hatbox.

❑ Boxes of all sorts and sizes can become amusing and talked-about storage containers (or articles). Old wooden ammunition boxes, biscuit tins, sturdy paper cartons and slatted pine fruit boxes can be painted or découpaged, and even shoe boxes made from very firm cardboard can be covered with fabric to become practical and attractive storage containers.

❑ Picture frames can be used as noticeboard surrounds.

❑ Small wooden safety ladders, providing they have a flat top, can become ideal bedside tables. Single-sided old ladders with frame and rungs of dowel can become discussion pieces when used as towel racks in a kitchen – lean them against a wall and you instantly have storage for as many towels as you could need.

❑ Storage is an essential element in any household, but don't be bogged down by the expected or expensive solutions. The whimsical, achievable, recycled, amusing and unexpected alternatives are just waiting to be discovered.

Light
and
Shade

*T*hese curtains and blinds are
so simple and so effective. There's no
sacrificing any of their charm. Now
tie your room's colour-scheme together
and cover your lampshades with
related fabrics. So easy, clever you.

The dramatic impact of this decorative screen is a clever balance for the matching circular tablecloth and over-cloth. (See instructions for making circular cloths on page 102)

Down to DETAIL

Decorative Screens

A screen can be a practical, inexpensive room divider or simply a focal point. As everyone's needs are different, the instructions are given as a general method. Choose your own trimmings to suit your taste and your room.

Before You Begin

❏ Join several purchased louvre doors with hinges to create a screen like ours. They may be left natural, painted to give a contemporary look, or carved, sponged and stencilled.

❏ To add fabric panels, you will need sufficient fabric to cover the length of the doors with a front and back panel and a fabric strip 80 cm x 22 cm for a bow for each door. Fabric panels are attached with a glue gun.

❏ To determine the size of your screen, decide where it will be located and how tall it should be to be useful.

❏ If door tops are to be shaped, design the shape on paper and transfer it to the door. You will need a fretsaw or a jigsaw to cut out the shape and sandpaper for smoothing rough edges.

MATERIALS
☐ louvre doors
☐ hinges
☐ screws
☐ screwdriver
☐ jigsaw or fretsaw
☐ sandpaper
☐ your choice of paint; stencils; stencil paints and brushes; sponge
☐ fabrics as desired
☐ glue gun

METHOD

1 Join doors together with hinges following manufacturer's instructions.

The taller the doors, the more support (and therefore hinges) they require.

2 To insert fabric panels, cut away top and bottom louvres from each door with a sharp chisel. If necessary, fill any holes with a suitable wood filler.

3 To paint and sponge a screen for a light, speckled effect, first paint with a base of acrylic paint and allow to dry. Using a slightly lighter colour and a natural sponge, dab paint-covered sponge over base coat of paint. Remove excess paint from sponge, by dabbing on to scrap fabric. When dry, stencil as desired, following Down To Detail instructions on page 114, or decorate screen with découpage as instructed on pages 136 and 145.

4 To cover screen with fabric panels: Measure width and length of louvres.

5 Cut a piece of fabric twice length plus 35 cm long by twice width. Press under 1 cm along long sides then again 2 cm. Stitch along inner folded edge. Fold fabric in half lengthways, wrong sides facing. Gather 2.5 cm down from fold, stitching through all thicknesses. Draw up gathers to width of louvres. Secure gathering threads. You now have a front and back panel.

6 Draw fabric through space left by bottom louvre until gathered area sits just under next louvre. Pull panels up over front and back of door and mark position of top louvre on front and back panel. Remove fabric panel from door. Fold excess fabric to wrong side 2.5 cm from mark on front and back panel. Gather across front and back at this mark, through all thicknesses securing folded fabric. Cut away excess fabric from 2 cm below gathering. Draw up gathers as for lower ruffle.

7 Replace fabric on door. Join front and back panels together at gathering line using glue gun or handsewing, attaching fabric to top louvre at the same time.

8 To make bows: Fold a 22 cm x 80 cm strip of fabric with right sides facing. Cut ends at an angle. Stitch around raw edges in 1 cm seam, leaving opening for turning. Turn and press. Tie bow. Glue or sew to top of screen, in centre of gathers.

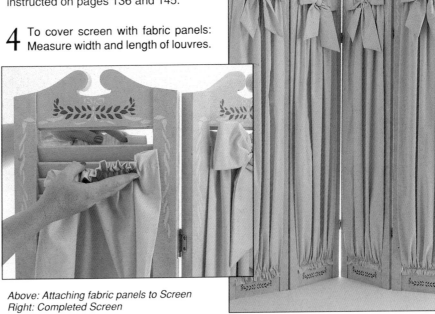

Above: Attaching fabric panels to Screen
Right: Completed Screen

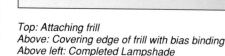

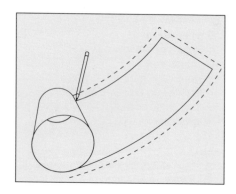

Top: Attaching frill
Above: Covering edge of frill with bias binding
Above left: Completed Lampshade

Lampshade

Brighten your home with this simple recycling idea. Give your old lampshade a new look with some of these clever suggestions for easy trims. It's more than likely that the shape of the lampshade suits the base, so measure the existing frame to work out quantities of fabric needed.

MATERIALS

- ☐ metal lampshade frame, stripped bare
- ☐ approximately 1 m of 115 cm wide fabric for cover
- ☐ approximately 1 m of 115 cm wide lining fabric
- ☐ fabric for bias binding and ruffles can be cut from scraps but if in doubt allow another 40 cm of fabric for ruffles
- ☐ PVA adhesive
- ☐ approximately 6 m narrow cotton tape or leftover bias binding
- ☐ strong sewing thread and handsewing needle
- ☐ approximately 2 m of plain bias binding in lining colour

METHOD

1 Wind tape or bias binding around both rings of frame until it is completely covered. Hold ends with pins until winding is complete then glue to secure.

2 Put a pin in tape at one point on shade to mark beginning and ending point. Spread lining fabric out flat and roll frame across fabric as shown. Mark position of frame as it moves across fabric leaving a 5 cm allowance on either end for seam allowances and 5 cm each at top and bottom. Repeat for main fabric. Cut out shape as marked (see diagram below right).

3 Fit lining around frame, pinning to tape for accuracy. Pin ends closed as a seam. Remove lining from frame, sew seam as pinned. Trim seam allowance back to 1 cm.

4 Place lining inside frame. Pin lining to tape with seam following line of one upright strut. Fold top and bottom edges to outside. Oversew to top and bottom rings by hand. Trim excess fabric. Repeat this process with main fabric, placing main fabric on outside and taking top and bottom edges to inside.

5 Cut sufficient 6 cm wide bias to cover top and bottom rings. Turn in 1 cm along both long sides, fold in half and glue over top and bottom rings, turning and neatly overlapping ends.

6 Cut sufficient 10 cm wide ruffle strips to measure at least one and a half or twice total circumference of top and bottom rings, depending on thickness of your fabric. Join ends of strip to form a circle. Fold strip over double with raw edges matching. Gather raw edges. Draw up gathers to fit inside bias-trimmed top and bottom rings. Glue into place. Glue bias binding over gathered edge, tucking under short ends at overlap.

Gathered Curtains

So you think sewing curtains is difficult? Not these. The method can be adapted for any size rectangular window and the simple, unlined style lends itself beautifully to all sorts of trimming – stencilling, bands of ribbon trim, appliqué or lace edges.

METHOD

See the stencil design on the Pull Out Pattern Sheet.

1 Press in 1 cm on long side edges, then again 4 cm. Stitch. Press in 1 cm at top and bottom, then again 7 cm. Stitch. Stitch again 3.5 cm from top. This row of stitching gives you room for inserting a rod, and will create a frilled effect above it.

2 Install brackets, slide curtain on to pole, adjusting gathers to fit.

3 To make tie: Fold strip in half length-ways with right sides facing and edges even. Stitch around edges, leaving opening. Turn and press. Mark hook position. Install hook and fashion tie-back into bow.

Pelmet

MATERIALS
☐ fabric strip twice length of curtain track x desired depth; frill fabric twice length of fabric strip x 10 cm deep
☐ piping length of fabric strip
☐ pinch pleating tape

METHOD

1 Hem short ends of pelmet and frill strips. Hem one long edge of frill and gather the other edge.

2 Stitch piping along raw edge of pelmet strip with right sides facing and raw edges even. Place frill over piping with right sides facing and raw edges matching. Stitch in previous stitchline.

3 Turn under 2 cm at pelmet top. Apply pleating tape following manufacturer's instructions. Draw up to fit.

Before You Begin

☐ See how to measure your window and estimate fabric quantities on the Pull Out Pattern Sheet. Trim quantities will depend on the size of your curtain. Add stencil and trims after sewing the curtain but before hanging.

☐ Decide whether to have two curtains opening in the middle, pulled to each side, or a single curtain. If you choose two curtains, halve the width and add an extra 5 cm to each for the centre hem allowances. Instructions are for one curtain. Make two using the same method.

☐ Curtain tie-backs are secured by brass hooks which come in many designs.

MATERIALS
☐ main curtain fabric
☐ 2 cm diameter dowel or metal curtain rod to suit your window width
☐ two support brackets and screws
☐ curtain tie-back hooks

Austrian Blinds

These blinds are the easiest of all to make, because accurate measurements are not so important. The impact depends a great deal on the fabric and its setting. Even the simplest fabrics such as voile or calico can look very stylish made up this way.

Before You Begin

❑ Austrian blinds need plenty of fullness for a luxurious look.

❑ There are usually two main types of blind tape available. Both have the rings, through which you thread the draw cords, already sewn on. One type of tape has small cords on either side which draw up to gather the blind. The other type has no gathering cords. Decide whether you want a gathered or flat effect up the corded lines. Look at our photographs to help you decide. Whichever design you choose, the tape and cord quantities are the same.

❑ Placing blind tapes close together, say 30 cm apart, will result in small scallops. Place them further apart for swag-like scallops. On average you will require at least three tapes, each one as long as your blind.

Fabric Blind

MATERIALS

❑ fabric piece twice width x twice length of window. If fabric needs to be joined to achieve width, use small flat seams
❑ tapes
❑ cord for each tape plus the width of blind (see illustration on page 27)
❑ if trimming edge with fabric ruffle, cut strips four times length plus twice width of blind x 22 cm
❑ brass cleat for fastening cords
❑ knob to cover knotted ends of cords
❑ small eye-hooks – one for each tape, plus one

METHOD

Neaten any exposed raw edges. Use 1 cm seams.

1 Cut out fabric to required size and join pieces if necessary.

2 Mark tape positions. Fold fabric along these lines and press for guidelines.

3 Join ruffle strips to make required length. Fold over 1 cm at short ends, stitch. Fold ruffle strip over double, matching long raw edges and with wrong side facing. Gather raw edge. Draw up gathers and sew ruffle to side and lower edges of blind, with right sides facing and raw edges matching. Start and finish ruffle 8 cm from top edge.

4 Fold in 1 cm on both side edges of blind above ruffle and stitch. Fold in 1 cm on upper edge, press, then fold another 7 cm. Stitch. Stitch again 3 cm from previous stitching.

5 Stitch tape along guidelines, starting just above ruffles and finishing just below top casing. Make sure you have a cord ring just above ruffle on each tape.

6 Fit blind on curtain pole, bunching it up to fit. Space tapes evenly.

7 Screw eye hooks into window frame just below pole position at top of tapes and another just below one rod bracket on the side through which you will thread blind cords.

8 If using tape which draws up, draw up gathering threads on tape and secure when blind is gathered as desired. Thread draw cords through rings on each tape, starting by securing cord in bottom ring and threading it as illustrated. Thread cords through extra hook in window frame.

9 Screw cleat into window frame at a convenient height. Pass cord ends through covering knob, knot together, trim ends. Pull knob down to cover knot. Wind cord around cleat to fix height of blind.

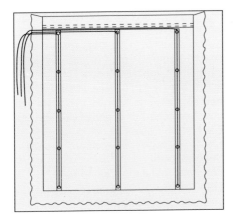

Lace Blind

The lace fabric we used has scalloped edges and as it was not wide enough for the window, two lengths were joined.

MATERIALS
☐ four times length of window in scalloped edge lace
☐ all other requirements are as for Fabric Blind

METHOD

1 Cut both scalloped edges off centre panel and set aside to be used later. Cut another length down the middle and join each half either side of centre panel. The scallops on the outside edges become the frill.

2 Trim top and bottom of blind with cut-off scallops. Cut a length of scallops to width of blind. Hem short ends. Using a 1 cm seam, sew scallops to top of blind with right side of scallops facing wrong side of blind. Press scallops to right side. Stitch across 7 cm down from top, then again 3 cm from previous stitching. Gather remaining scallops along both short ends and long side. Apply whole of gathered edge to bottom of blind to give appearance of a continuation of side frill.

3 Make blind in same way as Fabric Blind on page 26. Fabric, tapes, cords, brackets, rod, eye-hooks, knob and cleat instructions are all identical.

Below left: Threading of blind cords
Below: Fabric Blind

Crochet Blind

A delicate crochet window blind not only has a practical use but adds a touch of old-world charm.

MEASUREMENTS
90 cm wide x 76.5 cm deep (adjustable)

TENSION
Size of motif = 18 cm square

MATERIALS
☐ 300 g Coats Anchor Mercer Crochet cotton no. 20 in colour of your choice. (It is advisable to purchase total number of balls required at one time.)
☐ Milward steel crochet hook 1.25 mm (no. 3). (Use a size finer hook if your crochet is loose; if tight, use a size larger hook.)
☐ 1 m x 3 mm wide ribbon
☐ nine small ribbon roses
☐ eleven curtain rings
Note: Two motifs can be worked from 30 g of thread

ABBREVIATIONS
ch = chain; ss = slip stitch; dc = double crochet; tr = treble; dbl tr = double treble; trip tr = triple treble; quad tr = quadruple treble; quin tr = quintuple treble; lp = loop; rep = repeat; sp(s) = space(s); st(s) = stitch(es)

METHOD
First motif
Commence with 12 ch, join with a ss to form a ring.
1st row: 3 ch, into ring work 1 tr (3 ch, 2 tr) 7 times, 3 ch, 1 ss into third of 3 ch.
2nd row: 1 ss into next tr and into next sp, 3 ch, into same sp work 2 tr 3 ch and 3 tr (a starting shell made), * 3 ch, 1 tr into next sp, 3 ch, into next sp work 3 tr 3 ch and 3 tr (a shell made); rep from * omitting a shell at end of last rep, 1 ss into third of 3 ch.
3rd row: 1 ss into each of next 2 tr, 3 ch, * a shell into next sp, 1 tr into next tr, (3 ch, 1 tr into next sp) twice, 3 ch, miss 2 tr, 1 tr into next tr; rep from * omitting 1 tr at end of last rep, 1 ss into third of 3 ch.
4th row: 1 ss into each of next 2 tr, 3 ch, * 1 tr into next tr, a shell into next sp, 1 tr into each of next 2 tr, (3 ch, 1 tr into next sp) 3 times, 3 ch, miss 2 tr, 1 tr into next tr; rep from * omitting 1 tr at end of last rep, 1 ss into third of 3 ch.

5th row: 1 ss into each of next 2 tr, 3 ch, * 1 tr into each of next 2 tr, a shell into next sp, 1 tr into each of next 3 tr, (3 ch, 1 tr into next sp) 4 times, 3 ch, miss 2 tr, 1 tr into next tr; rep from * omitting 1 tr at end of last rep, 1 ss into third of 3 ch.
6th row: 1 ss into each of next 2 tr, 3 ch, * 1 tr into each of next 3 tr, a shell into next sp, 1 tr into each of next 4 tr, (3 ch, 1 tr into next sp) 5 times, 3 ch, miss 2 tr, 1 tr into next tr; rep from * omitting 1 tr at end of last rep, 1 ss into third of 3 ch.
7th row: 1 ss into each of next 2 tr, 3 ch, * 1 tr into each of next 4 tr, a shell into next sp, 1 tr into each of next 5 tr, (3 ch, 1 tr into next sp) 6 times, 3 ch, miss 2 tr, 1 tr into next tr; rep from * omitting 1 tr at end of last rep, 1 ss into third of 3 ch.
8th row: 1 ss into each of next 2 tr, 3 ch, * 1 tr into each of next 5 tr, a shell into next sp, 1 tr into each of next 6 tr, (3 ch, 1 tr into next sp) 7 times, 3 ch, miss 2 tr, 1 tr into next tr; rep from * omitting 1 tr at end of last rep, 1 ss into third of 3 ch.
9th row: 1 ss into each of next 2 tr, 3 ch, * 1 tr into each of next 6 tr, a shell into next sp, 1 tr into each of next 7 tr, (3 ch, 1 tr into next sp) 8 times, 3 ch, miss 2 tr, 1 tr into next tr; rep from * omitting 1 tr at end of last rep, 1 ss into third of 3 ch.
10th row: 1 ss into each of next 2 tr, 3 ch, * 1 tr into each of next 7 tr, a shell into next sp, 1 tr into each of next 8 tr (3 ch, 1 tr into next sp) 9 times, 3 ch, miss 2 tr, 1 tr into next tr; rep from * omitting 1 tr at end of last rep, 1 ss into third of 3 ch.
11th row: 1 ss into each of next 2 tr, 3 ch, * 1 tr into each of next 8 tr, a shell into next sp, 1 tr into each of next 9 tr, (3 ch, 1 tr into next sp) 4 times, 3 ch, miss 1 tr and 2 ch, 1 tr into each of next 3 sts, 3 ch, miss 2 ch and 1 tr (1 tr into next sp, 3 ch) 4 times, miss 2 tr, 1 tr into next tr; rep from * omitting 1 tr at end of last rep, 1 ss into third of 3 ch.
12th row: 1 ss into each of next 2 tr, 3 ch, * 1 tr into each of next 9 tr, a shell into next sp 1 tr into each of next 10 tr, (3 ch, 1 tr into next sp) 4 times, 3 ch, miss 1 tr and 2 ch, 1 tr into each of next 5 sts, 3 ch, miss 2 ch and 1 tr, (1 tr into next sp, 3 ch) 4 times, miss 2 tr, 1 tr into next tr; rep from * omitting 1 tr at end of last rep, 1 ss into third of 3 ch.
13th row: 1 ss into each of next 2 tr, 3 ch,

* 1 tr into each of next 10 tr, a shell into next sp 1 tr into each of next 11 tr, (3 ch, 1 tr into next sp) 4 times, 3 ch, miss 1 tr and 2 ch, 1 tr into each of next 7 sts, 3 ch, miss 2 ch and 1 tr, (1 tr into next sp, 3 ch) 4 times, miss 2 tr, 1 tr into next tr; rep from * omitting 1 tr at end of last rep, 1 ss into third of 3 ch.
14th row: 1 ss into each of next 2 tr, 3 ch, * 1 tr into each of next 11 tr, a shell into next sp, 1 tr into each of next 12 tr (3 ch, 1 tr into next sp) 4 times, 3 ch, miss 1 tr and 2 ch, 1 tr into each of next 9 sts, 3 ch, miss 2 ch and 1 tr, (1 tr into next sp, 3 ch) 4 times, miss 2 tr, 1 tr into next tr; rep from * omitting 1 tr at end of last rep, 1 ss into third of 3 ch.
15th row: 1 ss into each of next 2 tr, 3 ch, * 1 tr into each of next 12 tr, a shell into next sp, 1 tr into each of next 13 tr (3 ch, 1 tr into next sp) 4 times, 3 ch, miss 1 tr and 2 ch, 1 tr into each of next 11 sts, 3 ch, miss 2 ch and 1 tr, (1 tr into next sp, 3 ch) 4 times, miss 2 tr, 1 tr into next tr; rep from * omitting 1 tr at end of last rep, 1 ss into third of 3 ch.
16th row: 1 ss into each of next 2 tr, 3 ch, * 1 tr into each of next 13 tr, a shell into next sp, 1 tr into each of next 14 tr, (3 ch, 1 tr into next sp) 4 times, 3 ch, miss 1 tr and 2 ch, 1 tr into each of next 13 sts, 3 ch, miss 2 ch and 1 tr, (1 tr into next sp, 3 ch) 4 times, miss 2 tr, 1 tr into next tr; rep from * omitting 1 tr at end of last rep, 1 ss into third of 3 ch.
17th row: 1 ss into each of next 2 tr, 3 ch, * 1 tr into each of next 14 tr, a shell into next sp, 1 tr into each of next 15 tr (3 ch, 1 tr into next sp) 4 times, 3 ch, miss 1 tr and 2 ch, 1 tr into each of next 15 sts, 3 ch, miss 2 ch and 1 tr, (1 tr into next sp, 3 ch) 4 times, miss 2 tr, 1 tr into next tr; rep from * omitting 1 tr at end of last rep, 1 ss into third of 3 ch.
18th row: 1 ss into each of next 2 tr, 3 ch, * 1 tr into each of next 15 tr, a shell into next sp, 1 tr into each of next 16 tr, (3 ch, 1 tr into next sp) 4 times, 3 ch, miss 1 tr and 2 ch, 1 tr into each of next 17 sts, 3 ch, miss 2 ch and 1 tr (1 tr into next sp, 3 ch) 4 times, miss 2 tr, 1 tr into next tr; rep from * omitting 1 tr at end of last rep, 1 ss into third of 3 ch.
19th row: 1 dc into same place as ss, * (1 ch, miss 1 tr, 1 dc into next tr) 9 times, 1 ch, into next sp work 1 dc 3 ch and 1 dc, 1 ch, 1 dc into next tr, (1 ch, miss 1 tr, 1 dc into next tr) 9 times, (1 ch, 1 dc into next sp, 1 ch, 1 dc into next tr) 5 times, (1 ch, miss 1 tr, 1 dc into next tr) 8 times, (1 ch, 1 dc into next sp, 1 ch, 1 dc into next tr) 5 times; rep from * omitting 1 dc at end of last rep, 1 ss into first dc. Fasten off.

Second motif
Work as for first motif for 18 rows.
19th row: 1 dc into same place as ss, (1 ch, miss 1 tr, 1 dc into next tr) 9 times, 1 ch,

1 dc into next sp, 1 ch, 1 dc into corresponding lp on first motif, 1 ch, 1 dc into same sp on second motif, 1 dc into next 1 ch sp on first motif, 1 dc into next tr on second motif, (1 dc into next 1 ch sp on first motif, miss 1 tr on second motif, 1 dc into next tr) 9 times, (1 dc into next 1 ch sp on first motif, 1 dc into next sp on second motif, 1 dc into next 1 ch sp on first motif, 1 dc into next tr on second motif) 5 times, (1 dc into next 1 ch sp on first motif, miss 1 tr on second motif, 1 dc into next tr) 8 times, (1 dc into next 1 ch sp on first motif, 1 dc into next sp on second motif, 1 dc into next 1 ch sp on first motif, 1 dc into next tr on second motif) 5 times, (1 dc into next 1 ch sp on first motif, miss 1 tr on second motif, 1 dc into next tr) 9 times, 1 dc into next 1 ch sp on first motif, 1 dc into next sp on second motif, 1 ch, 1 dc into next lp on first motif, 1 ch, 1 dc into same sp on second motif and complete as first motif. Make five rows of four motifs joining each as second motif was joined to previous motifs. Where four corners meet, join third and fourth motifs to joining of previous motifs.

Lower edging

1st row: With right side facing, attach thread to first free 3 ch lp at lower edge, 3 ch, * (1 tr into next dc, 1 tr into next 1 ch sp) 9 times, 1 tr into next dc, 17 ch, miss eleven 1 ch sps, 1 trip tr into next sp, 4 ch, miss 1 sp, 1 quad tr into next sp, (4 ch, 1 quin tr into next sp) twice, 4 ch, 1 quad tr into next sp, 4 ch, miss next sp, 1 trip tr into next sp, 17 ch, miss eleven 1 ch sps, (1 tr into next dc, 1 tr into next sp) 10 times, 1 tr over dc joining motifs, 1 tr into next sp; rep from * along lower edge omitting 2 tr at end of last rep and working last tr into last free 3 ch lp, 3 ch, TURN.

2nd row: Miss first tr, 1 tr into each of next 17 tr, * 18 tr into next lp, 1 tr into next trip tr, 5 tr into next lp, 1 tr into next quad tr, (5 tr into next lp, 1 tr into next quin tr) twice, 5 tr into next lp, 1 tr into next quad tr, 5 tr into next lp, 1 tr into next trip tr, 18 tr into next lp, miss 2 tr, 1 tr into each of next 37 tr; rep from * omitting 19 tr at end of last rep and working last tr into third of 3 ch, 3 ch, TURN.

3rd row: Miss first tr, 1 tr into each of next 15 tr, * miss 2 tr, 1 tr into each of next 67 tr, miss 2 tr, 1 tr into each of next 33 tr; rep from * omitting 17 tr at end of last rep and working last tr into third of 3 ch, 3 ch, TURN.

4th row: Miss first tr, 1 tr into next tr, (3 ch, miss 3 tr, 1 tr into next tr) 3 times, * (miss 2 tr, 1 tr into next tr, 3 ch) 22 times, 1 tr into next tr, miss 2 tr, 1 tr into next tr, ** (3 ch, miss 3 tr, 1 tr into next tr) 7 times; rep from * ending last rep at **, (3 ch, miss 3 tr, 1 tr into next tr) 3 times, 1 tr into third of 3 ch. Fasten off.

Top edging

1st row: With right side facing, attach thread to first free 3 ch lp at top edge, 4 ch, * 1 tr into next sp, 1 ch; rep from * along top edge ending with 1 tr into last 3 ch lp. Fasten off.

To complete

Dampen and pin out to measurements. Thread ribbon through spaces of top edging then sew curtain rings securely in position. Decorate with ribbon roses as shown in illustration or as desired.

Simple Curtains

Making your own curtains is not at all difficult and very economical.

Before You Begin

❑ You will need to measure the window you wish to cover with curtains.

❑ To calculate your length, measure from the top of the curtain track to the floor or window-sill or, in the case of a curtain pole and rings, measure from the eye hook at the bottom of the rings to the floor. Allow an extra 20 cm in total for turning under at the top and bottom. Curtains will finish approximately 5 cm above the top of the track or eye hook of the ring.

❑ The width measurement will depend on the thickness of your fabric. For very sheer fabrics you will need up to 3 times the length of the curtain track. For medium-weight fabrics you will need 2¹/₂ times the length of the track while twice the track length is acceptable for heavier fabrics.

❑ Sheer fabrics are traditionally not lined. Medium-weight fabrics can benefit from lining, as lined curtains become good insulators and are most effective in controlling light. Try to make your curtain linings the same colour on all your windows, otherwise the exterior view could become a patchwork of multi-coloured linings. You will need the same width of lining as for your main fabric. Lining fabrics are often very wide, so you may need to buy less fabric than for your main fabric.

❑ Consult your curtain accessory shop about the most appropriate heading tape for your fabric. Which one you choose will depend on the type of track or pole you have installed, the weight of your fabric and the effect you want – normally standard gathered tape, pencil pleat or triple pleat (also called pinch pleat). Our curtains have a thick wooden rod over which wooden rings are threaded. These have a small ring at the bottom through which the heading tape hook is inserted. You will need a length of heading tape equal to the total width of your curtain plus 10 cm for side hems and ease. For example, if you use four drops of 115 cm wide fabric you will need 4.70 m of tape.

Top: The fabric-covered pole and painted-to-match curtain rings
Above: The back of the curtain showing the pleating tape and the way in which it is pleated using the special hooks available where you buy the tape
Above right: The simple curtain with pleated heading, fabric-covered curtain pole and fittings painted to match the fabric

MATERIALS

❑ sufficient main fabric for curtain (see *Before You Begin*)
❑ sufficient lining fabric (see *Before You Begin*)
❑ sufficient heading tape (see *Before You Begin*)
❑ sufficient rings or hooks matching sewing threads

METHOD

See the Pull Out Pattern Sheet at the back of the book for the window measurement diagram.

1 Cut your main fabric and lining into the lengths you have calculated in *Before You Begin*.

2 Stitch main fabric lengths together down the long sides until you have the complete curtain width. Do this for lining lengths as well. Turn under 1 cm on the outside edges of main fabric piece then turn under another 5 cm. Baste. Stitch along inner fold. Do this for lining piece as well, folding under 7 cm at sides.

3 Press both pieces. Place them together with wrong sides facing so that 1 cm of main fabric extends beyond the lining on both sides, and top and bottom raw edges are even. Turn over 3 cm of both curtain and lining *together* at top. Press and pin in place.

4 If using pencil pleating tape, unravel the draw cords of the first 5 cm of the tape. For triple pleating tape, such as

6 Turn up curtain hem. Pin and baste. Turn up the lining hem to sit 2 cm shorter than the curtain. Remove the curtain from the track. Stitch both hems. Press to finish.

Fabric-covered Pole

MATERIALS

☐ wooden curtain pole
☐ sufficient wooden curtain rings
☐ a pair of finials (end stoppers)
☐ sufficient fabric to cover (see *Before You Begin*)
☐ fabric or craft glue

METHOD

1 Cut a rectangular piece of fabric the length of the pole and the width of the circumference of the pole plus 3 cm for overlap.

2 If not using the selvage of the fabric, finish one long edge of the fabric by folding under 6 mm. Wrap the fabric around the pole with the folded edge covering the raw edge. Glue into place.

3 Finials can also be covered by using fabric cut on the bias, pleating out the fullness and cutting out these small pleats so that fabric lies flat with no gaps. The pattern will not match on these pieces, but it does not seem to matter! If you are worried by the possibility of gaps, you can paint the finials the same colour as the background colour of the fabric before you begin covering the pole.

4 You can cover all the rings with fabric too. Or you can simply paint them in a colour to complement your fabric.

Below: Sometimes all you need is a little imagination! You can make this elegant, draped pelmet simply by trimming a suitable length of fabric and draping it over your curtain track or pole as shown here. Take care that the right side of your fabric is always the one showing

Laura Ashley (Australia) Pty Limited

ours, turn in raw end of tape so that you have a hook channel just in from the edge of the curtain. Pin the upper edge of the tape to the curtain 1.5 cm down from the top. Stitch down all edges of the tape. If you are using pencil pleating tape, draw up the cords to gather the curtain and insert the hooks into the channels. If you are using triple pleating tape, insert the pronged hooks according to the manufacturer's instructions. This will give the pleated effect.

5 Hang the curtain and leave it to hang for twenty-four hours to allow the fabric to ease and 'drop'. After twenty-four hours, and while the curtains are still hanging, make the connecting 'ties' between the side edges of the curtain and lining .

Down to DETAIL

Café Curtains

This simple method of window dressing will afford privacy and at the same time allow plenty of light to enter the room. Café curtains can be casual or formal, soft and feminine or dramatically contemporary, depending on the fabric you choose. Plain fabrics can be stencilled, appliquéd or braid-trimmed.

Before You Begin

❑ Proportion is important when making café curtains. Generally, the lower curtains are at least half the length of the window and look best when they are approximately five-eighths of the length. The length of the upper curtain should complement that of the lower one but still allow a gap to let in light. It is usually one-quarter of the length of the window, or a little less.

❑ These curtains do not use stitch-on pleating tape, rather they rely on casings in the upper curtain and self fabric loops for the lower curtains which allow for insertion of the rods. The lower curtains

are two identical curtains which part in the middle.

❏ Remember to measure from the top of the rods when calculating fabric lengths for both curtains. Add a hem and casing allowance to each fabric drop (i.e. length of fabric) – 20 cm for the upper curtain and 26 cm for the lower curtain. For example, assuming that your upper curtain is to finish 30 cm from the top of the rod and your lower curtain is to finish 50 cm from the top of the lower rod, you will need to cut your upper curtain into drops of 50 cm, and your lower curtain into drops of 76 cm.

❏ Generally, you will find each curtain requires a total fabric width of 2¼ times the length of the rod. If you are using a sheer fabric, or lace, you may wish to increase this to 2½ times or even 3 times the length of the rod. For example, if your rod is 1 m long, you will need to seam together enough fabric drops to produce a total width of 2.25 m plus side and centre turn under allowances.

❏ To calculate fabric quantities for our curtains on your window follow the simple formulas below.
For the upper curtain the total length of the drops required to make up the required width, allowing 10 cm in total for side hems plus 20 cm per drop for casing and hem.
For the lower curtain the total length of the drops required to make up the required width, allowing 20 cm in total for side and centre hems plus 26 cm per drop for casing loops and hem.

MATERIALS
☐ sufficient fabric for upper and lower curtains (see *Before You Begin*)
☐ matching sewing thread
☐ strong handsewing needle
☐ curtain pole, brackets and rings

METHOD
For the upper curtain:
1 Join short ends of fabric drops to create the total width. Turn in 1 cm on the side edges, then turn another 4 cm and press. Stitch along the inner fold.

2 Turn over 1 cm on upper edge, then turn another 8 cm and press. Stitch along the inner fold. Stitch again 4 cm from previous stitching, creating the rod casing. The fabric above the casing will form a frill when the rod is inserted.

HINT
When choosing fabrics for your Café Curtains note that the broad stripe shown emphasises the hanging loops beautifully, but don't overlook trimming plain fabrics with broad bands of braid, strips of contrast fabric or cotton lace. Fabrics with printed borders of all descriptions can be effective too, especially when the border is used vertically at the centre opening of the lower curtain or repeated across both the top and bottom curtains.

3 Turn up 1 cm on the lower edge, then turn another 4 cm and press. Stitch along the first fold. Press.

For the lower curtains:
See the Pull Out Pattern Sheet at the back of the book for the template for the cut out.

1 The instructions are for one curtain. Make two the same. Join fabric drops, if necessary, to create the required width for the lower curtain. Turn in 1 cm on one side of curtain, then turn another 4 cm and press. Stitch along the first fold.

2 Fold 1 cm over to the wrong side on the top edge and press. Fold over another 25 cm on the top edge so that right sides are facing. Press.

3 Cut a cardboard template from the shape on the pattern sheet. Check that this is long enough to loop over your curtain pole, and adjust its size if necessary. Place the template at the top edge, 8 cm in from the hemmed side edge of the curtain. Mark the shapes across the curtain, about 10 cm apart or to suit your fabric pattern. Mark where you will place the final scallop, leaving 8 cm as on the other end and allowing for the side hem. Cut off any excess fabric.

4 Open out the marked top of the curtain. Turn in 1 cm along the side edge, then turn another 4 cm and press. Stitch along first crease. Fold the top of the curtain again. Stitch around the marked shapes and cut out. Trim and clip into curves for ease. Turn loops to the right side and press. At the back, bring the top of the loop to the base of the loop. Stitch through all thicknesses.

5 Thread the pole through the loops to hang the curtain.

6 If you wish to cover the curtain pole with matching fabric, this is quite easy to do. You can use your curtain fabric or you can choose a contrasting one. See the instructions on page 31 for how to cover your curtain pole.

Top left: The upper curtain showing the rod casing and frill
Centre left: The lower curtain showing the rod threaded through the loops

Festoon or Cloud Blinds

For a romantic look, nothing beats festoon blinds. The fabric you choose will set the style for your blind, from the soft and feminine look of sheer lace to the dramatic elegance of silk brocade. These are in simple homespun cotton for a contemporary feel.

Before You Begin

❏ To calculate your fabric requirements, measure the width and length of your window. You will need a piece of fabric twice this length by twice this width. If you need to join fabric to achieve this width, do so with small flat seams.

MATERIALS

For each blind:
- ☐ fabric (see *Before You Begin*)
- ☐ pencil pleating tape, twice the width of your window
- ☐ ring tape, four times your blind length plus 24 cm
- ☐ one cleat for fastening blind cords
- ☐ metal rod or dowelling for holding lower

edge, 1 cm in diameter to measure 2.5 cm shorter than the width of the window.
- ☐ eyelet screws – one for each length of ring tape plus one
- ☐ curtain track of your choice
- ☐ sufficient hooks for fastening blind to track

METHOD

See page 27 for the cord threading diagram.

1 Turn in 2.5 cm on the top and sides of fabric piece (or joined pieces). Press.

2 Unravel the draw cords of the first 5 cm of the pencil pleating tape. Pin the upper edge of the tape to the top of your blind fabric, 1.5 cm from the edge. Stitch down all edges of the tape, stitching the top hem as you go. Do not draw up the cords.

3 Turn under 1 cm on the lower edge and then turn another 4 cm. Press. Stitch bottom hem.

4 Stitch ring tape down side hems (fixing hems in place at the same time), and at two equally-spaced points across the blind from top to bottom hems. Leave an extra 6 cm of tape at the bottom of each length.

5 Loop this tape back on itself so that the end is just above the hem. Stitch. These loops are to hold the bottom rod.

6 Gather pencil pleating cord, until the blind gathers to the width of the track.

7 Attach eyelets to the window frame, just below the track, to correspond with the top of each strip of ring tape and another, just below one curtain track bracket, through which you will thread blind cords.

8 Cut a cord for each strip of tape, long enough to reach from the bottom rod, up the blind, through the eyelets, across the top and down to the side where the extra eyelet is, leaving sufficient length for knotting them together below the eyelet.

9 Thread the cords up from the bottom, tying the three bottom rings together as you go to form a permanent blousing effect. Attach the blind to the curtain track with the hooks. Insert the rod through the tape loops at the lower edge of the blind.

Roman Blinds

For a more tailored window treatment, consider these Roman blinds.

Before You Begin

❏ Roman blinds are traditionally fitted inside the window frame. They retain one or two pleats even when let down. Take this into account when measuring.

❏ To calculate your fabric requirements: You will need the desired width of the blind plus 10 cm for hems x the desired length of the blind plus 30 cm at the top for turning plus 12 cm for each timber lath plus 13 cm for the lower hem and lath pocket.

❏ Decide how many lath pockets you want to have by making a paper pattern of the blind. Fold in the 30 cm at the top and the 5 cm at the lower edge and then crease in the lath pockets. Do this until you are happy with the number and spacing of your laths – generally six or eight.

❏ Fabrics with strong patterns or ones that do not adequately screen the light, may need to be lined. Cut the lining fabric the same size as the main fabric. Baste the two pieces together, with wrong sides facing, and from here on treat them as a single layer, following the instructions below. Remember to choose a lining fabric in keeping with that on the other windows so your house is as attractive from the outside as it is inside.

MATERIALS

- ☐ sufficient fabric and lining (optional) (see *Before You Begin*)
- ☐ 5 cm wide contrast fabric strip or braid x four times the length of the blind, before stitching the pockets
- ☐ matching sewing thread
- ☐ sufficient 5 cm wide timber laths, as wide as the finished width of the blind (see *Before You Begin*)
- ☐ a mounting board the width of your window, 2 cm thick and 7 cm deep.
- ☐ one pair metal 'L' brackets
- ☐ tacks or a staple gun
- ☐ nylon cord about 6 mm thick for raising and lowering the blind
- ☐ sufficient eye hooks to have two for

each lath, two on the mounting board and one more at one end of the mounting board
- ☐ one metal cleat for tying off the cords

METHOD

See the Pull Out Pattern Sheet at the back of the book for the construction diagrams.

1 Turn 1 cm on both sides of the blind fabric piece to the right side. Press. Turn in 1 cm on long sides of contrast fabric strips. Press. Pin one strip to each edge of the blind, covering the pressed raw edge and having the pressed edges of the strip and blind matching. Stitch both long edges of the contrast strip to the blind. Stitch the other two strips one-third of the way in from the sides. Turn 1 cm on the upper and lower edges to the wrong side. Press. On the lower edge turn under 6 cm and stitch down, forming the last lath pocket.

2 Mark each lath pocket with two lines 12 cm apart. On the outside of the fabric, bring these two lines together. Pin and baste along marked lines. Stitch, forming the lath pockets. Carefully stitch the folded edge of each lath pocket down on to the blind. Insert the laths.

3 On the wrong side of the blind, screw an eye hook through the fabric into each lath about a quarter of the way in from the sides. Make sure that all your hooks run down the blind in a straight line.

4 Attach your mounting board to the wall above the window frame with metal 'L' brackets.

5 Tack or staple the top edge of the fabric to the top of the mounting board, close to the back (wall) edge so that the fabric covers the top of the board and hangs down the front of it, concealing the board altogether. Screw two eye hooks into the underside of the mounting board, each one in line with a row of eye hooks on the blind. Screw another eye hook into one end of the underside of the mounting board on the same side as you will mount the cleat for holding the cords on the window frame.

6 Secure a cord at the lowest eye hook on each side of the blind. Thread the cords up the row of eye hooks on the blind, including those on the mounting board, so that both cords emerge at the extra eye hook on one side of the mounting board. Knot the cords together below the level of the cleat.

Down to DETAIL

Leadlight Porthole

There is nothing quite like a well-designed and well-made leadlight window. Pinpoints of light and flashes of colour can transform a boring window with a poor view into a major feature. Leadlighting is perhaps one of those projects that should not be undertaken as a one-off project.

MATERIALS

- ☐ 15 mm 'H' section round lead cames for edges
- ☐ 4.2 mm, 5.2 mm and 5.5 mm 'H' section round lead cames for centre
- ☐ selected glass – in this case, German machine antique glass
- ☐ 50:50 solder stick
- ☐ horseshoe nails
- ☐ flux
- ☐ leadlighting putty
- ☐ whiting
- ☐ stove black

SPECIAL TOOLS NEEDED

Leadlighting requires specialised equipment. Making your existing tools do the job will not produce the best results. The tools are generally only available from stained glass materials suppliers.

- ☐ ordinary steel wheel cutter
- ☐ good quality tungsten carbide glass cutter, if using selenium oxide glass. If not self lubricating, organise a small container to hold the lubricant – a mixture of light oil and kerosene
- ☐ glass pliers
- ☐ cut running pliers
- ☐ grozing pliers
- ☐ electric soldering iron, 80 watt with 'hook nose' tip
- ☐ lead vice and pliers
- ☐ lathekin
- ☐ lead knife, such as Don Carlos pattern
- ☐ wire brush

METHOD

Note: Washing hands thoroughly after working with lead should be automatic, as lead is an accumulative poison.

1 Set up an area to work on that is flat and will not damage the glass. A workbench with a particle/chip board top is ideal. A felt covering will protect the glass from scratching. As work progresses the surface should be vacuumed of glass splinters frequently as these may damage or break the glass being cut.

2 Finalise your design. This is often the slowest part of the job, but many books on the subject have a number of designs that can be used or adapted. Try to avoid designs where tight curves

Right: An entrance showing a door with leadlight panels and a leadlight porthole
Below: Interior view of leadlight porthole

or sharp internal corners need to be cut, because you probably won't be successful. Plain shapes with relatively simple curves are easiest to cut and lead up.

3 Once the design is drawn, make several copies and colour them in with the colours you've selected. It may be worthwhile trying several combinations of colours to get it just right.

4 Measure the window. In this case, it is a 415 mm circular window. Deduct half the width of the lead (came), in this case about 7 mm, plus an additional 3 mm from the circle all round to allow for fitting. Large 'H' section lead is used on edges to allow for trimming should the pattern 'grow' slightly while being made. Therefore the pattern (cartoon) size is finalised at 400 mm in diameter.

5 Transfer your design to the full pattern size and make a full-scale drawing of the window. Do it in pencil first to ensure it is right. Then finally draw it in heavy felt pen to leave a line about 1.5 mm thick between the glass pieces. This automatically makes an allowance for the wall thickness of the lead section.

6 Make a couple of copies of the pattern, so that they can be used for numbering glass pieces, or cut into individual pieces and used as templates for cutting the glass (if you find that easiest), or if one gets damaged or torn.

7 Mount your main cartoon on a piece of particle/chip board or something similar, with plenty of room to work around the edges of the design. Normally, two battens are fixed to the board against which you can work. In the case of this circular design, mark out and cut a panel to fit against the battens, then mark out and cut a semicircle to hold the lead in place. In this example, glass was used as the panel, but you can use thin plywood.

8 Choose the coloured glass for each shape according to your design; buy it and have it ready to start. Similarly, have the lead ready, as well as horseshoe nails and all other needs.

9 Cut the first piece of glass to size. This should be a piece of scrap just for practice. Start the cut a small distance in from the edge of the glass. Apply steady pressure without stopping, and hold the cutter close to 90°. Draw it towards you,

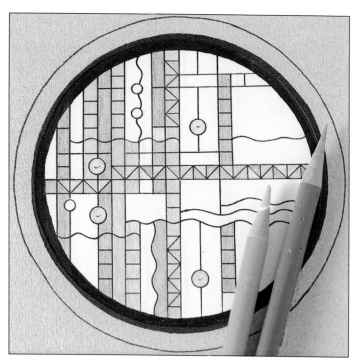

*Left: Drawing of the porthole, showing different colour sections
Below: Template of the leadlight porthole*

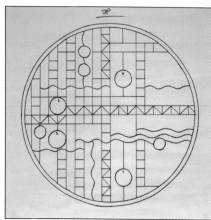

and let it roll over the edge near you.

10 To break the glass, hold it vertically and place your two index fingers under either side of the cut, and your thumbs on top of the glass – the knuckles should be touching. Rotate both hands down, or clockwise and anticlockwise, and the glass should break and 'run' along your score line. Shake off any splinters.

If the glass will not break, lightly tap under the score line with the hammer on the non-cutting end of the glass cutter. Hold the glass close to the score line to avoid breakage.

11 If you are still unsuccessful using your fingers, you may have to invest in a pair of cut running pliers to do the job. When cutting thin strips it may be necessary to use grozing pliers to grip the

narrow side, or you may injure your hand if you slip. Glass cut in this way will never be as neat as when it is cut by running.

12 When cutting the glass for actual leadlight, mark out from the cartoon directly, or the cut-out pieces. Cut the large pieces first as the offcuts may then be used for smaller pieces of the same colour. Aim at being economical – within reason.

13 Once it has been cut, hold each piece against your pattern and make sure it fits between the inked-in lines. If it overlaps it will need trimming with the grozing pliers. If it is too small it will need to be recut.

14 Generally leadlighters like to cut all the glass pieces to shape before starting the leading. The pieces can be laid on the spare cartoon, or each piece can be numbered on the face side with a corresponding number on the spare cartoon. The pieces can be carefully laid in a box until ready for use.

15 Before lead can be used, it must be stretched, and this is done with a lead vice and pliers. This must be done with care so that when you apply pressure, the lead does not snap, dumping you on the floor. Once stretched, the channels of the lead may need to be opened using a lathekin. You may be able to purchase prestretched lead.

16 Cut off the two damaged ends of the lead, and then cut sufficient length off the wider lead to place around the semicircle defined by the cut panel. The lead is cut using a sharp lead knife, in a rocking motion. The other half of the perimeter is the last piece in the jigsaw to be fitted at the end.

17 Select the piece of glass for the starting point. On our circle it can just about be anywhere on the bottom perimeter, but where successive pieces can be installed easily. The best place would be in the middle. This particular window was made by building up from the bottom, filling in all the lower area and then working up the centre and out to the sides.

18 Insert the first piece of glass, gently tapping it into place with the wooden end of the lead knife. Hold it in place with horseshoe nails, with the flat side of the nails against the glass.

19 Cut a length of the internal (thinner) lead slightly longer than the edge to be joined, and insert the adjoining glass into the lead. Hold it in place using the horseshoe nails. Mark the joint of the two glass pieces on the lead, taking care to get the angle right, and remove the lead. Make another mark just back from this first one, and cut the lead slightly short. This allows for the next lead, which crosses the first one, to sit properly with an accurate joint that will be easy to solder. Slowly continue in this fashion, fanning out across the window, building up the leadlight. Always hold each new piece or section with the horseshoe nails. Never use the nails against the lead as they will cause irreparable damage because of the softness of the lead.

20 When the entire leadlight has been made, the final outside wider came is fitted in place and you are ready to solder the joints. At this point, measure the panel for size.

21 Just before soldering, ensure that no flanges from the lead are bent onto the glass or out of shape, because once soldered, they will be set.

22 Soldering is done with an 80 watt iron, as this heats up quickly. Lower wattage irons can be used, but may be a little slower. The easiest tip to use is a 'hook nose' tip, or angled tip as pictured below. The tip should be properly tinned before use. Soldering must be carried out in the presence of flux, which removes oxide from the surface of the lead and provides a good surface for the solder to adhere to. Solid flux is recommended because it is easiest to clean up afterwards. Rub the flux over the joint to be soldered.

23 Start soldering at the point furthest away from where you are standing. Hold the iron close to the lead and take a small blob of solder from the stick. Place this on the joint. It should run on to the joint and, when the iron is removed, will soon set. Use a little at a time; you can always add more if the joint looks scantly soldered.

24 When all the joints are soldered, take a wire brush and brush off all traces of flux on the window. Any solder spilt on the glass or lead should be peeled off as well.

25 Turn the window over together with the base as the window is still not strong. Repeat the soldering on the back side. Once again, remove the leftover flux.

26 It's now time to putty the window. This must be done in one sitting, otherwise it will set and leave oil stains. Use prepared leadlighting putty, which has been made with carbon black. Wear old clothes as this is a messy job. Force

the putty under the lead flanges with whatever you find easiest, thumbs or the lathekin. Do not press down too hard on the glass as the panels can break very easily. Excess putty can be removed by carefully scraping with the lathekin or by using a horse-shoe nail alongside the lead.

27 At this stage, sprinkle whiting over the surface of the whole window and scrub vigorously to clean it. Don't press too hard, as the whole window is still a little soft and may distort. Repeat the process on the other side.

28 Let the window stand, rather than lie, for a few days to allow the putty to harden. After three days or so, decide whether you would like a grey or a black finish. If grey, simply polish the window with a bristle brush. If you want the lead to be black, apply some well-mixed black with a brush. After a few minutes, when the solvent has

evaporated, polish with a brush once again. Never use a cloth as it tends to shine the soldered joints silver.

29 Now install the window in the previously prepared frame.

Top: Cutting glass for the leadlight porthole
Above: Assembling the glass pieces and lead
Right: Soldering the lead joints with a `hook nose' soldering iron

Tracks and Rods
FEATURE

Your choice of curtain rods, poles or tracks will be based on the shape and function of your window, the effect you want to create – and your budget. If you live in rented accommodation, you should opt for rods or poles which are usually less expensive, easier to install and highly portable. Special extendable poles allow you to change the length to suit different windows – another plus for rent-payers!

Unless curtains are frequently drawn, poles are the answer for heavy drapes, framing a window, or lightweight privacy curtains. More sophisticated poles may be fitted with draw-cords, gliders and decorative finials (those pretty end-stops that stop the curtains from sliding off the pole). Prices will vary according to the style you choose.

Tracks range from simple, straight or curved styles to pricier, composite products which can support both curtains and a ruffled pelmet. These may have extension brackets to vary the distance between the curtains, walls and the pelmet.

If you are seeking a permanent arrangement, don't skimp on quality by using cheap, unreliable tracks. Remember to match hooks, gliders and end-stops to the style of curtain-heading tape

you have chosen. Pelmets hide a multitude of sins and save money because you can fit plainer tracks or rods than those required by exposed curtain heads.

Beautiful curtains must sit squarely on accurately positioned fittings. Arm yourself with a retractable fibreglass or metal tape measure and carefully measure window dimensions, frame size and the distance to the ceiling, floor and corners of adjacent walls. These measurements are essential when planning special effects, such as creating an impression of height on a shallow window. You can do this by hanging long curtains from poles or tracks raised well above the natural top of the window or even suspended from the ceiling.

Always anchor rods or tracks firmly with strong brackets, screwed to wooden battens or wall plugs. You will need to find out what's underneath your wall or ceiling plaster. If you arrange a free measure and quote from several reputable curtain makers (who will have to determine the construction materials to calculate costs), you'll be able to compare their prices and ask all your questions at no cost!

If you can avoid it, don't hang new curtains on old tracks or

poles. Choose fittings appropriate to the shape and style of your curtains. Heavy curtains may require special reinforcement, especially if they will be frequently opened and closed. Purchased kits should contain everything you'll need to complete the job: poles or tracks, strong brackets, sufficient hooks and gliders, and screws long enough to anchor brackets. Very long poles and tracks may need extra supporting brackets spaced at intervals between the usual end and centre brackets.

Choose fittings that frame your windows beautifully and do their job. Heavy curtains should completely retract to maximise light. For recessed windows, select flexible or curved metal tracks to fit the shape of the modern bay windows, hung with one continuous curtain or three separate curtains. Traditional bay windows, in three sections separated by wide corner frames, can use a single track or three separate curtain poles.

Instead of end-stops or finials, fit the last hook to a wall-mounted ring-fitting to hide track ends and avoid ugly gaps between curtains and walls. Never hang curtains straight across the face of a recessed window: they darken the room and detract from the charm of a traditional bay or dormer window.

Creating
a look

*R*e-create your favourite decorating style at home with clever combinations of colour, texture and accessories. You may have to start with your existing rooms and furniture and ring the changes with our tips. Of course, if you are able to buy new furniture and fittings, it will certainly make your job a lot easier.

IKEA

Country Form

Three Great Looks
FEATURE

Classic

You can fake the elegant lines and smooth textures of the classic look by using single-colour themes and rich-looking synthetic fabrics. Oval coffee and side tables, polished timber cabinets and wall mirrors, reflecting floor-length curtains and swags,

The Australian Wool Corporation

Dupont

Above: This elegant, classic living room shows the clever use of a subdued colour scheme and occasional furniture, lamps and ornaments to create the look
Left: The classic dining room features traditionally styled furniture, drapes and subtle lighting

develop this formal style. Repeat curtain colour in synthetic taffeta lamp shades, piped cushions trimmed with small tassels, or in graceful accessories like Grandma's favourite vase, a soft floral painting or a beautiful piece of glass. Plan formal arrangements of old-fashioned roses, camellias, gladioli and iris or stand spathiphyllum, strelitzia, flowering cyclamen, begonia or anthuriums in highly polished brass or timber planters. Conceal clutter in cupboards and light the rooms with traditional table or standard lamps, recessed spot lights, pendants or wall sconces – but keep it simple.

Contemporary

Simple lines and the smooth, cool textures of brushed or polished metals, glass, acrylic, polished timber and marble veneers reflect a no-fuss, contemporary approach. Upholstery options include leather or vinyl, linen or wool, lustrous satins or synthetics. The look is tailored and functional, without much fabric and absolutely no frills! Simple drapes and cushions in strong contrasting or neutral colours work with Roman and bonded blinds, slimline venetians or vertical drapes. Choose one or two accessories to develop the

theme, such as an abstract poster or print or a slim ceramic vase. Strike a green note with a single kentia palm, yucca or pony tail plant in a streamlined container. Compose simple floral arrangements of stark foliage and one beautiful lily or strelitzia in simple glass, ceramic or terracotta containers. Abundant natural light is a feature of the contemporary look, augmented with track lighting and floor or table lamps on slim adjustable stands. Use geometric pendants or spotlights to highlight important features in a room. Stereo and video equipment, books and collectables stand on open shelving or in glass cabinets, but take care to conceal the clutter in cupboards.

Country

Imitate the country folk who traditionally gather to make their own decorations with bright colours and lots of texture. Soften chunky pine or scrubbed timber furniture with tiny floral print fabrics or earthy homespuns, calico and wool. Treat used-furniture bargains with weathered paint techniques, or team rustic cane with frilly cushions. Select fabrics to complement existing colour schemes and add a touch of lace, a valance or handmade rag rug to achieve that country look. Accessorise with bright china plates hanging on walls; wreaths of dried grasses and seedpods framing small mirrors; toss a patchwork quilt on a sofa, bed or on a wall; hat and coat racks, watercolours and collections of almost anything from pebbles to milk jugs. Bunches of daisies, forget-me-nots or pansies and hanging baskets of ivy or maidenhair complement clustered pots of herbs, ferns and flowering geraniums or cineraria. Storage is open and cheerful. Have your shining pots stand on open dressers but camouflage modern appliances. Allow lots of natural light and, at night, turn on soft table lamps, cane-shaded pendants or electric 'oil' lamps.

Right: This living room features the fabric, accessories and comfortable feel of the country style
Below: Natural timbers and stoneware accessories decorate this country kitchen
Below left: Simple lines and an absence of clutter are the marks of a contemporary room

Laura Ashley (Australia) Pty Limited

Country Form

IKEA

45

Personal Touches

Put the mark of your own personality into your decorating scheme. Your home, whether it's a big house or a rented room, should say something about you and your life.

The possibilities for adding that special, personal touch are as endless as your imagination. If you have a hobby, why not display your finished work, and even those pieces you are still working on, on a table or dresser top. Sometimes a pleasing display of an assortment of objects that you enjoy looking at, makes a wonderful decorating and personal statement.

Don't be too worried about the tidiness of your display or even how odd it may look. Be adventurous and you will be surprised at how much your visitors will enjoy looking at it and what a great ice-breaker it can be when entertaining.

Above: If you have odd pieces of unusual china that you've acquired over the years, don't hide it away in a cupboard but display it for everyone to admire
Right: An eclectic mixture of old Eastern brass, weights and measures and a delightful carved wooden shoe combined with the texture of an old water filter are sure conversation starters when displayed on this wooden mantle
Far right: A sunny corner blossoms with this arrangement of much loved bits and pieces and a lovely old bowl full of rosy onions

46

Above: Soften the hard look of a modern stairway with a display of old bottles, jars and even wheels
Above right: Dress up an open shelf with a handsome collection of rolling pins
Right: A few pieces of beautiful Chinese blue and white porcelain add the perfect finishing touch to any room

47

A Roomful of Treasures

Long ago you were given a blue plate, then you bought another one at a local bazaar and then a friend gave you one for Christmas and, before you knew it, you had a collection! Your collection of plates, dolls, jelly moulds, tin cans, or whatever, offers great decorating possibilities if you display it well.

Perhaps you're a traveller and have brought back souvenirs that share a common theme – scarves, plates, luggage labels – you can frame or hang them on a dull wall. Ethnic collections can bring fascinating textures and colour to a room. Hand-loomed fabrics and carpets, primitive sculpture and hand-woven baskets will all complement each other.

Try to create a theme in certain rooms. An old favourite is a marine theme in bathrooms – shells collected from holidays long ago, framed shell prints and perhaps a mirror surrounded by shells. Libraries and studios lend themselves to collections of photographs, sporting trophies or memorabilia, and old prints. Kitchens are ideal for displaying utensils – old jelly moulds, ornate cake plates, bottle openers, scales with weights and measures, beverage bottles and old stoneware jars, all bring a rustic, cared-for and friendly look to a kitchen. If you are lucky enough to own one, an old timber dresser makes an ideal home for a kitchen collection. Collections of quite large objects, such as copper pans or baskets, can look wonderful suspended from the ceiling on hooks.

Above: A lovely collection of old millefleurs plates brings warmth to a plain white wall. See how the variety in shape and size adds interest to the display
Below: Kitchen ceilings are not usually very interesting to look at, except if they are like this one. A collection of stoneware milk jugs is suspended from timber beams

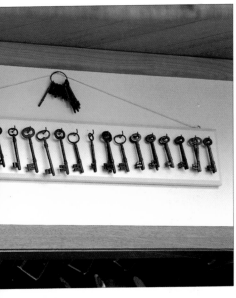

Top: A collection of antique ginger beer bottles lines open shelves in a country-style kitchen. The warmth and colours of the stoneware add a pleasing feature to the room
Above: For a great sense of fun, why not a collection of old keys of various shapes and sizes? Collected from junk shops, attics and church bazaars, they are mounted on a simple board using cup hooks

Above: This is a truly charming and unusual collection of vases in the shape of fancy hats, carefully mounted on a plain wall

Collections in entrance halls make a great decorating statement. This is often the first impression visitors get about the owners of the house and your first chance to show off! Our photograph of old-fashioned vases, shaped like hats, shows a colourful and whimsical touch, especially when complemented by a large bunch of spring blooms in a quaint old jug. Take care though, if you have small children and a large dog, a table in the narrow entrance hall may not be the ideal place to display a precious collection of china.

Some collections just evolve, or you can set out quite deliberately to assemble objects in a decorative group. Sometimes items from different eras can be combined successfully, but keep a colour or theme link between them. Old theatre programmes, nautical bits and pieces, books, paintings of a particular subject, coloured china, fashion accessories or toys are all varied and delightful when gathered and displayed in interesting collections.

ways with Walls

Walls need not be finished with plain paint any more. These days you have an almost endless variety of wallcoverings or wall finishes to choose from and they need not break the bank! You will find wallpapers for every room in your home from scrubbable vinyls for the kitchen to elegant flocked papers for your dining room and pretty florals for the bedroom. There are some surprisingly easy methods of using paint to create special effects, and the best news is that they will add only a little more to the initial cost of your paint. All you need is a lot of enthusiasm, a little energy and our easy-to-follow Down to Detail instructions for decorative painted finishes.

Down to DETAIL

Paint Finishes

The rough, cold cement floor of the living room, pictured opposite, now looks and feels like expensive inlaid stone blocks, costing nothing but your physical labour and a few tins of paint. Walls of a boring dark hall have been transformed into a gem-like Wedgwood box with the application of paint and some inexpensive plastic ornaments.

A room, apparently panelled silk, is, in fact, painted to appear that way. Pale, subtle colour glows in soft dragged lines on surfaces which previously were flat and dead and of no interest. With your labour, some paint and a lot of enthusiasm, you can turn your home into a treasure house of colour, texture and warmth.

Special paint effects were once the province of skilled professional decorators – but not anymore! You can texture and colour your walls, woodwork and furniture in ways that will make them unique.

You can achieve broken colour finishes by using two very basic methods: a paint glaze is either added over a background colour with a sponge or by spattering; or the paint glaze is rolled or painted onto the background colour and then partially removed using rags, combs, stippling brushes and so on. Different tools produce quite different effects with the paint – and the way you manipulate each tool is all-important.

The colour and pattern you choose can add that magical – and often missing – element of style to a room's colour scheme.

They create wonderful illusions – the overall effect can look luxurious and very expensive, yet the process can be as cheap as the cost of the paint!

These finishes are suited to articles made from just about anything – wood, glass, ceramics, highly glazed pottery, leather and plastic.

Plastic items bought straight off the shelf from a supermarket or department store – a plastic jug, tray or wastepaper basket – can be very successfully transformed and stylised with a painted finish.

So many of the everyday objects that surround us can be completely re-created using painted finishes – old table mats, vases and tin canisters to name a few. Don't forget that these things all fit into your larger design and home colour scheme and can, in fact, add that essential 'just right' finishing touch.

*Below left: A stencilled kitchen wall
Below: A Wedgwood green hallway with trompe l'oeil door
Opposite: A living room with ragged and dragged walls and a stone-finished floor
Inset: A detail of the painted floor*

Tools and Supplies

To achieve the best results, good tools and supplies are of the utmost importance. Buy them as you need them, beginning with the basics and adding to them as necessary.

- ❏ eggshell enamel (one part matt/flat enamel to one part satin enamel or one part matt/flat acrylic to one part satin acrylic)
- ❏ matt/flat enamel paints
- ❏ water-based artists' acrylics
- ❏ universal tints
- ❏ oil-based and water-based scumble medium
- ❏ turps (white spirit)
- ❏ shellac
- ❏ rollers
- ❏ methylated spirits
- ❏ roller covers
- ❏ roller pans (trays)
- ❏ wall stipple brush (rectangular)
- ❏ cutting-in (detail) brush, 50 mm
- ❏ 50 mm to 75 mm paint brushes
- ❏ dragging brush
- ❏ round stipple brush
- ❏ natural sponges
- ❏ calico (cut and washed) – buy new calico, cut in 20 m lengths, then wash it, put it through the dryer to remove lint, and cut it into short lengths

- ❏ containers for mixing
- ❏ large stirring sticks
- ❏ strainer bags (nylon tights)
- ❏ duster brush
- ❏ tack rags
- ❏ ladders
- ❏ lint-free dust cloths
- ❏ masking tape and tape dispenser
- ❏ razor blades

Cleaning tools

Most painting tools can be cleaned first by soaking in turps (white spirit) if oil-based, then by washing in hot, soapy water. If using water-based paints, hot soapy water followed by rinsing will do the trick. Rinse thoroughly – tools will harden and become useless if any paint residue is left after washing.

All brushes must be carefully rinsed after use. Have two or three tins of turps (white spirit) ready to use.

To soften a hardened brush, dip it into a saucepan of boiling water, detergent and ammonia – or immerse in paint stripper or brush cleaner for a short time.

The work area

The ideal work area is light, airy and spacious – with lots of shelving, cupboards and storage space. If this sounds too idyllic for your circumstances, don't despair – you can also get by with a very basic set-up.

If you are short on space, an efficient work area can be created by fitting out a cupboard with shelves and using a card table which can be folded away when necessary.

Remember, too, that many of the painting and varnishing materials that you will be using are highly flammable – so if you set up work in your kitchen, stay well away from the cooking area.

Ventilation is very important – you need a constant flow of fresh air to disperse any potentially dangerous fumes.

Keep your work area as clean as possible – stray dust and grime can ruin a freshly painted surface.

Good lighting is essential. Fit an extra light overhead if you don't have good natural light.

A set of shelves close at hand is an extra bonus for storage of tools and supplies which you need to lay your hands on quickly and easily.

Preparation

Preparation is crucial to a successful result. All walls should be sanded back and, where necessary, filled.

A wonderful filler for large holes in walls is cornice glue. This is in powder form and may be bought in bulk and made up following the instructions on the packet. It sands beautifully, so the patching is not evident. If this is not obtainable, any good wall filler will do the job.

Once the filler is dry and sanded so that the filling is imperceptible, the filled area must be sealed. If you do not seal the filled area, you will find it shows through as a grey patch when you apply the wall glaze.

Shellac is a sealing medium. It is thinned with methylated spirits and dries almost immediately, so that you can get on with the painting job straight away. If shellac is not available, use whatever sealer you can buy at your local suppliers. It is most important that the walls are well sanded and made as smooth as possible.

Once the wall is in as good a condition as you can possibly achieve and all sanding has been completed, wipe down with calico rags and vacuum the floor and walls. Then wipe all over with tack rags. These are made of cheesecloth, impregnated with linseed oil, and are invaluable for removing dust.

Before painting the walls, make sure that you mask all areas which are not to be painted – this will save hours of cleaning up later. Only buy good quality masking tape – never buy masking tape which does not bear a brand name or which is on sale because it is old stock.

Wall glazing

If you are restoring old walls – or new ones for that matter – great care must be given to the preparation. As with so many aspects

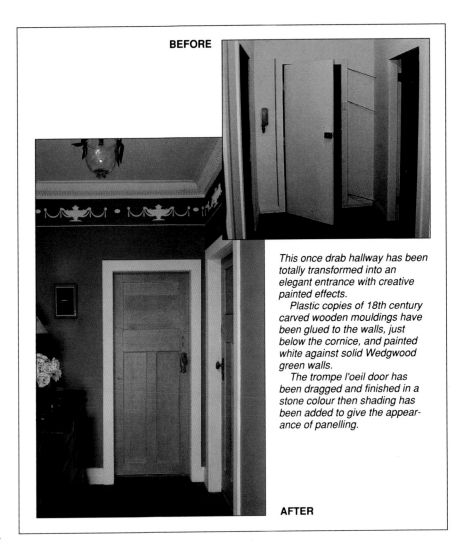

BEFORE

AFTER

This once drab hallway has been totally transformed into an elegant entrance with creative painted effects.

Plastic copies of 18th century carved wooden mouldings have been glued to the walls, just below the cornice, and painted white against solid Wedgwood green walls.

The trompe l'oeil door has been dragged and finished in a stone colour then shading has been added to give the appearance of panelling.

of interior and exterior decoration, the better the preparation, the better the final result.

You may now start painting the walls with eggshell sheen enamel. (The colour is up to you, but generally a room or a whole house can happily be prepared in white eggshell sheen enamel and then any colour or colours imposed over the white.) If you cannot buy this style of paint, you can easily make it yourself by mixing one part matt/flat enamel with one part satin enamel, thus creating the slight sheen one sees on an eggshell.

If you do not wish to work in oil-based paints, you can make the same eggshell sheen using acrylic house paints. However, a word of warning: when applying a decorative paint glaze to walls, the glaze is more workable and stays 'open' (does not dry out immediately) longer if it is imposed on an oil-based paint rather than on an acrylic paint. Acrylic paints are very absorbent and tend to soak up a decorative paint glaze in a very thirsty manner and make it much more difficult to work.

When applying the paint to the walls, you can use a brush or a roller. Rollers are very quick, but tend to leave behind the appearance of an orange skin. To overcome this orange-peel effect, lay on one section with the roller – about 610 mm at a time then

AFTER

This pine chest of drawers was sealed with shellac and painted cream.

Panels were painted on the drawers and finished by applying crackle medium.

The top has a faux marble finish, adding the classical finishing touch to the piece.

BEFORE

quickly come back over the wet paint with a good bristle brush and 'lay-off', that is, pull the brush from the ceiling down to the skirting board through the paint, removing the orange-peel pattern in the paint. If you do this carefully the paint surface should be absolutely smooth.

Doors, architraves, skirting boards, windows, etc, should be prepared in the same way, using a brush to apply the paint. After the application of two coats of eggshell sheen enamel the walls may look opaque. If this is the case, you are then ready to get on with the decorative glaze. If, however, there are patches on the wall which have a slightly grey appearance, you must apply more coats of eggshell sheen until the wall is absolutely opaque.

Once the walls are a solid colour, they are ready to receive the decorative glaze. One word of warning here: if, in spite of all

your hard work, you have not been able to achieve an absolutely even, smooth surface on your walls, there are some glazes which will not be suitable. For instance, the dragged finish requires a very smooth, even surface, allowing the brush to glide over the wall without meeting any bumps.

Before applying your decorative glaze you must mask skirting boards, cornices, architraves and doors if you are to achieve a first-class, professional finish. Use a low-tack tape, made for French polishers, which is half low-tack and the other half brown paper. The half that is brown paper will provide extra protection to the masked areas. Be careful at the corners where it does not bond well to itself; you will need a length of ordinary tape over it to make sure the bonding is secure at that point.

Taking the trouble to mask off

areas properly is well worth the effort. Your finish will be crisp and clean on all the edges and you will have no cleaning up to do. Ignore this step and you will spend many tedious hours removing unwanted paint.

Before commencing work on the walls, spend some time practising on sample boards so that you get the feel of creating the paint finish. If you have a wall or two on which to practise, such as a lavatory or laundry area (they can always be repainted!), try the finish on those walls before embarking on a more ambitious project.

Woodwork

In Victorian and Edwardian houses, the colour in woodwork was often made by aniline dyes suspended in either shellac or varnish. This dye will bleed through almost any paint finish.

To determine if the colour is, in fact, aniline, take some steel wool and methylated spirits and rub the finish vigorously. If the

This once raw concrete floor has been painted to suit the soft colours and textures of the room and to give the impression of stone-tiling.
The concrete was first sealed with shellac, then three colours were ragged and sponged on to create the texture and appearance of stone.
The floor was then finished with 'lining' to make the tiling pattern.

finish starts to come away and some colour appears to be remaining in the wood, you can be sure it is aniline. Similarly, if the finish is varnish with aniline, steel wool soaked in turps (white spirit) used in the same way will give you the same answer.

The only material which will contain these dyes is an aluminium paint. This paint is readily available for painting roofs and is invaluable for covering aniline. Follow the directions on the tin for application. Make sure the background is completely covered with the aluminium paint before proceeding to the next step of applying the eggshell sheen enamel.

Furniture

If the piece of furniture has been well painted, varnished or French polished, there is no need to strip it. If, however, it is a mess of dripping paint, remove the offending cover first.

If the first case applies, sand back the piece until it is smooth.

Fill any areas which require filling, then seal filled areas with shellac or a proprietary sealer. Sand the sealed area until it is smooth, wipe with a calico rag and then a tack cloth, and then begin painting with either oil or acrylic eggshell sheen enamel, usually white.

If the piece of furniture has been stripped, then it must be treated as raw and first sealed with shellac or a proprietary sealer. Sand as above and wipe off – then coat with the usual coats of eggshell sheen enamel to an opaque coverage.

You are then ready to apply the decorative paint glaze.

Glazes

In painted finishes, glaze does not mean shiny. A glaze is a semi-translucent coat of paint painted onto an opaque background. The paint is broken open with a tool, such as a cloth, plastic bag or brush, allowing the opaque background to shine through, thus creating depth and dimension. Consequently, these finishes are often referred to as 'broken' paint finishes. If you wish to have a shine on the finish, this is done by applying varnish – either satin or gloss.

Varnish is the final coat that gives protection and an extra depth to painted finishes, depending on the number of coats applied. Of the many types of varnish available, gloss marine varnish offers the most protection. When matured and wet-sanded it has a smooth surface that withstands heat very well. Marine satin and matt/flat varnishes are also hardy finishes, as are the old-fashioned resin-

Mixing the eggshell sheen enamel

Applying the eggshell sheen enamel

based varnishes.

Most varnishes tend to yellow slightly, but some can be deliberately tinted to correct this. Some yellowing is fine over most colours except white and pale pastels. A little umber mixed in varnish to be applied over a red antiquing glaze gives an excellent result.

Surfaces in constant use require a great deal of protection and can be varnished in a number of ways, depending on the desired appearance. All varnishes, particularly high gloss, should be left to mature.

Scumble medium or antiquing glaze

Scumble medium is a semi-translucent medium composed of linseed oil, turps (white spirit), whiting and extenders to create a longer drying time.

Scumble medium is an essential part of glazing. It adds translucency to the paint, extends the drying time – which means you have more time to work with the paint once it has been applied –and enables the paint to hold the imprint of the tool. If you did not use scumble medium and performed, say, a stipple, you would find the paint had closed up into an opaque colour within an hour or two.

Oil-based and water-based scumble medium have the same characteristics, although obviously made from entirely different materials.

To prepare for stippling apply the glaze to the skirting board

Bounce the brush up and down into the glaze to create a stippled effect

Stippling

If using water-based mediums, add one part glaze to two parts water. You must always use your common sense when thinning, as the viscosity of paint and scumble medium can vary dramatically. The glaze should always sit on the background as a cover not a texture. If you find there is texture in the glaze, it is too thick and you will need to thin it.

It is recommended that stippling is kept for the smaller areas of a room. One of the most difficult finishes to perform expertly is a stippled wall. Stippled doors, skirting boards, architraves and cornices look wonderful.

MATERIALS

- ☐ one part matt/flat enamel
- ☐ one part scumble medium
- ☐ one or two parts turps (white spirit)

SPECIAL TOOLS NEEDED

- ☐ roller or brush to apply the glaze
- ☐ rectangular wall stipple brush

METHOD

1 Quickly apply the glaze to the background, leaving a ragged edge (this is in case the edge dries out and you get a seam line – a ragged seam line is less obvious than a straight join).

2 Now bounce the brush up and down into the glaze. Keep wiping off the brush so that any excess glaze is removed from the brush and not returned to the paint surface.

3 When the area is completed, remove the masking tape and allow the glaze to dry overnight. The result is the soft look of an unvarnished finish. If desired, a coat or two of satin varnish may be applied.

Dragging

The technique of dragging is perfect for doors, skirting boards and architraves. If working on such architectural timber, use a 50 mm cutting-in brush (house-painter's brush). A plain door can be transformed into a panelled piece, simply by masking out each panel, dragging and then moving on to the next section.

To prepare for dragging, use a paint roller to roll the glaze on evenly

Jam the dragging brush into the glaze, feathering the brush out away from the surface you are working on

MATERIALS

Oil-based glaze:
- ☐ one part matt/flat enamel
- ☐ one part scumble medium
- ☐ one to two parts turps (white spirit)

Water-based glaze:
- ☐ two parts acrylic paint
- ☐ one part water-based scumble medium (don't use water unless the glaze is very thick)

SPECIAL TOOLS NEEDED

- ☐ roller to apply glaze
- ☐ wall-dragging brush with strong bristles

METHOD

1 Dragging requires two people working: one to apply the glaze with a roller and the other to work up the ladder. Roll the glaze evenly onto the wall in strips about 900 mm wide. Roll the outside edge constantly so that the glaze doesn't get a dry edge – this shows as a darker stripe.

2 Jam the dragging brush into the glaze between the cornice and wall and then evenly drag down the wall. If you are

on a ladder, just walk down the ladder without hesitating – hesitations will cause irregular stop-marks in the finish.

3 As you work down towards the skirting board, feather the brush out, away from the wall. Wipe the brush, turn it over to the other side, jam it into the glaze at the skirting board and pull it up the wall over the same area you have just dragged down.

4 Feather away from the wall near the cornice. This should be enough for good, strong drag marks. Continue around the room until each wall has been dragged.

Sponging

Low contrast is best for this finish, otherwise the room can look as though a demented animal has run across the walls! It is essential that you use real sea sponges as they impart a soft, subtle shape not possible with synthetic sponges.

MATERIALS

Oil-based glaze:
- ☐ one part matt/flat enamel
- ☐ one part scumble medium
- ☐ one to two parts turps (white spirit)

Water-based glaze:
- ☐ one part matt/flat acrylic
- ☐ one part water scumble
- ☐ three parts or more water

SPECIAL TOOLS NEEDED
- ☐ sea sponges
- ☐ 50 mm cutting-in brush
- ☐ round stipple brush

METHOD

1 Dip the sponges in water and wring them out – this makes them soft and malleable. Load one sponge with the glaze and apply to the wall in a random pattern – working an area about 900 mm wide at a time from floor to ceiling.

2 Dip a second sponge into turps (white spirit), or water if using a water-based glaze, and start to soften the harsh edges of the glaze. Move the glaze around a little, taking some into the background space where there is no glaze at all. This creates a feeling of depth, and creates another tone. Make sure that you work quickly and do not allow the glaze to dry up or you will have harsh join marks where you apply the next section.

3 Corners are a little tricky and it is wise to use a cutting-in brush or a round stipple brush to help you get into the join. The last thing you want is a strong white line running down the corners of the room. If you think the finish is too strong, follow up with an overglaze (see page 60).

Parchment Finish

This finish is best performed with the second glaze in oil-based paint and mediums. It requires two processes, but can be completed in one day. It gives a lovely, textured effect to the walls.

MATERIALS

First glaze:
- ☐ thick white acrylic paint, straight out of the tin

Second glaze:
- ☐ one part oil-based paint
- ☐ one part scumble medium
- ☐ one part turps (white spirit)

*Above left: To prepare for sponging load one sponge with glaze and apply it randomly
Left: Dip a second sponge into turps (white spirit) or water (if using a water-based glaze), and use it to soften the first glaze*

SPECIAL TOOLS NEEDED
- ☐ 75 mm bristle brush
- ☐ washed lint-free calico rags

METHOD

1 Take the bristle brush and apply the first glaze to the wall in a random, slightly basket-weave pattern. Allow as many brushstrokes as possible to remain in the paint.

2 Take a rag which has been wrung out in water, and move the paint around slightly, taking some into the previously untouched area. When you have finished, most of the wall should have varying areas of paint on it. There should be about 15 per cent only where the background is showing through. Allow to dry for one to two hours.

3 Take another rag and dip into the second glaze. Apply to the wall, patting on and rubbing, using a circular swirling motion. If you find you have applied too much glaze, or it is too dark, dip another cloth into turps (white spirit) and remove some glaze.

4 When dry, this finish has texture and irregular areas of colour where the first glaze has sopped up the second glaze. Make sure your application is reasonably even so that you do not have too much variation in the degree of colour.

Crackle Finish

MATERIALS
- ☐ eggshell sheen enamel
- ☐ masking tape
- ☐ matt/flat acrylic paint
- ☐ crackle medium

SPECIAL TOOLS NEEDED
- ☐ brush and/or ruler
- ☐ plant sprayer and water
- ☐ oil-based or water-based varnish

METHOD

1 The furniture to be decorated must be prepared with as many coats of background colour in eggshell sheen enamel (or eggshell acrylic) as are needed to be opaque. It is essential that the background is not porous and the background paint is absolutely dry before crackle medium is applied.

2 If you intend to use the crackle medium as an inset, such as on these drawers, first mask out the area with masking tape. Once the tape is down (always run your thumbnail along the edge to ensure good bonding), apply the crackle medium. It is viscous and should be allowed to flow onto the surface rather than be painted on in the normal manner.

3 Make sure that the piece is horizontal, as the medium runs if on an angle and can make a mess. Allow the medium to dry. This can take from one to two hours to

To complete the chest of drawers shown on page 56, first mask out the area for crackling with masking tape

Apply the crackle medium, allow it to dry, cover with the paint, then lightly mist with a fine water spray

Cut out the masking tape with a blade or you risk peeling off the newly painted finish

overnight, depending on the weather. Don't proceed to the next step until you are sure the medium is absolutely dry (it dries very flat and is often hard to see).

4 The paint used over the medium must be matt/flat acrylic. You can use a household acrylic paint, but sometimes good quality artist's acrylics are even better. Often a deep-tint base household paint will not crack so well because it is too heavily pigmented. You need to try your paint and medium on a sample board first. If you want coarse, graphic crackling, use the paint straight out of the tin, with random brushstrokes. There must be no pressure on the brush. The loaded brush must glide over the medium. Keep reloading the brush. Crackling occurs in the direction of the brushstrokes.

5 If you want the fine, cobwebby crackling to show, thin the paint approximately two parts paint to one part water. Once you place the loaded brush, or roller (for ease of application in this instance), on the dried crackle medium surface, it must merely glide over the surface and be reloaded constantly. Speed is of the essence. So, very quickly apply the loaded brush to the surface, keep reloading and reapplying, using absolutely no pressure. Having applied all over, cover with the paint then lightly mist three to four times with a fine mist of water from a plant sprayer.

6 The crackling occurs as the paint dries, which is almost immediately. If you wish to protect this finish, use oil-based or water-based varnish. Water-based varnish can reactivate the crackle medium, so be careful not to overwork it. However, once dry and matured for a few days, water-based paint is very strong and, unless the piece of furniture receives a lot of wear, it is not essential to varnish.

7 A fabulous crackled, aged surface can be obtained on walls by using this medium. To be held satisfactorily on a vertical surface, the medium must be thinned one part crackle medium to one part water. It can then be painted on to a wall (must be non-porous) and will dry without running.

8 The big trick with this wall finish is that the acrylic paint which is used over the top of the medium must be thick, otherwise crackling will not occur over the thinned crackle medium.

9 Once the medium is absolutely dry, the acrylic paint may be applied. It looks best if random brushstrokes are used and, again, the brush must glide over the surface so that the crackle medium beneath is not disturbed. In this case, the paint should be applied with a brush, not a roller. Crackling usually occurs in the direction of the brushstrokes, so bear this in mind as you work. Don't forget to cut out the masking tape with a blade, or you will peel the finish off the wall.

Overglaze

This will soften or brighten a finish.

MATERIALS
Oil-based glaze:
- [ ] one part matt/flat enamel
- [ ] one part scumble medium
- [ ] one or two parts turps (white spirit)

Water-based glaze:
- [ ] two parts acrylic paint
- [ ] one part water-based scumble medium (don't use water unless the glaze is very thick)

SPECIAL TOOLS NEEDED
- [ ] brush or roller
- [ ] stipple brush
- [ ] pieces of lint-free calico

METHOD
1 The finish on which you wish to apply the overglaze should have been allowed to dry overnight. Apply the overglaze with a brush or a roller, stippling to remove any brush or roller strokes, and then start texturing with a piece of washed, lint-free calico.

2 Allow some of the background to shine through. Do not cover the background completely with the overglaze – the application is simply to soften or enliven. Make sure you pick up any drips with the calico.

3 The overglaze will be absorbed into the background quite easily and you will find it adds a lovely amorphous quality to the original glaze.

4 Oil-based scumble medium is sensitive to ultraviolet light in that it yellows if covered. If you wish to move your pictures after they have been hung for a year or so, you may find that there are yellow patches on the wall. Once these areas are again exposed to ultraviolet

light, these yellow patches will disappear in about a month. The same applies to a furniture surface which has been finished with the scumble medium.

Ragging

MATERIALS
- ☐ base coat
- ☐ oil-based top coat (see Parchment Finish)
- ☐ turps (white spirit)

SPECIAL TOOLS NEEDED
- ☐ brush or roller
- ☐ lint-free cotton rags

METHOD
This is a very quick and effective way to achieve an interesting effect on a plain wall, using a scrunched-up, lint-free rag or even a plastic bag.

Top: Apply the darker colour to the surface to be painted
Above: Before the paint dries, break up and lift off the colour using a scrunched up clean, lint-free rag, leaving behind the ragging effect

1 You may find some team effort worth while here, as the effect depends on the top coat of paint being 'lifted off' just after it is applied. While one person is painting the top coat, the other member of the team can follow behind doing the ragging. If the top coat is allowed to dry too much, the effect will be spoiled as not enough of the base coat will show through after ragging.

2 Just after the top coat is applied, it is 'lifted off' by dabbing with a rag or something similar, exposing the base colour and creating an interesting crushed effect. The base coat can be of emulsion or acrylic paint or oil-based. Oil-based paints give a richer look than emulsion.

3 For the top coat, use oil-based paint thinned with turps (white spirit), or emulsion or acrylic paint, thinned with water. You can contrast colours or tones of the same colour, by applying a top coat that is darker than the base.

Simple Marbling

Marbled skirting boards can become a very attractive, decorative feature in an otherwise simple or understated room.

MATERIALS
Oil-based glaze:
- ☐ one part matt/flat enamel
- ☐ one part scumble medium
- ☐ one part turps (white spirit)

Water-based glaze:
- ☐ one part matt/flat acrylic
- ☐ one part water-based scumble medium
- ☐ one part water

SPECIAL TOOLS NEEDED
- ☐ 50 mm cutting-in brush
- ☐ 50 mm round stipple brush
- ☐ feather
- ☐ newspaper

METHOD
1 If you are working in a room 3 m x 3 m, you will need about forty pieces of tabloid newspaper. Fold each piece in half diagonally and then fold each side into a series of 25 mm concertinas.

2 Paint the glaze onto the skirting board and quickly stipple to remove the brushstrokes. Now, with an up-and-down movement of the newspaper, break open

Paint the glaze onto the skirting board and quickly stipple to remove any brushstrokes

Using an up-and-down movement, work with newspaper, folded in concertina fashion, to break open the glaze, revealing the pale paint base beneath

Work over the fractured area with a feather, loaded with a little white glaze, to make a pattern of veins in the marble

the glaze to reveal the pale paint base beneath. Move the paper sideways on the glaze, thus creating fractures, leaving virtually none of the surface untouched. The trick with this is that all the surface has movement to it.

3 Make sure that the finish runs at a diagonal of about 45°– it must not be upright. As each piece of newspaper becomes clogged with glaze, discard it. When the whole area is fractured, you can work it over with a feather, loaded with a little white glaze to add some veins. However, this finish will stand out very well on its own without the application of the veins.

Down to DETAIL

Stencilling

Stencilling is one of the oldest decorative effects and can be as simple or ornate as you wish. Traditionally, stencils were cut from oiled cardboard or even brass sheets and were regarded as a craftsman's tools. Today you can still use brass and cardboard stencils but inexpensive plastic stencils are now readily available in an enormous variety of contemporary and traditional designs. You can also design and cut your own stencil using a plastic sheet and tracing your chosen design with a chinagraph pencil or a fine, indelible, felt-tipped pen.

Before You Begin

❑ It is important to use the correct brush for stencilling – an ordinary paint brush will not do. Stencil brushes are flat-topped and are used by dabbing the brush down on to the area to be coloured, rather than stroking. This prevents paint being pushed under the stencil edges and smearing the design. You can use small natural sponges.

❑ As for your paints, it is best to use acrylic or special fast-drying stencil paint. If mixing colours to achieve a desired tint, mix enough for the entire room, as it is difficult to duplicate a particular colour

mix. Take care too that your paints are very creamy in consistency, so they will not clog the brush or sponge, but not so thin that they will run under the stencil edges. If you are stencilling in more than one colour and are concerned that the colours should not run into one another, paints can be dried quickly with a hairdryer on low force and medium heat.

❑ If stencilling with more than one colour, it is a good idea to cover with masking tape those parts of the stencil design to be painted in the second colour. Wait for the first colour to dry before stencilling with the second one and so on. This will stop one colour from bleeding into the other.

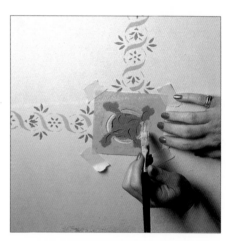

Top: Applying the first colour of the stencilled border to the wall
Above: Applying the second colour to complete the stencilled design

Stencilling a Border

MATERIALS

- ☐ suitable paint
- ☐ stencil brushes
- ☐ manila cards
- ☐ linseed oil
- ☐ turps (white spirit)
- ☐ sharp craft knife
- ☐ cutting board
- ☐ pencils
- ☐ plumb line
- ☐ spirit level
- ☐ chalk
- ☐ masking tape

METHOD

Make the stencil in the same way as for the Stencilled Floorcloth on page 74.

1 Paint the wall in the normal way. Then, using a plumb line and spirit level, mark the position of your border, marking both horizontal and vertical base lines.

2 Place the stencil on the wall, aligning its edges with the drawn lines and marking each corner of the stencil with easily-removed blackboard chalk. Continue placing the stencil along the guidelines, marking the corners along the entire length of the border.

3 Attach the stencil to the wall with masking tape. If you are using more than one colour, cover over any areas to be painted in another colour with masking tape to avoid paint overlapping.

4 Be sure to remove any excess paint from your brush or sponge before applying it to the wall. You will find surprisingly little paint is needed. Work in circular movements from the centre of each cutout area to the edges. Part of the charm of a stencilled decoration is the variations that occur in paint application, so don't feel compelled to paint until a solid block of colour appears, or to match one motif exactly to the next.

5 When the paint is dry, unmask the stencil and clean it if necessary. Then move the stencil to the next set of chalk marks and paint as before. Continue in this way until the border is completed.

Use this stencil design at any size you like. Simply enlarge it on a photocopying machine to your preferred size

Decorating with Wallpaper

There are not many do-it-yourself activities that will give you more satisfaction than wallpapering. And it really is easy!

Vinyl-based wallpapers (which come prepasted and ready to put straight on the wall) make paper-hanging so easy that even first-timers can produce quite professional results.

Wallpapering is particularly satisfying because the rewards are so immediate and dramatic. In just a day or two you can transform a tired bedroom, a bland living room or a problem hallway. What's more, the wallpaper comes off the wall as easily as it went on, so in a few years if you feel like a change – hey presto and it's a whole new look.

Use wallpapers and borders to inject life, colour, warmth and style into the gloomiest of rooms. Create a feeling of coolness in a room that becomes overheated easily and add warmth and cosiness to rooms that miss out on the sunlight.

Let your lifestyle and individual sense of design help you choose your wallpapers – and what a choice! Whether you are looking for a sophisticated city-style look for a new flat or a country cottage look for a house, there's a huge range of superb designs to cater for your taste. You can mix patterns and plains or even florals with stripes, paper below the chair rail or above it! It's up to you. One thing is certain – you'll have lots of fun!

How to choose your wallpaper

Most shops carry large 'libraries' of pattern books with entire ranges in a variety of colourways. However, you don't want to spend hours and days wading through sample books. This usually leads to confusion and much frustration!

Instead, take details of the rooms to be decorated, including their size; colour and style of the drapes, carpets and other furnishings; the direction windows face; colours of adjoining rooms. A good retailer will be able to show you an imaginative range of options. Don't be afraid to select something that reflects your personality and individuality. You could try one of the superb flocks: brilliant if you're lucky enough to have a chandelier. You might prefer a grasscloth – real or imitation – with its horizontal weave and texture which creates the illusion of the room being larger than it really is.

Still not sure? As well as pattern books, many retailers carry stocks of sample rolls and may allow you to take these home to see how the paper looks in the room it is destined for.

WHICH WALLPAPER TO CHOOSE?

❏ **Vinyl** is today's most popular wallpaper. Made from polyvinyl chloride (PVC) it is resistant to water and can be scrubbed with a soft bristle brush to remove most marks. It is usually prepasted.

❏ **Vinyl coated** papers have had liquid PVC applied to them, giving a more durable, washable surface.

❏ **Embossed vinyl** has been moulded to give a raised pattern and has a tough paper backing.

❏ **Blown vinyl** has a relief design effect, created by expanding the vinyl during manufacture.

❏ **Duplex** wallcovering consists of two sheets of paper which have been bonded for strength. It can be sponged but not scrubbed.

❏ **Natural papers**, such as grasscloth and silks, cork, wood veneers, burlap, are all made from natural materials applied to paper backings. Hanging them usually requires some degree of expertise.

❏ **Flock wallcoverings** are regarded as an elegant background for traditional decorating schemes. Finely chopped wool, rayon or nylon is applied to the design and coated with adhesive, for a luxurious velvet effect.

❏ **Relief papers** are usually white and not to be confused with the embossed vinyls or flocks. Relief papers include anaglypta, a great favourite in Victorian times. Anaglypta is made by bonding two sheets of paper then passing it through deeply-embossed rollers.

❏ **Mylar foil** is made from a resin. It looks like real foil but won't show creases after hanging.

❏ **Foil** is a thin, flexible metal sheet (often aluminium), laminated on to a backing of paper or fabric. Excellent for accent areas such as one wall of a bathroom or in a small hallway.

❏ **Murals** range from maps of the world to scenes of autumnal forests and tropical islands which can cover an entire wall, creating a feeling of spaciousness in small rooms.

Getting Started

Preparing the surface is important and well worth the effort. You should aim for clean, non-porous surfaces because porous surfaces 'steal' moisture from the paste, affecting its adhesive qualities. Different wall surfaces will require different kinds of preparation. Check with your local wallpaper shop for any specific instructions for your walls.

If possible, remove blinds and curtains, wall lights and, of course, prints and pictures! Give yourself the maximum room in which to work by moving furniture to another room or placing it in the centre. Use drop sheets to protect your floor coverings: old bed sheets are ideal.

If you intend papering the ceiling as well as the walls, do this first. If not, paint the ceiling and all woodwork before you begin papering.

Which room first?

Most people wallpapering for the first time choose a small room, such as the bathroom, in which to start…just in case! This is a mistake – you'll have a cistern, shower recess, bath, wash basin, cabinet and all sorts of other odd-shaped fittings to contend with and work around.

It's much easier to begin in a bedroom or lounge where the walls are uninterrupted, allowing you to quickly polish your skills. By the time you reach the bathroom, you'll be an expert!

Borders

Friezes or borders are very popular and have led to a revival of interest in all wallcoverings. To begin with, borders are inexpensive and simple to apply and remove. Success with a border will inspire a feeling of confidence and soon you'll want to paper an entire room.

The tools you'll need are the same as for wallpapering and the same rules apply for wall preparation as for wallpaper.

Measuring is easy too. It's all done in linear metres, so you simply measure the distance around a room. If it is going around a door, then measure the sides and top too. Most borders are sold in 5 or 10 m lengths so

Lifestyle

you get plenty for your money! They are often prepasted so you can use the water trough as you would with full-sized wallpaper.

Perhaps the most dramatic use of borders is at chair rail height. You can then paper below and paint above or vice-versa, or use two different but complementary wallpapers and have the border intersecting them.

You can apply a border over the top of wallpaper to provide focal points, or use a border to give added importance to a prized mirror, painting or print. You can even apply them to ceilings for a very distinctive designer look!

How much wallpaper do you need?

Walls		Distance around the room (doors and windows included)																	
METRES		8.53	9.75	10.97	12.19	13.41	14.63	15.85	17.07	18.29	19.51	20.73	21.95	23.16	24.38	25.60	26.82	28.04	29.26
	FEET	28'	32'	36'	40'	44'	48'	52'	56'	60'	64'	68'	72'	76'	80'	84'	88'	92'	96'
2.13 to 2.29	6' 10" to 7' 6"	5	5	6	6	7	7	8	8	9	9	10	10	10	11	11	13	13	14
2.30 to 2.44	7' 7" to 8' 0"	5	5	6	6	7	7	8	9	9	10	10	11	11	12	13	14	14	15
2.45 to 2.59	8' 1" to 8' 6"	5	6	6	7	7	8	8	9	9	10	10	12	12	13	14	15	15	15
2.60 to 2.74	8' 7" to 9' 0"	5	6	6	7	7	8	9	9	10	10	11	13	13	14	14	15	15	16
2.75 to 2.90	9' 1" to 9' 6"	5	6	7	7	8	8	9	10	10	11	11	13	14	14	15	15	16	17
2.91 to 3.05	9' 7" to 10' 0"	6	6	7	8	8	9	10	10	11	11	12	14	14	15	16	16	17	17
3.06 to 3.20	10' 1" to 11' 6"	6	6	7	8	9	9	10	11	11	12	13	14	15	16	16	17	18	18
		Number of rolls required																	

Framing Up

Bare walls just cry out for the decorator's touch and pictures are the obvious solution. The right frame for your picture and the arrangement of a group of plates can make all the difference. These are some very clever decorator's tricks for framing your prints or paintings.

Above: This charming collection of old black and white prints is not what it seems. If you look closely, you will see that the pictures, the frames and the ornate hanging bows and drapes are in fact applied directly to the wall
Left: Give new life to an old picture frame rescued from the junk shop with the use of a little gold paint and some fancy ribbon
Above centre: Another frame salvaged from the junk heap hides behind this border of glued-on shells
Above left: Frame a group of china plates by stencilling a pattern of bows and tassels on the wall behind
Far left: Follow through the folk-art theme of these hand-stitched samplers with rustic styled frames like these. It is important that your frame reflects the style and feeling of the art

Lifestyle

Forbo Pty Ltd

what's Afoot?

*W*hatever you choose for floor coverings, it will be a substantial investment, so don't rush into it. Quality ranges from the very basic to the luxurious, and there are attractive options at both ends of the scale and in between.

All about Floors
FEATURE

Carpets

Laying fitted carpets (wall-to-wall or broadloom) should be left to professional carpet layers but large carpet squares, rugs and carpet tiles are portable, easy to lay and can be repositioned to spread the wear. Fibres can be man-made or natural: acrylic and polyester, nylon, wool or wool blends. Nylon is durable and versatile, wool is a natural insulator and less prone to static electricity; stains, dust and burns are less noticeable. Popular wool-nylon blends display the advantages of both fibres. Pile also affects wear and appearance. Loop-pile is tougher than the plush surface of beautiful cut-pile carpets which mark easily. Combination cut-and-loop or sturdy cut-and-twist offer interesting patterns and textures. Modern, easy-care rubber-backed carpets are available in attractive colours and patterns featuring a variable density of pile for different purposes. They're durable and comfortable to stand on.

Right: Slate floors in one of the many beautiful colours available are an ideal choice for a kitchen floor
Below: Pure wool fitted carpet enhances the open plan of this lovely living/dining room

Ceramic tiles

This is the perfect choice for anyone needing a low maintenance, easy-to-clean flooring but their highly glazed surface may be slippery when wet, something to remember when choosing bathroom or kitchen tiles. Ceramic tiles retain heat in winter yet stay deliciously cool in summer. They come in different sizes, from the very small to the very large. Generally, large tiles should be installed by professionals, as should those on awkward floors where you need to cut tiles to fit around built-in units and plumbing. The amount you save by laying them yourself can easily be swallowed up in the cost of replacing badly cut or damaged tiles. Remember too, that ceramic tiles give you no second chance for that dropped plate or vase. If you are a bit of a 'butter fingers' or have small children, this may not be a wise choice for you.

Slate

The colours and textures of slate enhance any setting. It stays cool in summer and warm in winter. You'll need a diamond-tipped saw to cut slate but its irregular texture will camouflage accidents. You must allow time for slate bedded in sand and cement to dry thoroughly, then sweep away mineral salts before sealing. Clean with a mop and warm water.

Lifestyle

Cork tiles

A relatively short-term option for kitchens and playrooms, cork cushions tired feet and once sealed is easily cleaned with a moist, soft mop. Cork is less durable than vinyl and is generally only good for one 'recut' (resand) and reseal before needing replacement.

Rubber tiles

Brightly coloured, high-tech tiles that are easy to lay and cut into patterns. Noise-absorbing, they are ideal for playrooms, kitchens and other high traffic areas. Rubber is non-slip and impervious to moisture. It's kind to tired legs and easy to clean.

Terracotta tiles

Richly coloured, clay-based terracotta is an attractive choice and a sound investment, requiring little maintenance after sealing: just clean with a soft mop and a few drops of white vinegar in water. See the caution about early sealing of slate floors – the same applies to tiles. Do take care when working with tools or moving furniture as a dropped hammer or other heavy object can damage any highly glazed floor tile.

Above: For a truly dramatic effect, you can lay ceramic tiles in patterns like this one
Above right: The natural warmth of polished timber floors enhances any room setting

Coir, seagrass and sisal matting

Tough, grassy fibres wear well, have great texture and lovely natural colours. They're do-it-yourself favourites but moisture can cause mildew, rotting and unpleasant odours. Matting should last around ten years with regular cleaning to prevent fibre damage from built-up grit and sand in the matting.

Wood

Timber floors are beautiful and, once sealed, they are easy to clean, very durable and can be left unadorned or strewn with rugs. Timber strip floors are constructed from either hardwood (wears forever and comes in striking natural colours with little grain) or softwood (less durable but features lovely grain and knots, best for light traffic areas). Noise-absorbing parquet flooring panels are easy to lay and ideal for kitchens or family rooms. They wear quickly in high traffic areas and may need recutting and resealing about once every three years. Sweep timber floors with a soft broom and never use detergents or solvents on them. A few drops of fabric conditioner in a bucket of warm water, applied with a soft, moist (not wet) mop, can give a lovely finish.

Vinyl

Choose either tiles or sheets (in different widths) in a multitude of colours and patterns, including superb slate or marble look-alikes. Vinyl tiles are thinner and more brittle than sheets but are easier to fit around difficult angles, and errors are less expensive because you only damage one or two tiles rather than a whole sheet. Their coarse finish scratches easily, recovers slowly from dents and needs more maintenance: not a good choice for busy rooms. Vinyl sheets are denser and more resilient: they recover faster from furniture and heel impressions. Some sheets feature cushion backing while some have a built-in sealant. Sheeting is more pliable than tiles and easier on the legs in kitchens and playrooms.

Laying a Vinyl Tile Floor

Vinyl tiles are an excellent surface for kitchen floors, easier to lay than sheet vinyl and easier to repair by replacing individual tiles.

Before You Begin

❏ To do the job properly it is essential that the floor underneath is perfectly flat, achievable only with concrete slabs that have been steel-trowelled or finished with self-levelling cement, or with rougher slabs and floorboards that have been covered with underlay sheets. This second option is more accessible to most people.

❏ Underlay sheets are most likely to be of either masonite or fibre-cement, the latter being easier to lay, immune to water damage and giving a better, more rigid surface.

❏ Floor boards must be flat. If boards are badly warped the whole floor must be rough-sanded before the underlay can be fixed. Floor sanders can be hired and are worth the expense. Remove lumps from concrete with a cold chisel.

Note: Manufacturers supply information sheets that cover all aspects of this kind of job.

❏ When setting out the tiles, try to avoid tile edges falling within 80 mm of underlay joins. Avoid narrow pieces near walls and always use the cut edge against walls or cupboards rather than against other tiles.

❏ Use only the adhesive recommended by the tile manufacturer and follow instructions carefully.

❏ Use tiles laid loose to establish the longest perpendicular line through the room that will give an equal distance to the closest walls on either side. Use a chalk line, or a tight string line suspended between two nails.

MATERIALS
❏ tiles
❏ suitable adhesive
❏ underlay sheets
❏ nails

SPECIAL TOOLS NEEDED
❏ knife
❏ hammer
❏ notched trowel
❏ string or chalk
❏ disposable cloth
❏ steel ruler
❏ tape measure

METHOD

1 Start laying the underlay sheets in a corner of the room, keeping sheet edges about 3 mm away from the walls. Lay out all the sheets on the floor and cut where necessary before fixing any to the floor.

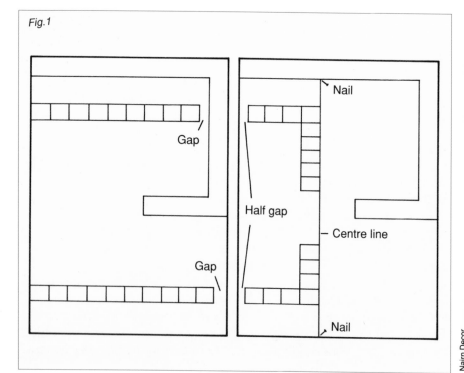

Fig. 1

Nairn Decor

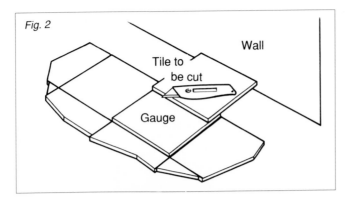

Fig. 2

Wall

Tile to
be cut

Gauge

2 Nail the sheets in place, ensuring that nail heads are flush with the surface of the sheets before laying the tiles. It may be necessary to sand the joints between the sheets if the floor beneath is really rough.

3 Sweep the floor carefully. Loose-lay tiles along and out from the centre line (Fig. 1), establishing what size the border tiles will be. Any one of these centre tiles can be laid first.

4 Using a notched trowel to spread the adhesive, prepare an area equal to about six tiles along the centre line. Place the tiles as close to their proper position as possible to avoid having to slide them. As each tile is laid, press it down with the palm of your hand and rub the surface firmly. You must assume that the tiles are cut perfectly square during manufacture so you should not allow any cracks to appear between them as they are laid. Immediately remove any adhesive which has spread on the floor or smeared the tiles.

Note: Boxes of tiles should be well-mixed before the first one is laid because you cannot assume that the colour will be constant from box to box. Selecting boxes with the same batch number when purchasing tiles gives some insurance.

5 When cutting tiles around the edges, lay the tile to be cut over the adjacent tile, making sure the pattern is the right way up. Then lay another full tile over the top and push it hard against the wall. You will now have a thickness of three tiles. Using the top tile as a gauge, score the second tile with your trimming knife (Fig. 2). Remove the top tile and cut through the second tile and it will fit perfectly into the space. Repeat this process until all edge tiles are in place.

6 Walk around for a while on the tiles or hire a roller, making sure that all adhesive is removed and that all tiles are sticking down well. Wait twenty-four hours before moving heavy items, such as the fridge, into place on your new floor.

Left: Easy-to-lay tiles make a great surface for kitchen floors

Above: Detail of the floorcloth showing all of the painted elements, including the borders, the chequerboard and both floral designs
Left: The stencilled floorcloth

Stencilled Floorcloth

Painted or stencilled floorcloths were popular in the 18th and 19th centuries as a cheap and colourful way to decorate the floors. Traditionally made of canvas and painted with housepaint, the cloths had a brittle surface which had a tendency to crack and discolour over a period of time. The availability of modern, fast-drying acrylic paints, and even specialised fabric inks, makes floorcloth decoration easier and gives greater durability.

Before You Begin

❏ When choosing your paints, it is advisable to use opaque inks, especially when printing on to a dark background.

❏ We recommend you make two chequerboard stencils because of the amount of stencilling to be done. The inks

tend to build up on the stencils during use, thus reducing the size of the design.

❏ For small areas, use either a small stencil brush or even a cotton bud.

❏ You can cut separate stencils for each part of the design or mask off areas to be painted in a different colour with masking tape if using a single stencil.

❏ Primed artists' canvas can be used and does not need undercoat.

❏ Planning on graph paper helps with dimensions and corner placement.

❏ The background or undercoat for this floorcloth uses a transparent base for opaque screen printing inks (available through screen printing suppliers) but matt acrylic varnish or PVA adhesive glue (1 part glue : 5 parts water) can also be used.

MATERIALS

The materials and measurements given here will make a floorcloth with finished measurements of 160 cm x 1 m.

For the floorcloth:
- ☐ 1.50 m of 180 cm wide heavy cotton canvas
- ☐ screen printing inks or acrylic paints in your choice of colours

74

- matt varnish (polyurethane) to seal the finished surface
- contact adhesive
- coloured pencils in the same colours as your paints
- 1.5 cm wide masking tape

For the stencil:
- one 11.5 cm square manila card for the corner flower design; one 22 cm square manila card for the centre flower design; two 20 cm x 40 cm manila cards for the chequerboard design
- linseed oil
- mineral turpentine (white spirit)
- fine lead pencil
- eraser for removing pencil markings
- stencil brushes (small and medium sized) or sponges
- craft knife or sharp blade
- board or piece of glass on which to cut stencils

METHOD

See Pull Out Pattern Sheet at the back of the book for the small floral and the chequerboard stencils. See page 181 for the large floral stencil.

For the stencils:

1 Draw two diagonal lines from corner to corner on each of the four blank pieces of manila card. The intersection of these lines indicates the centre of each manila card.

2 Coat both sides of each manila card generously with a 50:50 mixture of linseed oil and mineral turpentine (white spirit) and allow to dry. Remove any excess oiliness by wiping with a soft cloth.

3 To trace the stencil designs on to your oiled manila cards, position the corner flower design in the centre of the 11.5 cm square card and the centre flower design in the centre of the 22 cm square and trace.

4 Draw a grid of 2.5 cm squares on the other two pieces of card, leaving a 5 cm border all around the edge of each card. Try to keep the chequerboard measurements as accurate as possible. Cut out alternate squares of the chequerboard pattern. At the 5 cm border line, cut a notch in each edge of the stencil cards, as shown on the Pattern Sheet. These notches will help you align the chequerboard pattern.

For the floorcloth:

1 Cut the sheet of canvas to measure 180 cm x 120 cm. This includes hem allowances of 10 cm.

2 Lay the canvas out on a large flat surface, and weight or tack down the edges. Measure in 10 cm from each side and draw a fine pencil line. This is your hem marking.

3 Place masking tape *outside* this rectangle with your tape edge along the pencil line. Using your undercoat or background colour, paint the canvas inside this taped rectangle and allow it to dry.

4 Place a second piece of tape butting up against the inside edge of the first row of tape. Place a third row of tape, butting its edge up to the inside edge of the second. Remove the middle row of tape and put it aside for later use. This process will give you the correct size and location for painting the perimeter stripe. Cut away the tape overlap at the corners to give an uninterrupted border line.

5 With green paint/ink, paint the stripe between the rows of masking tape. Allow to dry. Before removing the masking tape, trace around the inside edges with a fine pencil line. This will be where you will begin your chequerboard pattern.

6 Position your 11.5 cm square piece of manila card in a corner with two sides of the card butted up against the inside edge of the masking tape. Trace around the outside of the card with a fine pencil line and repeat this procedure in each corner. This area will be used for stencilling the corner flower design.

7 Position your chequerboard design with the notches in the short side edges aligned along the fine pencil line. Using a coloured pencil to match colour 1, trace around the inside of your stencil in the areas where you wish to use that colour. Position the stencil for colour 2 and using an appropriately-coloured pencil, repeat the procedure.

8 Place the first chequerboard stencil back on the canvas, with the coloured lines as your guide and using a stencil brush or sponge, apply the appropriate colour with a dabbing motion. Allow the paint to dry and repeat the process using the second chequerboard stencil and the second colour.

9 When the chequerboard pattern is dry, position the corner flower stencils, matching the edges of the card to the edges of the chequerboard pattern. Paint in the first colour. Place the same stencil in the diagonally opposite corner and paint in the same colour. Paint the second colour in the other corners.

10 Position three rows of masking tape as before, this time *inside* the edge of the chequerboard design. Once again, remove the centre row of tape, and paint the green stripe as before.

Centre design

To make a placement line for the central flower stencil, draw a line lengthways, down the centre of the floorcloth. Place the larger flower design stencil diagonally on this line, with the stem towards the centre and as close as possible to the inner border pattern. Place a small mark on the cloth where one corner of the card is nearest the centre. This is important, as it shows you where to position the card for the next flower, which is one step closer to the centre. Apply the paint with a light dabbing motion. Repeat this procedure, starting from the opposite end. You should then have four flower motifs along the centre line, with their stems towards the centre.

If you prefer to cluster the flowers in the centre, draw two centre guidelines, one lengthways and the other across the width. Simply place the stencil in each quarter with the stem towards the centre.

To complete:

1 When all the stencilling is completed and the ink is dry, carefully iron the floorcloth with a hot, *dry* iron. You must either iron the floorcloth on the wrong side or use a pressing cloth.

2 Fold under the hem allowances and glue them in place, mitring corners. Place something heavy on the glued edges to ensure a good bond while it is drying.

3 Coat the right side of the floorcloth with two or three coats of clear lacquer (acrylic or polyurethane) to protect and seal. If you are planning to store your floorcloth, it is best rolled not folded.

Floor Finishes
FEATURE

If your floors are looking a bit sad and worn, don't decide immediately on covering them with fitted carpets. Often the solution to unattractive floors is a creative one, rather than a bank-breaking exercise!

Whichever method you choose, you will first need to fill all the knot holes with a proprietary wood filler and seal the finished, treated floor boards with clear polyurethane paint.

Bleaching

Bleaching will result in a much lighter floor colour that can be sealed with polyurethane paint. The method is most suitable for floors that have not been stained, as stain soaks into the fibres of the timber and is difficult to eliminate completely although bleaching can lighten an existing stain. If the timber has been treated with stain and a polyurethane sealer in the past, it must be first sanded back to the stained timber.

Ensure good ventilation while you're working, as the fumes from bleach can be irritating.

METHOD

1 Paint the floor with liquid bleach and allow it to soak into the timber. Continue to coat the floor with bleach until the desired lightness is achieved. This may be a slow process. After bleaching, wash the floor down with a 50:50 solution of white vinegar and water to neutralise the bleach. If the timber swells during bleaching, it is easily overcome with light sanding.

2 Seal with clear polyurethane paint following the maker's instructions.

Staining

Staining does not have to be restricted to the traditional wood shades – you can be quite adventurous with your colour choices!

METHOD

1 Select the stain colour of your choice. If the floor is new, or has been freshly sanded, apply the colour as the manufacturer directs.

2 If you have an existing stained and sealed floor, you will need to sand the floor back to a raw state, then proceed to stain with a new colour as the stain maker directs.

Floor finishes from left to right: Bleached; limed and stencilled; stained and stencilled; limed; stained

3 Once you are satisfied with the colour achieved, seal the floor with clear polyurethane paint following maker's instructions.

Stencilling

This decorative method of painting floors has stood the test of time! Creative people have long painted their floors, not only to save money, but to be able to enjoy a continuation of the design theme in their room. So often the floor is regarded only as a platform for the room, when it could be a decorative feature in its own right. Stencilling can be done over a previously stained and sealed floor.

Borders work very well on floors, especially as a frame for feature rugs. They can emphasise areas of the room, by giving visual definition to various sections, such as around fireplaces.

METHOD

1 Sand back the surface of the floor where the paint is to be applied sufficiently to give a rough feel. This roughness will allow the stencil paint to adhere to the floor without the risk of it flaking off.

2 Following our directions for stencilling on page 62, mark out where your decorated areas will be. When you are happy with the placement, draw in your guidelines and stencil in the designs.

3 When the stencilled areas are completely dry, seal with clear polyurethane paint following the maker's instructions.

Painted Floors

This method of revamping a floor works very well in low-traffic areas, or in rooms that have a large central area covered by a rug. You can paint high-traffic areas, but you must be prepared for the paint to wear away quickly in these areas. You may choose to paint with acrylic paints, wiping off the paint shortly after application in the direction of the grain using a lint-free cloth.

METHOD

1 Paint can be applied over existing stain and sealer, but you will need to sand back any obvious rough areas before starting to paint.

2 Be sure that you don't fall into the trap of painting yourself into a corner! Start painting at the furthest corner from the door, and work back towards the door.

3 Making certain that the floor is dust-free, paint the floor with several coats of oil-based paint. Sanding back lightly between coats of paint will encourage the better adherence of subsequent coats of paint.

4 Finally, seal the floor with one or two coats of clear polyurethane paint, following the maker's instructions.

Plaited Rug

Use up all your fabric scraps and leftovers to make this versatile floor rug. Folding and plaiting joined strips of fabric makes an economical and attractive floor covering.

Before You Begin

❏ Using fabric folders to prepare your fabric strips is not absolutely necessary but will make life a lot easier. These folders come in a kit from craft shops. They are slightly triangular in shape and funnel-like. The fabric strip is pulled through the folder and comes out with its edges folded to the centre and the width of the strip is crushed to a usable size. If working without fabric folders, press both edges of fabric strips to meet in the middle. Crush slightly as you plait.

❏ For most fabrics, 12-15 cm wide strips are ideal for plaiting.

❏ Fabric requirements can vary enormously for different thicknesses, but as a rough estimate, 1 m of 115 cm wide fabric will plait into a 30 cm square.

❏ Choose coordinating fabrics that blend well together and be sure to include a plain colour for contrast. While you will be plaiting with three lengths at a time, you can use more than three colours if you wish by joining lengths of different fabrics together.

If you use colours from your fabric scrap box, be sure to keep the variety spread throughout the rug and not allow banks of any one colour to predominate.

❏ Always plait with three lengths – four becomes too difficult to manage. Weighting the already plaited end while you work, allows you to pull gently and adjust as you plait. You could jam the end in a drawer, tie it to some nearby object or have someone hold it for you. You will soon find your own tension and best method for coping with the bulk and the strips waiting to be plaited. Some people find it easier to keep one of three strips shorter than the others.

MATERIALS
- ❏ fabric – generally cotton and wool types are best for floor coverings
- ❏ cotton twine for binding
- ❏ three fabric folders (if available)
- ❏ large, blunt flat-ended needle that may also curve at the end

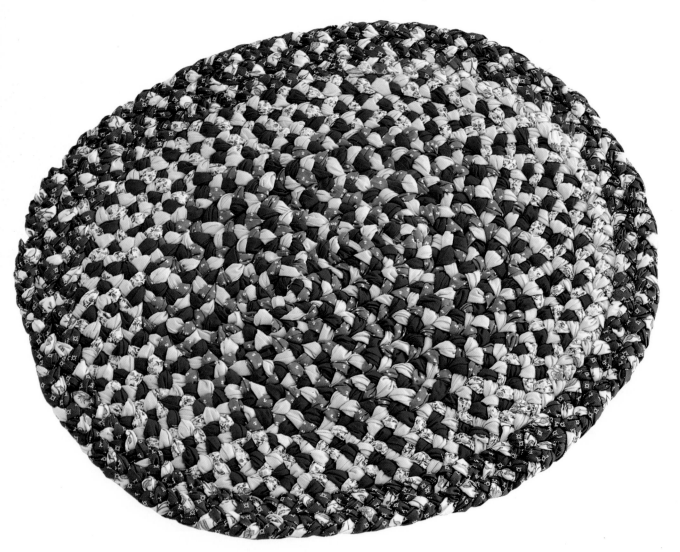

Two-deck-cushion sofa

Ottoman with attached cushion

Barrel-back chair

about the hours you spent replacing the 'insides' of your chair, but they will certainly notice the colour and style of the covers you have chosen.

Choosing the right fabric for the job and the room is crucial to a successful project, but the great variety of fabrics available can be daunting for the home decorator. The four natural fibres – cotton, wool, silk and linen – are all widely used in home furnishings:

❏ Cotton, which is mass produced and generally economical, is a popular choice for curtains, slipcovers and cushions.

❏ Wool is very hard-wearing, flame resistant, light and relatively waterproof. It is popular for furniture coverings.

❏ Silk is the glamour fabric but because of its relatively high cost is usually reserved for trimming, cushions or luxury pieces.

❏ Linen is one of the world's

oldest domestic fibres and because of its long-wearing qualities has always been a popular choice for home furnishings.

Many man-made or synthetic fibres are also available these days and are often blended with natural fibres. This reduces the fabric cost as well as taking advantage of the good wearing and washing qualities of polyester and viscose.

Colour and pattern

The choice of colour and pattern for a particular covering project will be determined by a number of factors. Are you decorating a whole room or will your new cover have to fit in with existing pieces? Is your room big enough to cope with that large splashy floral or will it be overwhelmed? Do you already have a strong pattern in that room? Do you

need to warm up a room with yellows, pinks and reds or do you need to cool it down with a blue or mauve?

Remember that colours can be affected by the light in a room, both natural and artificial. Before buying metres of fabric, take home a sample piece, drape it over your sofa or chair and leave it there for a day or two. Then you can judge the effect of the light in the room and how you think it will fit in with curtains, wallpaper and other colours and patterns in the room. Generally the larger your room the more you can get away with in colour and pattern. There are exceptions, of course, but as a rule of thumb, it will help you to avoid decorating disasters.

Matching patterns where fabric pieces join can be a nightmare. If you are not experienced, or endowed with the patience of

Job, you are probably best to stick to plains or all-over small prints, which do not need matching. Stripes do need careful matching but provide their own easy-to-follow guidelines. Florals or medallion patterns are more difficult because the motif has to be centred on seats and backs, wasting a lot of fabric. Checks are the hardest of all, having to be matched in all directions at once. Check before you buy whether the fabric you like will present matching problems. Lay two lengths side by side as though they were joined, then move one slightly up or down. Now stand back and see the difference. You can do the same test if patterns are to meet 'end-to-end' or 'side-to-end'.

Golden rules for choosing fabric:

❏ Be sure that the fabric you choose is suitable for the job you are doing. Don't let your enthusiasm cloud your judgement.

❏ Be sure your purchase is economically sound. Don't overspend on areas that don't warrant it but do buy the best you can afford, especially for high-use areas. If you have fallen for an incredibly expensive cushion fabric that you really can't afford, perhaps you could use just a little of it as a feature and team it with a less expensive background fabric.

❏ If you are going to sew soft furnishings at home, be sure that your sewing machine is up to the job. Remember, you may have to sew through four and five layers of fabric.

❏ Make sure you check on wearability, stretch and colourfastness before you buy. Generally the tighter the weave, the less the fabric is likely to stretch out of shape.

Fabric Know-How

Whether it's inexpensive cotton used extravagantly, patchwork quilts, lush silk drapes or antique tapestries born again as small cushions, fabrics make a statement about you and generally set the decorating theme.

You don't have to spend a lot of money – often it's the creative use of inexpensive fabrics that is the most effective. Remember, whether you're considering furniture or fabrics, good design doesn't have to cost any more than poor design.

The great variety of fabrics available to choose from can be daunting to the fledgling home decorator. Apart from traditional knowledge about fabrics and their properties, manufacturers today often have helpful information printed on the sample cards, telling you of a fabric's washing abilities and its potential for fading. They will refer to the 'wearability' of the fabric – or in other words, how strong it is! Pay attention to this valuable information. Fabrics are only guaranteed by the manufacturer if used in recommended situations.

The four natural fibres, cotton, wool, silk and linen are all familiar in home furnishing. Cotton has long been the leader for sheets, towels and most curtains. It's mass produced and this helps to make it inexpensive to manufacture into fabrics of many weights and textures. Wool is the basis of traditional and modern floor coverings. Wool is the best fabric insulator while being hard wearing, flame retardant, light and fairly waterproof. It is long-lasting, but take care with laundering. Silk has the glamour role, providing traditional fabrics for upholstery, tassels and braids, cushions and luxury rugs. Silk is a very fine and strong fibre, a good insulator, quite expensive compared to other natural fibres, and is the most lustrous fibre of all. Linen is the world's oldest domestic fibre. Sheets and household napery have always been made from linen, with its main appeal being its sheer endurance – it never seems to wear out!

Today you still have the choice of natural fibres, but also have access to the wide range of man-made or synthetic fibres. The most commonly used of these fibres are polyester, acrylic and viscose – all produced by chemical processes and all with valuable qualities.

Synthetic fibres are often blended with man-made fibres in fabrics. This serves two purposes – the cost is reduced, and very often the synthetic fibres give added strength. Synthetic fabrics usually wash very well, the fibres do not absorb dirt and moisture, and are long wearing. They also provide insulation and effective light control.

Slipcover Set

This easy-cover project may be the perfect opportunity to convert six odd chairs into a matched set!

Before You Begin

❏ This slipcover pattern is designed for chairs which are flush across the top of the backrest with no protruding knobs – all the lines and surfaces of the chair should be as straight as possible. Bowed backs and curved seats will not allow the fabric to hang properly.

❏ Choose your fabric carefully. You will need a sturdy material that doesn't present too many problems with matching patterns on adjacent surfaces. There is no set pattern because the dimensions of each chair are different.

Below: Take advantage of the great range of fantasy fabrics available
Bottom left: Cutting and construction diagrams

Laura Ashley (Australia) Pty Limited

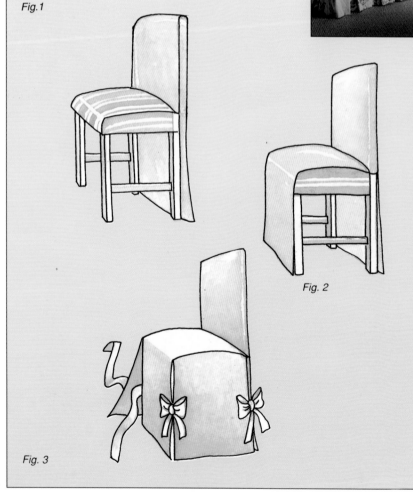

Fig. 1

Fig. 2

Fig. 3

❏ Measure your chair to calculate the amount of fabric and the pattern pieces to cut. Measure and cut the following:

Pattern piece 1: *length x width of chair* – length from the seat up the back and down to the floor (allow for the chair frame width at the top of the backrest) by the chair width (allow for the chair frame width at the sides). Cut one.

Pattern piece 2: *Depth of seat x width of chair* – the seat depth plus the distance to the floor by the chair width. Cut one.

Pattern piece 3: *Depth of seat + width of frame x height of seat from floor* – seat depth plus width of the timber frame by the seat height from the floor. Cut two.

Once you have established these measurements you can calculate the amount of fabric required.

❏ Choose a contrasting or complementary fabric for the lining as it is sure to show at the joins. If you like, the slipcover can be lined with the main fabric for an all-over look.

❏ For added comfort, include a layer of wadding between the main fabric and the lining.

BEFORE

❏ Using your measurements, draw the pattern pieces onto suitable paper, brown wrapping paper is a good choice, marking in significant points.

MATERIALS
☐ sufficient fabric and lining (see *Before You Begin*)
☐ matching sewing thread
☐ fabric or ribbon for ties

METHOD

1 Cut out the pattern pieces from main and lining fabric, allowing 1.5 cm all round for seams. Take care to match and centre any fabric pattern at this point.

2 On pattern piece 1, sew together from the top of the backrest to the seat (Fig.1). Press.

3 Sew pattern piece 1 to pattern piece 2 at the seat back edge (Fig. 2). Attach a pattern piece 3 at each side (Fig. 3). Press.

4 Make eight 30 cm ties out of scraps of cover fabric. Pin one end of each tie on the right side of the fabric just below seat height on the front and back edges, keeping raw edges even.

5 Make the lining in the same way as the cover. Place the lining and cover together with right sides facing. Sew around the outside, leaving an opening for turning and catching the ends of the ties in the seam. Turn the cover right side out, taking care to push the corners out completely. Press.

AFTER

Top: This easy-cover project has transformed a plain dining chair (Top left)
Above: Detail of side split and tie

87

Sofa Bed and Pillows

In the wink of an eye, this very clever sofa changes into a double bed for those unexpected guests. It would look just as good covered in a geometric print, denim or traditional mattress ticking.

Before You Begin

❑ The size of your sofa bed is pretty much up to you. We have used a double-bed size piece of foam, cut into four pieces. You may prefer to buy the four pieces already cut, if these are available.

❑ We have used foam that is approximately 15 cm thick. If your foam is a different thickness, adjust your fabric measurements accordingly.

MATERIALS

☐ piece of foam approximately 137 cm x 183 cm x 15 cm thick

☐ 7 m of 180 cm wide plain desuti, lightweight canvas, denim or heavy calico

☐ 5 m of 4 cm wide firm, cotton webbing tape or twill tape

☐ two pillows

☐ one double bed feather or polyester-filled continental quilt

☐ 12 mm wide coloured cotton tape, enough to stitch around the outside edges of the quilt and down each channel and around the pillowcases. One side of an average double quilt will use about 35 m

METHOD

1.5 cm seams allowed throughout.

1 Measure the foam and mark crossways cutting lines to divide it into four equal blocks – each approximately 137 cm x 46.5 cm x 15 cm. To cut foam, it is best to use an electric carving knife or jigsaw and to raise the foam up on house bricks.

2 Make paper patterns of the sides, ends, top and bottom surfaces. Add 1.5 cm seam allowances all around each piece. Cut eight side panels, eight end panels, eight top/bottom panels. Cut two pillowcases, each 1.75 cm x 50 cm.

3 Mark each one of the four foam blocks A, B, C and D.

To cover blocks A and D:

1 Take two side pieces and two end pieces and join the short ends together to form a strip then join the ends to form an open rectangular box (Fig. 1).

2 On the right side of the fabric, sew a length of webbing tape to one long edge of one side piece, starting and ending 1.5 cm from both corner seams, with the tape lapping over the edge of the fabric by about 2 cm (Fig. 1).

3 Pin the top panel to the box, matching corners to seams and stitch all around. Pin the bottom panel to the other side of the box and sew on three sides – leaving the taped side open (Fig. 2).

To cover block B:

1 Join side and end panels as for A and D (Fig. 1). Sew one length of webbing tape to one long side panel as for A and D.

2 Take a top edge of the opposite long panel and stitch it to the webbing protruding from block A, still leaving the seam open. Attach the top and bottom panels, still leaving the taped edge open. Turn the cover right side out.

To cover block C:

1 Join side and end panels into an open box as for B but do not sew on any tape. Stitch top and bottom panels to sides, leaving open one top edge and one diagonally opposite bottom edge of the long side panels. Join to cushion D in the same way as A and B. Turn CD right side out. This gives you two hinged pairs AB and CD (Fig. 3).

2 Handstitch the AB pair of cushions to the CD pair, by inserting the tape from B into the still-open seam in C, so that they will fold in an M or W shape when viewed from the end (Fig. 4).

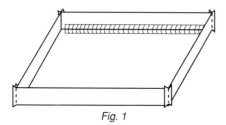

Fig. 1

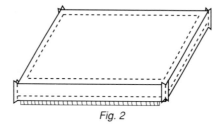

Fig. 2

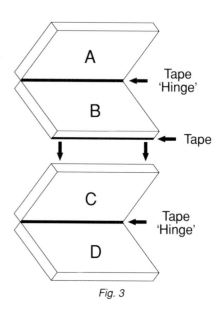

Fig. 3

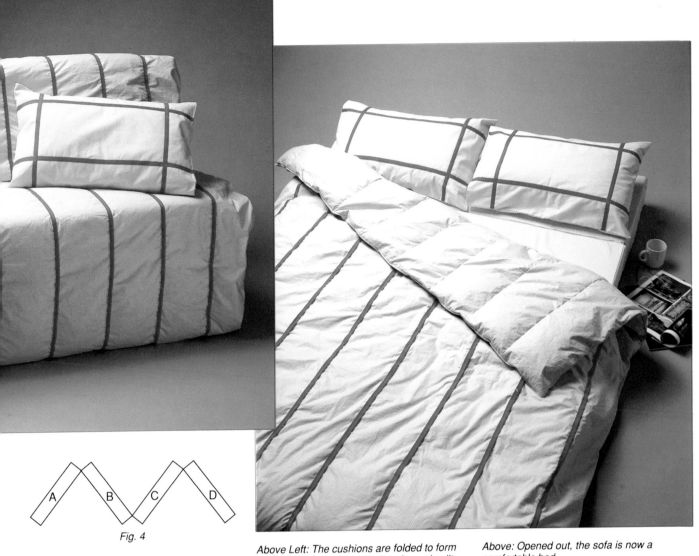

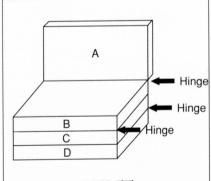

Fig. 4

Above Left: The cushions are folded to form the sofa and covered with the trimmed quilt

Above: Opened out, the sofa is now a comfortable bed

3 Ease the foam blocks inside the covers at the hinged openings. Fold under each opening seam allowance and slipstitch it to the tape, so that the cover fits snugly and the connecting seam is closed.

4 Placed about 10 cm from the wall, the top cushion flips up to form the back of the sofa and converts easily to a double bed.

For the pillowcases:

1 Turn under 6 mm on the short ends of the fabric. Turn under another 1 cm. Stitch down and press. Fold 5 cm under on one end. Stitch in place. Fold 15 cm under on the other end. Pin side seams. Match the two ends together and press. Remove pins.

2 Measure 12 cm from both folds and top and bottom edges. Mark these lines with dressmaker's chalk. Pin col-oured tape around the rectangles as marked. Stitch tape into place, mitring its corners as you go. You will have a border of tape on both sides of the pillowcase.

3 Fold the trimmed pillowcase as shown on page 177 with right sides facing. Stitch sides. Take care to secure the stitching well at the open end. Turn to right side and press.

Throwover quilt

We have decorated an inexpensive, purchased quilt for use with the sofa bed. During the day it provides an attractive cover and at night can be slipped into a single bed quilt cover. Stitch coloured tape around all the edges and down the channels of the quilt. You can stitch this on one side only or on both, as you prefer.

HINT

An easy way to see how the sofa hinges, is to tape together four empty audio cassette cases, marked A, B, C and D, according to the diagrams. You will find it helpful to refer to this while you are making the sofa.

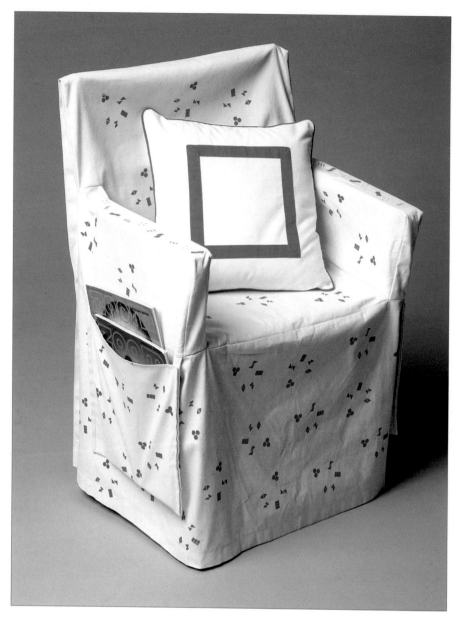

Director's Chair Cover

The director's chair has found a place in many households at one time or another. Reasonably priced, comfortable and easy to store, it can undergo endless transformations. This is a great way to dress up a director's chair. Whether you choose a plain fabric such as ours or a bold print, these inexpensive chairs will take on a whole new look.

Stencilled Director's Chair

Before You Begin

❏ Remove the existing covers from your chair and use them to estimate the fabric for new covers. Don't forget to leave seam and hem allowances. It is sometimes possible to buy replacement covers for director's chairs, ready for decorating. Before you buy, check that they will fit.

❏ The manila card for making your stencils is generally available from stationery suppliers. You can, of course, use firm plastic sheets if you prefer.

MATERIALS

☐ sufficient fabric, such as a lightweight canvas
☐ screen printing inks
☐ stencil brushes or sponges (one for each colour)
☐ two pieces of manila card, one 11.5 cm square for the flower motif and one 22 cm x 40 cm for the chequerboard
☐ mineral turpentine (white spirit)
☐ linseed oil
☐ craft knife or sharp blade
☐ board or sheet of glass for cutting stencil on
☐ eraser
☐ coloured pencils (as close as possible to the colours you are using)
☐ fine lead pencil

METHOD

See Pull Out Pattern Sheet at the back of the book for the stencil patterns.

1 Using the old covers as your pattern, cut new back and seat covers for the chair. Finish the edges, with overlocking, zigzag stitching or as you prefer, to prevent fraying, and mark the hem turnings. Do not sew the seams at this stage.

For the chequerboard stencil:

1 Mix mineral turpentine (white spirit) and linseed oil to 50:50 proportions. Apply fairly generously to both sides of the 22 cm x 40 cm manila card. Allow to dry. Remove excess oiliness with a soft cloth.

2 Draw a 2.5 cm squared grid on the card, leaving a 5 cm wide border all around the edge. Keep the chequerboard measurements as accurate as possible.

Cut a notch at the edges of the card where the 5 cm border lines meet the edges. These notches will be your placement guides.

3 Cut out alternate squares on the first line. Leave the second line. Cut the third line as for the first. Continue in this way until you reach the opposite border.

4 Measure 2.5 cm from each hem marking and draw a fine vertical pencil line. This will be the placement line for the edge of your stencil design.

5 Position your stencil on the fabric so that the notches are aligned along your pencil line. Using a coloured pencil in your first colour, trace around the inside of the stencil in the areas where you wish to use that colour.

6 Reposition the stencil for your second colour and repeat the above step, using the second colour pencil.

7 Position the stencil on the fabric, using the coloured lines as a guide. Paint in the first colour. Allow it to dry before stencilling with the second colour.

For the floral stencil:

1 Using the floral stencil on the pattern sheet, or your own design if you prefer, stencil the chair back panel. You can place the design any way you want, repeating the design on the chair seat also if you wish.

2 Prepare the 11.5 cm square stencil card in the same way as for the chequerboard stencil. Draw two diagonal pencil lines, connecting opposite corners of the card. This marks the centre of your stencil. Trace your design on to the centre of the card. Cut out the stencil. Using coloured pencils in the same colours as the paints you have chosen, draw around the elements of the stencil design.

3 Paint your design with a dabbing motion, completing one colour and allowing it to dry before painting with the other one.

4 When the paint is dry, iron the covers on the wrong side with a hot dry iron for about four to five minutes. This will set the inks so that they can be washed without the risk of your design disappearing.

5 Pin the hems at the marked turnings and check the fit before sewing. Stitch the seams as marked. Replace the covers on your chair.

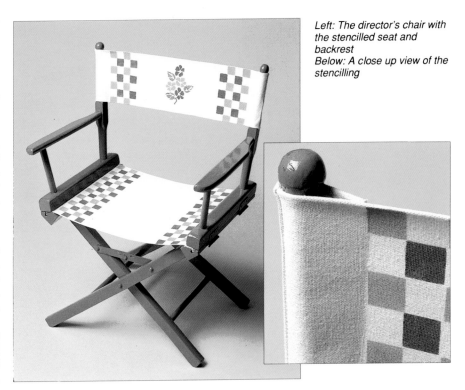

Left: The director's chair with the stencilled seat and backrest
Below: A close up view of the stencilling

Chair Cushions

Chair cushions are an easy way to add comfort and style to wooden chairs. Choose a washable fabric to complement your colour scheme.

MATERIALS

For each cushion:
- ☐ two 50 cm x 45 cm pieces of sturdy fabric
- ☐ polyester fibre for stuffing

For piped cushion:
- ☐ 1.50 m of corded piping (see page 174)
- ☐ 2 m x 14 cm fabric strips for ties

For walled cushion:
- ☐ 3 m of corded piping (see page 174)
- ☐ 50 cm x 6 cm fabric strip for wall
- ☐ 2 m x 14 cm fabric strips for ties

For frilled cushion:
- ☐ 4.60 m x 10 cm wide frill
- ☐ 2 m x 6 cm wide strip for closure strip and ties

Note: 1 cm seams allowed. Same pattern outline applies for all cushions.

Piped Cushion

METHOD

Pattern Outline:
See the pattern on the Pull Out Pattern Sheet at back of book.

1 Cut out two cushion pieces. Mark positions of small quilted squares. Make piping and attach to right side of cushion front as instructed on page 174.

2 Cut strips into four 50 cm lengths. Fold each in half with right sides facing and stitch around one long and one short end. Turn, press. Place ties at markings on right side of front, matching raw edges. Stitch along piping stitching line.

3 Place cushion back and front together with right sides facing. Stitch around edge following piping stitching line, leaving opening for stuffing at centre back. Turn cushion to right side.

4 Stitch around four little squares securely at markings. Stuff cushion, being sure to distribute stuffing evenly. Close opening by hand.

Walled Cushion

METHOD

1 Cut two cushion pieces as for Piped Cushion. Mark positions of small quilted squares. Make piping as instructed in Down To Detail on page 174.

2 Stitch piping around right side of each cushion piece.

3 Starting at a back corner, pin wall around one cushion piece over piping stitching line, matching raw edges. Determine where back seam should be in wall. Mark seamline, trim away excess fabric if necessary. Stitch seam. Stitch pinned edge of wall to cushion, following piping stitching line.

4 Make ties as for Piped Cushion. Pin ties on to remaining cushion piece.

With right sides facing, align remaining cushion piece on raw edge of wall, pin and stitch following piping stitch line, leaving an opening at back for stuffing. Turn and press. Quilt four squares securely as marked. Stuff cushion evenly. Fold in wall seam allowance at opening, pin to piping stitch line. Stitch.

Frilled Cushion

METHOD

1 Cut two cushion pieces as for Piped Cushion. Mark positions of small quilted squares.

2 Join frill strips where required. Fold frill over double with wrong sides together and raw edges matching. Gather raw edges together. With right sides facing and raw edges matching, stitch frill around sides and front of one piece. Place remaining piece over top, with right sides facing. Stitch around trimmed edges in frill stitching line. Turn and press.

3 Cut two 40 cm pieces from tie strip. Fold over double with right sides facing. Stitch one long side and short end. Turn and press. Stitch quilting squares securely as marked.

4 Centre remaining strip across back of cushion, matching one long side to one raw edge of cushion and frill ends. Stitch matched edge. Stuff cushion evenly. Fold over 1 cm on raw edges of strip. Fold strip over double and pin to close back of cushion, enclose raw ends of frill and form ties extending on each side. Stitch around ties over all folded edges. Press.

5 Stitch 40 cm ties firmly to extension ties where frill meets cushion.

Magic Quilt

These magic quilts fold up and tuck into a sewn-on pocket, making a pillow! Every sofa needs pillows and something warm to snuggle into – how convenient to unwrap the pillow and find a cuddly rug inside! Make another one for the family car.

Before You Begin

❏ Make your magic quilt from pre-printed cushion panels, joined to make the correct size, or a pre-printed quilt panel with extra fabric for the pillow section. You can, of course, make a quilt from plain fabric.

❏ Remember to allow enough fabric for two sides of quilt, plus two sides of pillow piece. The average large quilt measures approximately 1.55 m x 1.20 m, with a pocket 45 cm square.

❏ Folding the quilt may sound complicated but it's really very simple if you follow all the steps. This process can work

for any size quilt, just remember to have the pillow big enough for the quilt.

MATERIALS
❏ fabric
❏ polyester wadding to fit quilt and pillow

METHOD
Use 1 cm seams throughout.

1 Join cushion panels, if necessary, to create quilt front and back.

2 Baste wadding to wrong side of quilt front. Place back and front together with right sides facing. Stitch around outside edge, leaving an opening for turning.

Top: Folding Quilt
Above left: Open Quilt
Above: Quilt folded as a pillow
Cat toy is made following instructions on page 116.

Turn and press. Close opening by hand. Topstitch edge of quilt if desired.

3 Make pillow piece using same method as for quilt. Attach to back of quilt at centre of one short end by stitching around two sides and base where edges match, leaving top open. Note: If using different fabrics on front and back of quilt, be sure to make pillow in same way.

4 To fold quilt: Place quilt with front fabric facing you. Fold in one-third of quilt at each side on top of the centre third. Pull pillow from back of the quilt over to front so that it encloses lower section of folded quilt and exposes front fabric of pillow piece. Smooth out corners of pillow piece. Go to top of quilt and proceed to turn down folded quilt in sections of size of pillow piece, until last section folds neatly into pillow piece.

Table *tops*

*T*hey say that one of the pleasures of eating good food lies in the enjoyment of the eye as well as the appetite. A lovely setting of table linen will put the finishing touch to your meal – as well as your dining room decor!

Choose a colour and style that complements your china and your dining room or kitchen colour scheme.

Stencilled Cloth and Napkins

❏ Measure your table to decide on the size of your cloth by running a tape measure across the table and over the sides to the depth you wish for the overhang. Be sure to include in your fabric allowance, the tabletop measurement and overhang for all four sides. Sometimes fabric can be so wide that you do not have to join pieces to reach the required size. If this width is not obtainable, join strips so that the seams run along near the table edges, rather than one seam down the middle of the table.

❏ It is best to choose a one hundred per cent cotton fabric with a smooth finish for a tablecloth and napkins. Cotton launders well and is pleasant to handle. If you prefer the wearing qualities of man-made fibres, try using a polyester/cotton mixture.

❏ There are many ways to locate the stencil design on your tablecloth, depending on the size of the cloth and the design, and your own preference. You could place the design at each place setting, as a continuous border around the edge of the cloth or positioned to sit in from the edge of the table, as in the one shown. Bear in mind when positioning your design, that the edge of the tablecloth is not likely to be visible when you are seated at the table so much of the effect could be lost.

MATERIALS

For the tablecloth:
☐ Allow sufficient fabric to cover table top and desired overhang, plus 5 cm all around for hem

For each napkin:
☐ 60 cm square of fabric

For both:
☐ matching sewing thread
☐ manila card for the stencil
☐ mineral turpentine (white spirit)
☐ linseed oil
☐ lead pencil
☐ sharp craft knife
☐ board for cutting stencil
☐ stencilling paints
☐ stencilling brushes
☐ masking tape

METHOD
1 cm seams allowed throughout.

For the tablecloth and napkins:

1 Fold the fabric as shown in the diagram below, having the edge 'A' measure 8 cm and the hems all 1 cm.

2 Stitch across the corners, trim seams. Turn the border to the right side.

3 Pin and baste inner edge in place. Stitch down and press.

For the stencilling:

1 Mix mineral turpentine (white spirit) and linseed oil in a ratio of 50:50. Coat both sides of the manila card quite liberally with the mixture. Any excess oiliness can be wiped off with a soft cloth.

2 Draw the design on to the card. Cut out the stencil with a sharp craft knife.

3 Position the stencil on the cloth and napkins. Paint in first one colour and then any other colours one by one. Cover with masking tape any area that you wish to paint a different colour.

4 To set the colours, press on the wrong side of the fabric with a dry iron on a setting suitable for the fabric.

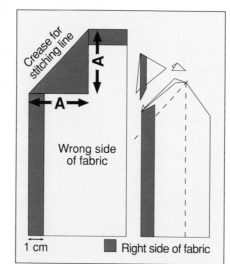

Above: Folding and stitching diagram for mitred corners
Right: The linen cloth and napkins stencilled to match the china pattern

Primary Brights

If you can sew straight, these place mats and napkins are just right for you. The skills involved are as simple as can be, and you will be delighted with the imaginative colour combinations possible. You could choose your own colours and even patterns to mix and match – black and white, pattern and plain, or simply crisscross the base with pretty braid.

Before You Begin

❏ One hundred per cent cotton fabric is ideal for making table linen. It washes well and is available in a wonderful array of colours. If you prefer a synthetic fabric for its wearing qualities, choose a cotton and polyester mixture for the best of both worlds.

Place Mat with Coloured Bands

MATERIALS

For each place mat:
- ☐ piece of fabric 50 cm x 34 cm for the base
- ☐ polyester wadding 50 cm x 34 cm for the base
- ☐ piece of fabric for the contrast backing 56 cm x 40 cm
- ☐ five strips of contrast fabric each 34 cm x 4 cm
- ☐ three strips of contrast fabric each 50 cm x 4 cm
- ☐ matching sewing threads

METHOD

1 cm seams allowed throughout.

1 Baste fabric base to wadding around the edges and through the centre to hold the fabric smoothly in place.

2 Fold in 6 mm on the long edges of each contrast fabric strip. Press. Using dressmaker's chalk, divide the base into 6 cm squares separated by 2 cm wide contrast bands and a 2 cm wide contrast border all around. Pin bands into place on base, weaving them over and under each other as shown. Stitch along both edges of each strip to secure in place.

3 Place trimmed base on to the centre of the contrast backing piece with wrong sides facing. Baste together around the edge of the trimmed base. Note that the backing piece extends 3 cm beyond the trimmed piece on all sides. This extension will form the contrast border. Turn in 1 cm on all edges of backing piece. Mitre the contrast backing corners as shown on page 96, having A measure 4 cm.

4 Fold extensions of the backing to the right side, enclosing the edges of trimmed piece. Stitch around the inner edge of the border, close to the fold and through all thicknesses.

From left to right: Bound napkin; quilted and bound place mat; bound napkin; place mats with coloured bands and matching napkins

Napkins with Contrast Borders

MATERIALS

For each napkin:
☐ 50 cm square of main fabric
☐ four 50 cm x 7 cm contrast fabric strips for borders
☐ matching sewing thread

METHOD

1 cm seams allowed throughout.

1 Cut the ends of the fabric strips to perfect diagonals. Fold in 1 cm on the inner (shorter) edge. Press.

2 Seam the strips together at the corners to form an open square. Press the seams open.

3 Place the right side of the contrast border square over wrong side of the main fabric piece, with raw edges matching. Stitch all around the outer edge. Trim the corners to reduce bulk. Turn the border to the right side and press. Stitch around the inner edge of border, through all thicknesses.

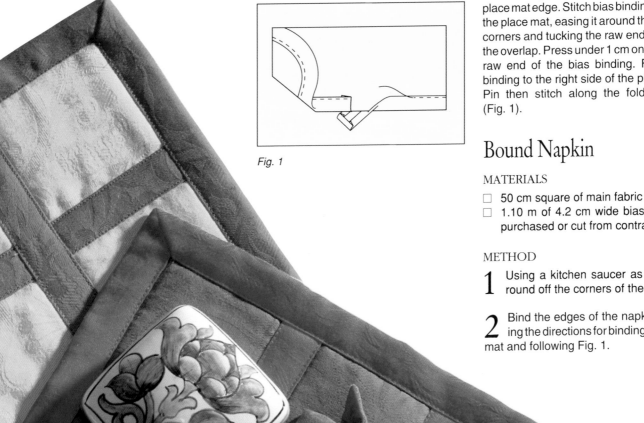

Fig. 1

Quilted and Bound Place Mat

MATERIALS

☐ two pieces of main fabric, each 50 cm x 34 cm
☐ polyester wadding 50 cm x 34 cm
☐ 1.80 m of 4.2 cm wide bias binding, either purchased or cut from a contrast fabric
☐ matching sewing thread

METHOD

1 cm seams allowed throughout.

1 Place the wadding between the two main fabric pieces, so that the fabrics are right side out. Baste around the edges. Using a kitchen saucer as a guide, round off the corners.

2 Using the photograph as a guide, divide the place mat into squares and mark with dressmaker's chalk. Stitch along the chalk rows to quilt.

3 Position the bias on the wrong side of the place mat, with right sides facing and with your stitching line 1 cm in from the bias binding edge and 1.5 cm from the place mat edge. Stitch bias binding around the place mat, easing it around the curved corners and tucking the raw end under at the overlap. Press under 1 cm on the other raw end of the bias binding. Fold bias binding to the right side of the place mat. Pin then stitch along the folded edge (Fig. 1).

Bound Napkin

MATERIALS

☐ 50 cm square of main fabric
☐ 1.10 m of 4.2 cm wide bias binding, purchased or cut from contrast fabric

METHOD

1 Using a kitchen saucer as a guide, round off the corners of the napkin.

2 Bind the edges of the napkin following the directions for binding the place mat and following Fig. 1.

Pretty Pastels

Create your own heirlooms! These place mats and napkins are sewn from lightweight pure linen – a timeless fabric that lasts and lasts.

Before You Begin

❑ All place mats and napkins, except B, are the same size and made in the same way. They differ only in the manner of trimming. The place mat and napkin B are trimmed first, then made following the Basic Sewing Method.

MATERIALS

For each set:
☐ piece of fabric 60 cm x 40 cm for the basic place mat
☐ piece 60 cm x 60 cm for basic napkin

For set A:
☐ embroidery thread

For set B:
☐ six different coloured sewing threads

For set C:
☐ a motif from a floral, cotton fabric
☐ matching sewing thread

For set D:
☐ silk braid or embroidery floss, suitable for hand-stitched couching
☐ matching sewing thread

For set E:
☐ embroidery floss in the appropriate colours for your design

BASIC SEWING METHOD
1 cm seams allowed throughout.

1 Mitre corners as shown on page 96, having A measure 7 cm.

2 Fold the fabric as shown on page 96, pressing in hems and stitching lines. Stitch across corners, trim seam, turn to the right side. Press.

3 Stitch around inner folded edge. Press carefully using a warm iron and damp cloth or ironing spray.

For trimming set A:
See the Pull Out Pattern Sheet at the back of the book for the place mat and napkin embroidery design.

1 Trace the design on to one corner of the mat and napkin. Embroider the outline using embroidery floss in your chosen colours and buttonhole stitch.

2 When the embroidery is complete, carefully cut away the fabric inside the embroidered outline using small sharp scissors.

For trimming Set B:

1 Press a crease 5 cm in from all edges on both the place mat and the napkin. Using this crease as your starting and finishing point, stitch six rows of twin-needle stitching across the mat and napkin using six different colours. Be sure to stitch your corners so that the stitching remains on the right side.

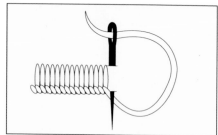

Fig. 1: Buttonhole stitching

C

B

D

2 When the stitching is complete, finish corners and borders following the Basic Sewing Method on page 100.

For set C:

1 Cut out a floral motif from a print fabric, allowing 6 mm fabric excess around motif.

2 Position appliqué pieces on the place mat and napkin. Baste. Stitch around the edge of each piece, 6 mm from the edge using a small zigzag stitch. Cut away the excess fabric, close to the stitching. Adjust your sewing machine stitch to a wider satin stitch. Stitch again over the previous stitching, enclosing raw edge as you stitch. Do this for each appliqué piece, using matching sewing thread.

For set D:

1 The couching design is worked at random on to the place mat and napkin, forming a border around the centre. If you are using a sewing machine with a braiding foot attachment, follow the manufacturer's instructions for its use. If stitching by hand, use small, evenly spaced stitches. You may like to use a metallic embroidery thread for stitching.

2 Lay the silk braid along the fabric, forming the curled design, and stitch over it, securing it to the fabric. (see below)

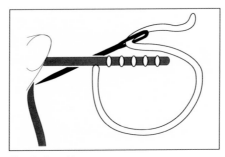

Fig. 2: Couching

For set E:

See the Pull Out Pattern Sheet at the back of the book for the pansy design.

1 Trace the pansy design from the pattern sheet on to the fabric using dressmaker's tracing paper.

2 Embroider the design as shown using long and short stitch (Fig. 3) for the pansy petals and leaves and satin stitch for the centre of each flower as shown (Fig. 4).

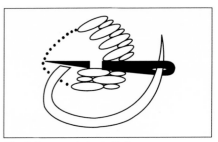

Fig. 3: Long and short stitch

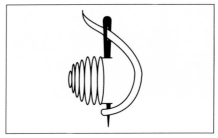

Fig. 4: Satin stitch

From left to right: Place mat and napkin sets – set C; set B; set D; set A; set E

Circular Tablecloths

Circular tablecloths are a pretty disguise for unattractive items that need to be nearby. There is no great mystery to making circular tablecloths. The secret lies in measuring and cutting accurately and then the sewing is just a straight line.

Left: Add flair to a plain cloth

Before You Begin

❏ Measure from centre of table, down to floor. Let's say this is 90 cm, just for this exercise. Add extra for hems if you plan to turn edge under rather than add a ruffle or lace. Take all hem trimmings into consideration when taking your basic measurement and add or subtract accordingly.

❏ Purchase four times this basic measurement of fabric plus 10 cm unless your fabric is as wide as twice the basic measurement, or your table is very small.

MATERIALS
☐ sufficient fabric
☐ trims and ruffles as desired

METHOD

1 Join your fabric to make one large piece, large enough for circle (Fig. 1, page 103). To do this you will need to cut two pieces each twice basic length plus 10 cm. Leave one piece aside. Cut other piece down through middle, parallel with both selvages.

2 Join selvages of these cut pieces to selvages of large uncut piece (Fig. 1, page 103).

3 To cut out cloth, fold prepared fabric in half (Fig. 2, page 103). Fold in half again.

Left: Plain cloth topped with a square Overcloth
Below: Overcloth with bows covers the plain tablecloth

102

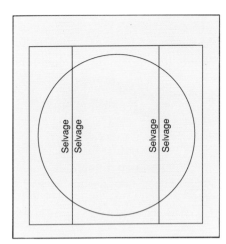

Fig. 1

4 Place one end of tape measure at folded point and swing tape around, marking out arc of a circle, making a line at the basic measurement point. Cut through all thicknesses along this line.

5 To finish hem, measure around cloth circumference to determine quantities for ungathered lace or bias binding. Use at least one and a half times this measurement if gathering lace or a fabric ruffle. A simple hem can be finished by turning under 1.5 cm on the edge and stitching narrow piping cord into the hem, using your machine zipper foot.

Overcloth

Before You Begin

❏ Plan how large you want the overcloth to be. Make sure the proportion is right for your circular cloth.

Fig. 2

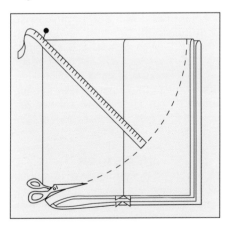

❏ Allow a minimum ruffle length of one and three-quarter times the outside edge of cloth. Strips of contrast or border fabric for ruffles can add a decorative note.

MATERIALS
❏ square of fabric for cloth
❏ strip of fabric for ruffle

METHOD

1 Join ruffle strips to make up required length. Gather one long edge. Turn over a narrow hem on other edge. Press and stitch.

2 With right sides facing and raw edges matching, stitch ruffle around cloth. Neaten all raw edges with zigzag or overlocking. Remember to pleat ruffle slightly at corners to prevent it curling inwards.

Overcloth with Bows

MATERIALS
❏ circle of fabric – you may need to join fabric as instructed on page 102

❏ fabric strip for ruffle
❏ bias binding
❏ elastic

METHOD

1 Make ruffle and attach as for Step 1 of Overcloth.

2 At quarter points on circumference, stitch a casing from bias binding 2.5 cm wide x 7 cm long. Thread elastic through casing making sure that outer end of elastic is sewn to casing at cloth edge. Leave top end of casing open. Stitch another length of elastic just above top of casing. Draw up elastic. Tie ends together to gather casing. Release elastic when washing and pressing cloth.

3 Using contrast or main fabric, cut lengths approximately 20 cm x 50 cm. Fold over double with right sides facing. Cut ends to a V. Sew around raw edges, leaving an opening for turning. Turn and press. Tie into bows and sew securely to cloth, over gathering.

Tea Setting

Beautiful embroidery is a feature of this dainty linen afternoon tea set. Keep the shapes and other trims very simple to allow the detail of the embroidery to stand out.

Before You Begin

❑ The embroidery diagrams are full-size. Use the whole design for the tea cosy and the traycloth but only use the single flower below the dotted line for the napkin.

MATERIALS
☐ Anchor Stranded Cotton, 2 skeins each: Rose Pink 048, 050; Muscat Green 0279; 1 skein each: White 01; Rose Pink 052, 054; Muscat Green 0280; Antique Gold 0890
☐ 60 cm of 114 cm wide cream medium-weight embroidery fabric
☐ 30 cm thick wadding
☐ 30 cm of 115 cm wide cotton fabric for lining
☐ bias binding to match one colour in Stranded Cotton
☐ Milward International Range crewel needle no. 7
☐ tracing paper
☐ dressmakers' carbon paper

METHOD
Cut following fabric pieces: one 35 cm x 30 cm for tea cosy, one 50 cm x 35 cm for traycloth and one 35 cm x 35 cm for napkin.

Tea Cosy

Pattern Outline: — — — — — —
See Pull Out Pattern Sheet at back of book.

1 Trace off floral design and transfer it to centre of one long side of one fabric rectangle, 6 cm from lower edge.

2 Work embroidery, following stitch diagram and key. All parts similar to numbered parts are worked in same colour and stitch. When embroidery is complete, press carefully on wrong side.

3 Trace tea cosy pattern from Pattern Sheet. Cut embroidered fabric to that shape. Cut two pieces of wadding, two pieces of lining and one piece of fabric for back to same shape. Trim 1.5 cm from all around wadding pieces.

4 Baste wadding to wrong side of embroidered piece and back. Baste lining over wadding.

5 Place front and back together with lining sides facing. Bind curved edge of tea cosy, joining front to back as you go. Bind all around lower edge in same way.

Traycloth

1 Trace off floral design and transfer it to fabric rectangle, 5 cm from left-hand edge and 6.5 cm from lower edge.

2 Work embroidery, following stitch diagram and key. All parts similar to numbered parts are worked in same colour and stitch. When embroidery is complete, press carefully on wrong side. Bind edges of fabric rectangle, rounding off corners.

Napkin

1 Trace single flower and transfer it to lower left-hand corner of fabric square, 4 cm from both edges, omitting flower stem shown in solid black in stitch diagram.

2 Work embroidery, following stitch diagram and key. All parts similar to numbered parts are worked in same colour and stitch. When embroidery is complete, press carefully on wrong side.

3 Bind edges of fabric rectangle, carefully rounding off corners.

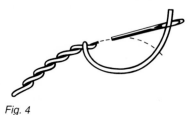

Fig. 4

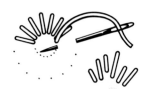

Fig. 1

STRAIGHT STITCH
Single-spaced stitches are worked in either a regular or irregular manner (Fig. 1). Sometimes stitches vary in size.

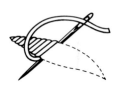

Fig. 2

SATIN STITCH AND OPEN SATIN STITCH
For satin stitch, work straight stitches close together across shape (Fig. 2). Running stitch or straight stitch can be worked under satin stitch to form a padding and give a raised effect. Take care to keep a neat edge.

For open satin stitch, work stitches slightly wider apart and do not have padding underneath.

Fig. 3

LONG AND SHORT STITCH
This is a form of satin stitch where stitches are of different lengths. It is often used to fill in a shape which is too large or too irregular to fill in with satin stitch. It can also be used to achieve a shaded effect.

For a first row, stitches are alternately long and short and closely follow shape outline. For a second row, stitches are worked to fit in for a smooth appearance (Fig. 3).

STEM STITCH
Work from left to right, taking small regular stitches along line of design. Thread always emerges on left side of previous stitch (Fig. 4).

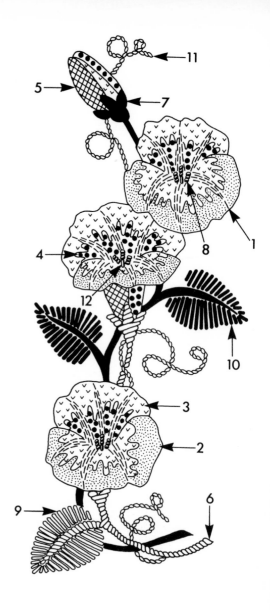

Full-size Drawing

KEY & STITCH GUIDE

Use three strands throughout

Long and short stitch:

1 01
2 048
3 050
4 052
5 054

Satin stitch:

6 0279
7 0280
8 0890

Open satin stitch:

9 0279
10 0280

Stem stitch:

11 0279

Straight stitch:

12 0890

Bindings
and
Borders

Today's fabrics provide wonderful opportunities for truly personalised household furnishings. You only have to wander through your local fabric shop to notice the ranges of coordinating and related fabrics available. Stripes to go with all-over florals, small prints to coordinate with florals, and perhaps another smaller floral to tie the whole thing together.

It's easy to be your own designer when coordinating these fabrics – use our examples for some inspiration. If no matching patterned fabrics are available, look at plains, small prints and stripes that match colours in other printed designs and develop your own coordinated look. Providing the colours match, quite varied prints can look very effective when combined, especially if you sprinkle some plain bindings and fabrics amongst them.

Braids can work magic on plain fabrics too, and rows of stitched ribbons, braids and laces in a toning shade can make a simple cushion cover into a wonderfully romantic decorating feature.

These coordinated looks are an attractive but expensive feature of some manufactured furnishings. You will see how easy it is to achieve these effects for yourself for very small financial outlay and some planning and imagination.

Place Mats and Napkins

Nothing sets the scene quite like attractive table linen. These designs are delightfully easy to make, and adapt to all sorts of fabric designs. Choose cotton or polycotton fabrics for easy care.

Place Mat with Self-fabric Border

MATERIALS
- ☐ main fabric 50 cm x 64 cm
- ☐ fabric 36 cm x 50 cm for centre panel
- ☐ wadding 42 cm x 56 cm
- ☐ 1.35 m bias binding or 3 cm wide fabric strip, folded in half lengthways

METHOD
Seam allowances of 1 cm allowed.

1 Centre wadding on wrong side of centre panel. If desired, quilt through all thicknesses with intersecting, diagonal lines of stitching.

2 Baste centre panel in centre of main fabric piece with wrong sides facing, leaving an 8 cm border around panel. Press under 1 cm on raw edges of main fabric piece and mitre corners to give a 7 cm border. See diagram on page 109 for how to mitre corners.

3 Turn border corners to right side. Tuck binding under pressed edge, leaving 5 mm of binding protruding. Stitch pressed edge down into place, stitching through all thicknesses.

Place Mat with Contrast Border

MATERIALS
- ☐ two pieces main fabric and one piece wadding each 44 cm x 58 cm long
- ☐ 2.10 m contrast fabric border of your chosen width
- ☐ bias binding or 3 cm wide strips fabric, folded in half lengthways

METHOD
1 Place main fabric pieces with wrong sides facing and baste wadding between them.

2 Cut two 44 cm long and two 58 cm long strips from border fabric. Press under 1 cm on one long edge of each strip. Cut ends to perfect diagonals and join together with mitred corners.

3 With right sides facing and raw edges matching, stitch border to main piece. Trim corners. Turn and press. Tuck binding under pressed edge of border. Stitch pressed edge down into place, stitching through all thicknesses.

Napkin with Contrast Border

MATERIALS

- square fabric 47 cm x 47 cm
- four strips border fabric 47 cm x 8 cm (vary width to suit fabric pattern)
- bias binding or 3 cm wide strips fabric, folded in half lengthways

METHOD

1 Press under 1 cm along one long edge of each contrast border strip. Cut ends to perfect diagonals and join together with mitred corners.

2 Place border and square together so that right side of border faces wrong side of square. Stitch together around outside edge. Trim corners. Turn to right side and press.

3 Tuck binding under pressed edge of border. Stitch pressed edge into place, through all thicknesses.

Napkin with Bias Trim

MATERIALS

- square fabric 47 cm x 47 cm
- 1.90 m bias binding

METHOD

1 Press bias over double, lengthways. Baste binding around edge of napkin, enclosing raw edge. Fold over one short end of bias. Overlap other raw edge at meeting point (see diagram).

2 Stitch through all thicknesses, being sure to catch both upper and lower edges of bias in seam.

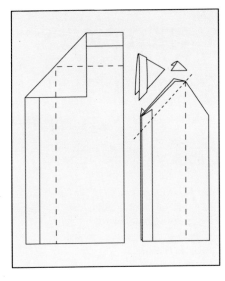

Above: How to sew a self-fabric mitred corner
Below: How to attach bias binding

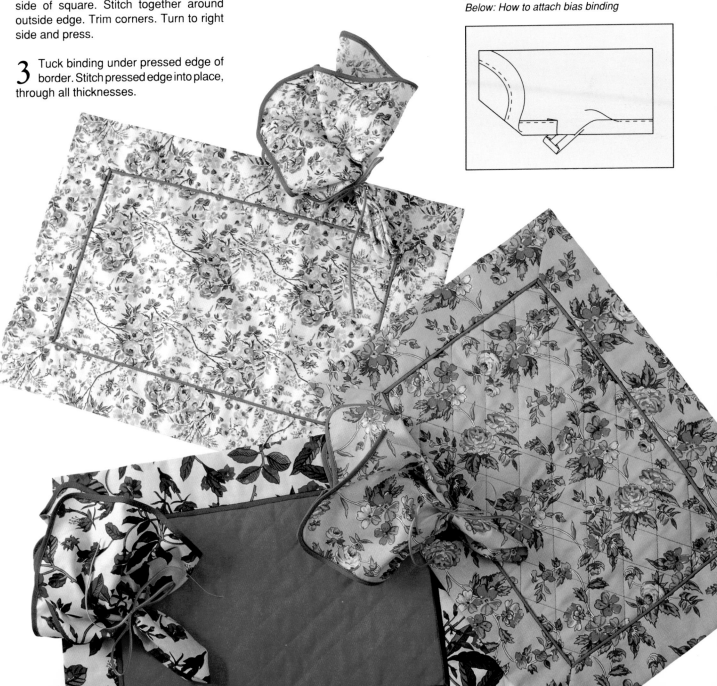

Centrepieces

There are many times when you need to decorate the centre of your table, and often these occasions arise when there's nothing pretty in the garden. All you need is a little ingenuity.

Candles in Pots

MATERIALS

- ☐ small terracotta pots, can be same size or various sizes
- ☐ wide-based candles to fit pots
- ☐ dried flowers
- ☐ ribbons
- ☐ silver foil
- ☐ sand to support candles and flowers, if needed

METHOD

1 If using sand, line base of pot with foil, place candle in pot and pour in sand. If not using sand, melt candle base slightly and place in pot, making sure it is secure.

2 Tuck bunches of dried flowers around base of candle.

3 Tie a bow around pot if desired. Place pots in a row down length of table or group them in centre.

Christmas Centrepiece

❑ Gather up all your materials before you begin and experiment with the design.

❑ A decorative option to consider is to spray the holly leaves gold prior to using. Dried oak leaves, real holly leaves or even plastic berry sprays look lovely tucked into the trimmings.

MATERIALS

- ☐ florists' foam wreath
- ☐ fresh or artificial holly leaves
- ☐ staple gun or strong sewing pins
- ☐ bunches of ribbon, tied into bows
- ☐ several candles
- ☐ gold spray paint
- ☐ masking tape

METHOD

1 Cover wreath with masking tape, wrapping it as you would a bandage. Spray with gold paint and allow to dry.

2 Make indents for candles evenly around wreath with tips of scissors. Attach holly leaves around and down sides. Spray with gold paint. When paint is dry, push candles into indentations.

3 Tie bows from ribbon. Push pin through knot of ribbon. Pin ribbon bows in amongst holly.

Painted Fruit on a Silver Tray

MATERIALS

☐ assorted fruit and leaves
☐ silver tray
☐ gold spray paint

METHOD

1 Wash and dry fruit thoroughly, removing any dust and moisture.

2 Place fruit and leaves individually on newspaper and spray with gold paint. Allow to dry and spray again if required.

3 Arrange fruit decoratively on a silver tray. Tuck spare leaves into folded napkins for a special touch.

Fruit Centrepiece

MATERIALS

☐ cone-shaped florists' base
☐ conifer or holly cuttings
☐ red apples
☐ metal meat skewers
☐ suitable tray

METHOD

1 Push one end of skewers through cone and push apples on to other end. Use as many skewers as you need to form a pleasing arrangement.

2 Tuck holly and conifer cuttings around apples. Place arrangement on the tray.

Country
Charm

*T*hese traditional, homely crafts
will bring joy and a whimsical touch
to your home. There are cats for the
doorstep and for your breakfast table,
simple ways with crazy patchwork
and a welcoming topiary tree covered
with pretty dried flowers.

Down to DETAIL

Stencilling

Stencilling is an old and lovely craft with many applications. It is the process of applying paint through a cut-out design. Stencils can be used on tablecloths, sheets, pillowcases, walls, furniture, clothing – the list is virtually endless.

Before You Begin

❑ Stencilling fabric is usually easier if you use a pure cotton. As the finish in some fabrics repels paint, wash your fabric thoroughly before applying any paint.

❑ For cutting out a stencil, use firm, clear plastic sheeting, such as plastic dividers for binders, or sheets of thick manila cardboard, coated with a mixture of 50 per cent turpentine and 50 per cent boiled linseed oil. Hang sheets up to dry and wipe thoroughly before using.

❑ Experiment first on scraps for fabric absorption and colour strength. Don't judge a colour until it is dry. To heat-seal colours, iron the back when dry or use a very hot hair dryer on the paint surface.

❑ Choose a paint that is appropriate for the surface you are stencilling. If working on wood, select a quick-drying paint with only a little water.

❑ If repeating a pattern, for example around a wall or across fabric, measure out each position before painting. Reposition the stencil accurately each time.

❑ Use masking tape to hold the stencil in place while you are painting. Be sure to keep tape clear of area to be stencilled.

❑ Stencil brushes are flat and thick, with a level 'surface', because the best way of applying paint is by tapping the brush down on to the space to be painted. Brush strokes can blur the outlines. Before painting, remove excess paint from the brush with a rag.

MATERIALS
❑ plastic or thick manila cardboard for the stencil
❑ sharp craft knife or scalpel for cutting stencil
❑ bread board or similar for a cutting surface
❑ stencil brushes
❑ paints
❑ masking tape
❑ fabric for practice and testing colours

METHOD
See stencil design on Pull Out Pattern Sheet at back of book.

1 Place clear plastic over motif to be copied and trace around design, or trace off design and transfer to cardboard. Cut stencils out using sharp knife.

2 Define stencil areas that will be the same colour by covering all other areas with masking tape. Continue to do this until whole stencil has been coloured.

3 Taking care to paint the elements in the logical order (main colour first then details), start painting from the outside, gradually filling in the entire area until you are happy with the depth of colour.

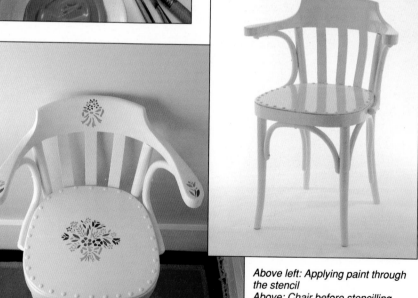

Above left: Applying paint through the stencil
Above: Chair before stencilling
Left: Finished chair

It is easy to isolate any part of a stencil to use on its own, or to repeat it to build up the total design. For very simple stencils, use only one colour, or one main colour and a very small amount of a second one. This makes stencilling simple indeed.

See instructions for making these simple curtains on page 25.

GLUES USED IN THIS BOOK

The variety of glues available throughout the world is extensive. We have used three different types of glue.

1   A glue gun, into which you insert pellets of hardened glue which are then expelled in a hot, melted form. This glue dries very quickly.

2   PVA (polyvinyl acetate) adhesive, available under numerous brand names. It is milky in appearance, dries clear and shiny and is non-toxic.

3   Spray-on glue. It is usually ozone friendly, but its fumes make it advisable to use in a well ventilated room. It dries quickly and allows for the item to be repositioned.

Country Cat Door Stopper

A welcoming country cat at your door – why not? These happy feline friends are so simple to make you can sew one for every room. If you replace the brick with stuffing, it makes a charming toy.

Before You Begin

❏ If the toy is for a child under three years, embroider all the features.

MATERIALS
- ❏ 40 cm x 115 cm wide firm cotton fabric
- ❏ 35 cm x 52 cm quilting wadding
- ❏ polyester fibre for stuffing
- ❏ house brick
- ❏ pair safety eyes
- ❏ embroidery threads for facial features
- ❏ embroidery thread for whiskers
- ❏ 40 cm of 3 cm wide ribbon (or a self-fabric tie) for neck bow
- ❏ small bell
- ❏ craft glue

METHOD
Pattern Outline: ▬▬ ▪ ▬ ▪ ▪ ▬ ▪ ▪ ▬ ▪
See Pull Out Pattern Sheet at back of book. Neaten all exposed raw edges. 1 cm seams allowed.

1 Place legs, head and tail pieces together in pairs, right sides facing. Stitch together, leaving opening for stuffing at chin and at straight, short edges on legs and tail. Clip curves, turn and press.

2 Stuff with fibre. Close head opening by hand. Turn 1 cm along open edge of legs and tail to wrong side.

3 Make darts in body pieces. Place body pieces together with right sides facing and stitch around side and top edges. Turn to right side and press. Wrap brick in wadding and place inside body piece. Fold in edges neatly under brick and handsew to secure. Stitch legs and tail into place by hand.

4 Attach safety eyes following manufacturer's instructions, or embroider eyes, nose and mouth.

5 Thread 9 cm lengths of dental floss or several strands of embroidery thread, stiffened with glue, through nose at markings for whiskers. Knot close to fabric to secure. Tie ribbon or self-fabric tie into bow. Attach just below chin by hand. Stitch bell securely in place.

116

Country Cat Place Mat

Make one of these delightful breakfast companions for everyone in your family. For an added dash of fun, make each one in a different, but toning, country print.

Before You Begin

❑ Cut out the place mat following the pattern on the Pattern Sheet for the Country Cat Door Stopper (page 116) but cutting the placemat 32.5 cm x 25 cm.

MATERIALS

For each place mat:
☐ tracing paper and pencil
☐ 25 cm of 115 cm wide country print cotton fabric
☐ 25 cm fine polyester wadding
☐ embroidery threads
☐ matching sewing threads
☐ clear drying craft glue

METHOD
See Pull Out Pattern Sheet at back of book. 6 mm seams allowed.

1 Trace off pattern for cat's body, head and legs from Pattern Sheet.

2 Using tracing as your pattern, cut two bodies, two tails, two heads and four legs from fabric, and one body, one tail, one head and two legs from wadding.

3 Pin wadding to wrong side of one head, one tail and two legs. Place remaining fabric pieces on pinned pieces with right sides together and raw edges even. Stitch around outside edges, leaving an opening for turning. Trim seams to eliminate bulk and clip corners for ease. Turn and press. Handsew openings closed.

4 Pin wadding to wrong side of one body piece. Quilt body piece in diagonal rows using a quilting guide, if you have one, or following evenly spaced lines of masking tape.

5 Place legs and then tail on body, overlapped as shown. Trim away any of leg that shows beyond tail and eliminate bulk wherever possible. Topstitch legs and tail in place, stitching 6 mm from edge.

6 Topstitch around head 6 mm from edge. Embroider facial features. Eyes and mouth are done in tiny chain stitches and mouth is satin stitch. Make whiskers from strands of light-coloured embroidery thread, stiffened with craft glue. Stitch whiskers through from one side of nose to other, making a tiny knot on either side to secure strands. Cut whiskers to an appropriate length.

7 Place remaining body piece on top of trimmed piece with right sides together and raw edges even. Stitch around outside edge, leaving an opening for turning. Trim seams, turn and press. Handsew opening closed.

8 Stitch head to body, stitching over line of topstitching.

9 Embroider a bow at neck, using tiny chain stitches in two colours to form stripes. Take care to curve stitches to look like ribbon.

Découpage Cat Boxes

For the ultimate cat-lover, these boxes can hold a variety of treasures including a brush, collar, bells, fluffy balls and toy mice.

MATERIALS
☐ firm white paper
☐ pencil
☐ tracing paper
☐ sharp scissors
☐ paints or coloured felt pens
☐ PVA adhesive
☐ soft paintbrush for gluing
☐ suitable boxes
☐ clear spray lacquer

METHOD

1 Trace cat outlines and colour them in with paints or felt pens. Cut out cats with sharp scissors.

2 Experiment with layout of cats on your box until you are happy, then spread adhesive over area cats will cover. Lay cats on glued surface, then paint another coat of adhesive over top. Continue placing cats, overlapping if desired, and covering with adhesive each time.

3 When adhesive is completely dry, spray with several coats of clear spray lacquer.

Crazy Patchwork

This is the easiest patchwork method known! You need a little patience assembling the pieces, but accuracy is not essential to achieve the overall effect! First make up your patchwork fabric, then make this cheerful cat teapot cosy and cushion.

Before You Begin

❏ Choose fabrics of the same type and weight to make laundering easier.

❏ Place the fabric pieces together in groups to see how they look side by side and alter the combinations until you are pleased with the effect.

❏ Where fabrics overlap, neaten the edge of the upper one – either by turning it under or by covering it with ribbon or lace. The neatened edge is then laid flat, overlapping the raw edge of the adjoining piece.

Patchwork Fabric

MATERIALS

❏ scraps of coordinating fabrics. These can be combinations of prints, contrasting textures, lace and ribbons, or bright shiny plains and prints.

METHOD

Allow 1 cm for seams, turnings and hems.

1 Decide on your patchwork pattern. Neaten all visible raw edges as described. Pin or baste pieces together.

2 Stitch through all thicknesses. Continue adding pieces until the required fabric size is achieved. Cut out pattern pieces for your particular project.

Patchwork Cushion

MATERIALS

❏ patchwork square 40 cm x 40 cm
❏ 3.20 m of 10 cm wide ruffle
❏ 3.20 m of 7 cm wide lace or 3.60 m strip of 9 cm wide lace fabric, hemmed along one long edge
❏ two pieces backing fabric, each 40 cm x 23 cm
❏ 30 cm zipper
❏ 40 cm square cushion insert

METHOD

Make cushion following directions for Frilled Piped Cushion on page 172.

1 To make lace-trimmed ruffle: Join short ends of lace and of fabric ruffle strips together. Hem both strips along one long side.

2 Place lace over fabric, matching raw edges. Gather ruffle strip and lace along raw edges, through all thicknesses. Place ruffle around cushion front with right sides facing and raw edges matching. Stitch through all thicknesses.

3 Make cushion back as instructed in Down To Detail on page 174.

Left: Patchwork Cushion
Below: Don't be alarmed if the wrong side of your work looks as messy as this

Cat Teapot Cosy

MATERIALS

☐ patchwork fabric rectangle 52 cm x 35 cm for front and back
☐ 52 cm x 35 cm lining
☐ 30 cm of 115 cm wide coordinating fabric for tail, legs and head
☐ polyester fibre for stuffing tail, legs and head
☐ 52 cm x 35 cm wadding
☐ embroidery thread and safety eyes
☐ 40 cm of 3 cm wide ribbon; small bell
☐ craft glue

METHOD

Pattern Outline: ━ ‧ ━ ‧ ‧ ━ ‧ ‧ ━ ‧ ‧ ━
See Pull Out Pattern Sheet at back of book. 1 cm seams allowed.

1 Make your Patchwork Fabric as instructed on page 119.

2 Cut out pattern pieces from patchwork fabric as directed. Cut front and back pieces from wadding as well.

3 Place leg and tail pieces together in pairs with right sides facing. Stitch around outside edges, leaving short straight edge open. Clip curves, turn to right side and press.

4 Stuff legs and tail. Take care not to stuff too firmly. Pin opening closed.

5 Place head pieces together with right sides facing and raw edges matching. Stitch around outside, leaving opening for turning at chin. Clip curves and trim angles. Turn to right side and press. Stuff. Close opening by hand.

6 Place front and back body pieces and body lining pieces together, with right sides facing and raw edges matching.

Stitch around curved edges of body and of lining pieces. Clip curves.

7 Place body and lining together with right sides facing and raw edges around lower edges matching. Stitch around lower edge, leaving a 12 cm gap for turning. Turn through opening, pushing lining up into body. Inside lower edge (on lining side) handsew lining to seam allowance to prevent lining rolling out.

8 Handsew tail and legs firmly into position. Overlap legs slightly at front and handsew to secure.

9 Embroider nose and mouth. Insert eyes following manufacturer's instructions. Stiffen embroidery thread with glue for whiskers. Stitch whiskers on either side of nose; knot close to fabric to secure. Attach bow and bell. Handsew head in place, securing at back and sides.

Topiary Tree

In days past, clever gardeners clipped trees, shrubs and hedges into wonderful shapes. Today the tradition lives on in these versatile, decorative trees you can make yourself – in any size.

Before You Begin

❏ Remember balance is important. Don't put a very tall tree into a small pot.

❏ The trees become quite top-heavy once completed; consider this when securing the base in its container.

❏ For miniature trees, use small polystyrene balls instead of florists' foam block and sharpened meat skewers or dowelling for the stem. They look wonderful as table centrepieces for special occasions.

❏ Topiary trees are ideal for special occasions and can be covered with small balloons, leaves or flowers.

MATERIALS
- ☐ assorted ribbons; strips of tulle; decorative fabric; dried flowers and leaves; nuts; shells; seed pods
- ☐ florists' foam block or ball
- ☐ nails; tissue paper; paper
- ☐ length of dowel or an attractive branch for stem of tree
- ☐ pot or container
- ☐ spray paint, if desired
- ☐ small quantity of quick-dry cement
- ☐ medium-weight florists' wire
- ☐ small wire cutters and pliers

METHOD

1 Hammer nails into sides of one end of stem and sharpen other end.

2 Lay paper across drainage hole in pot and stand nailed end of stem in pot. Fill pot with cement and allow to dry.

3 Wire up all trimmings into bunches and wind wire around stems. Paint any trimmings now. Tie bows or layer ribbon and wire layers together. Strips of tulle and fabric can be used as ribbons.

4 When cement is dry, pull centre of foam block firmly down on to sharpened, top end of stem. Start inserting wired trimmings into foam block, first building up a circular perimeter to act as a guide. This will prevent you subsequently having some bunches too far into or out of the circle. Remember to build up this perimeter from all angles – try to imagine you are creating a smooth, round ball.

5 When all bunches are inserted, scrunch up tissue paper or similar to hide cement and place pot into basket.

6 Rim of pot can be decorated with glued-on nuts, shells, dried flowers or seed pods.

Above: Pushing wired bunches of trimmings into foam ball
Right: Topiary Tree

Terracotta Pots

Simple, everyday terracotta pots are perfect for stencilled or painted trims. The naturally warm tones of the clay work well with a variety of colours in traditional motifs, reminiscent of folk art images.

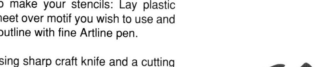

Before You Begin

❏ Examine the shape and features of your pots for inspiration. Many of them have grooves and lines which lend themselves to painting.

❏ Use both freehand and stencils for painting your pots. Stencils can be bought, or made quite simply from firm, clear plastic sheets.

❏ Don't neglect the inside of your pot. If you plan to use it for a plant holder, then paint just inside the rim. If you want to use it only as a decorative item, you can make the inside just as interesting to look at as the outside.

❏ Painting stencils is quite easy if you follow a couple of simple rules – keep the stencil still and firmly pressed against the side of the pot (masking tape can be useful here) and do not load your brush with too much paint at one time. Stencilling a curved surface can be a bit tricky, but is not impossible if you take it slowly.

❏ If you decide to keep your pots indoors, spray them with a clear lacquer to preserve and protect the paint and to give your pot a 'glow'.

MATERIALS
☐ sheets of firm, clear plastic
☐ fine Artline pen
☐ sharp craft knife
☐ medium round paintbrushes for lines
☐ small, natural sponges or stencil brushes for stencils
☐ acrylic paints
☐ old saucers to hold paint

METHOD
See Pull Out Pattern Sheet at back of book for additional designs.

1 To make your stencils: Lay plastic sheet over motif you wish to use and trace outline with fine Artline pen.

2 Using sharp craft knife and a cutting board, cut around outline, cutting away those areas you wish paint to cover.

3 Make sure your pots are clean and free of dust or grit. Place stencil in desired position against pot and fill in colour using a sponge or stencil brush.

4 Paint in any lines and grooves with the round brush.

Down to DETAIL

Folk Art Stool

The folk art tradition began in the 15th and 16th centuries when ordinary folk began to imitate the fine painted furniture and decorations they saw in their churches and the homes of the gentry. Naturally, the style and subjects of the painting have not remained static in all those years and differing regional styles have also developed.

Apart from linen cupboards, tables and chairs, folk artists painted dowry chests and storage boxes. One family treasure, the 'bride's box', was usually painted with a loving-couple motif, often surrounded by a romantic saying.

MATERIALS

- [ ] lidded stool in raw wood
- [ ] wet and dry sandpaper, 240 and 120
- [ ] tracing paper
- [ ] carbon paper
- [ ] pencil and ruler
- [ ] Roymac series 2800, flat brush size 8
- [ ] Rowney S40, round brush size 3
- [ ] brush for applying polyurethane varnish
- [ ] Matisse Water-Based Clear Sealer
- [ ] polyurethane varnish, oil-based
- [ ] Matisse Professional Artists' Acrylic Background Paint: AB Antique Blue
- [ ] Matisse Professional Artists' Acrylic Colours (Flow formula): AW Antique White, T Terracotta, P Pink (T + AW), YO Yellow Oxide, MB Mars Black, G Green (Y + MB)
- [ ] Matisse Oil Patina, BU Burnt Umber
- [ ] soft cotton cloth

METHOD

See pages 127 and 128 for the painting designs.

1 Sand stool with 240 and then 120 grade sandpaper. Seal with Matisse Water-Based Clear Sealer, following manufacturer's instructions. Allow to dry.

2 Rule a pencil line 40 mm in from each edge on top and long sides of stool. Paint one coat of AB around these marked panels, sides and inside legs. Allow to dry.

Raw wood stool – sanded and ready to paint

3 Mix a dark green paint colour with the round brush and paint a 2-3 mm line

around inner edge of panels and 20 mm inside edge of stool ends. Allow to dry.

Measure up and draw in panels for top and sides

Sanding the edges of the stool

4 With 120 grade sandpaper, dipped in clean water, sand lightly on edges and corners of stool where normal wear patches might appear. Wipe off scrubbings with a clean, damp, cotton cloth as you go.

Above: Transferring the oval design
Right: Folk art painting can be used to decorate many different objects

5 Trace in inner and outer outlines of oval-shape for stool lid and transfer them to centre of stool top. Paint them in a dark mix of G. Allow to dry then draw in flowers and leaves.

6 Paint leaves over dark G oval in a medium G. Paint S strokes of leaves with a shading of YO on inside and MB on outside. Paint in flowers, following Painting Flowers guide below. Allow to dry

Painting the side panel

7 Trace floral design for sides of stool. Transfer designs to stool. Paint in leaves, stems and calyxes, using medium G and round brush. Paint in flowers following Painting Flowers guide below. Allow to dry.

Adding the antique finish

8 Leave painting to dry for a day or so. Make a pad or wad with a soft cloth and place a line of BU about 10 mm long on it. Wipe evenly over entire stool with pad, adding another 10 mm line of BU as necessary. Wipe back colour to desired depth, leaving it darker at edges and lighter in centres. Allow to dry completely. Drying time will depend on thickness of oil patina and degree of humidity.

9 Apply several coats of polyurethane varnish, allowing each coat to dry before applying next coat.

PAINTING FLOWERS

Roses
Using round brush and T, paint a large circle and one comma petal on dark side. Mix T and G and paint a dark hollow in mouth of rose, blending in top edge to soften line. Load brush with P, then dip it into fresh AW. Starting at mid-front of rose, under hollow, press point of brush down so colours blend and make a comma stroke by lifting brush slowly as you follow edge of hollow up and around. Make another comma under first one. Repeat for other side of rose, varying amount of white as shown. Paint three more commas under bowl of rose in same way.

Blue flowers
Load brush with AB and then dip it into fresh AW. For each petal, paint one curved stroke to left and another to right giving a variegated colour. Centre is a circle of T with a highlight of YO.

Yellow flowers
These are painted in same way as blue flowers, using YO and AW. Centre is T with a shadow of dark G.

S Stroke

Comma Stroke

126

Painting design for stool sides

127

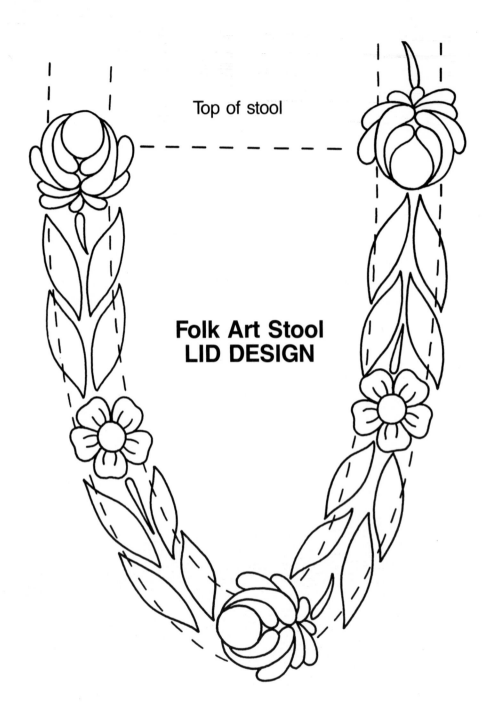

Top of stool

**Folk Art Stool
LID DESIGN**

Painting design for stool top

Stencilled Rug

These stencilled rugs are easily made with the creative use of masking tape to form a stencil. The instructions cover the general method and some tips for decorative options and methods.

Before You Begin

❏ Decide on your design before you start painting. It can be as complex as an all-over tartan pattern covering the whole rug, or a simple border of two lines around the perimeter of the rug. Practise on big sheets of paper until you get it just right. Whichever way you decide to proceed, make sure you prepare the simple equipment first, as it is difficult to alter patterns once you have started to paint.

❏ Use a sponge for colouring the rug. While paintbrushes are suitable, the results are not as even. Be adventurous with your use of colour – often these rugs provide a way of tying together a previously difficult colour scheme.

❏ Use acrylic, water-based paints. You can use the same paint as for your walls or even children's school paints. Oil paints can be messy and take too long to dry.

❏ Don't have too much paint on the sponge. Transfer some paint to a saucer – this allows you to scrape the sponge lightly across the saucer's edge to remove excess. Gently dab the paint in the areas to be coloured – you will soon see how much pressure is necessary to create the effect you desire. The surface of the matting will prevent total absorption – another good reason not to have too much paint on the sponge as it could run off into spaces not sealed by tape and spoil your outline.

MATERIALS
☐ seagrass, coir or similar matting made from natural grasses
☐ masking tape of different widths
☐ acrylic paints
☐ small natural sponges
☐ rug-sized sheets of scrap paper for practising your patterns

Above right: Applying paint with a sponge
Right: Sticking down masking tape
Below: Stencilled Rug

METHOD

1 Choose a design. Press masking tape securely on to matting to outline it.

2 Completely fill in the areas to be coloured with paint. Allow to dry thoroughly, then peel off masking tape.

3 You can paint over rug with a clear lacquer semi-gloss paint to seal it but this is not absolutely necessary.

Country
kitchen

*T*raditionally, a country kitchen
shines with the warm patina of
polished timbers, slate or tile floors and
an abundance of those small 'country'
touches. These include wreaths of dried
flowers; bowls of fruit and vegetables;
collections of old china or cooking
implements displayed on open shelves
or in an old dresser, and a pot holder,
curtains, place mats and so on, made
from a pretty, small-print fabric.
You may not be in a position to scrap
your existing kitchen and start again
but you can add those clever details
that will give your kitchen decor a
country feel. Try your hand at the old
craft of paper pricking and then apply
it to your kitchen shelves. Sew our
collection of fabric bits and pieces and
don't forget the matching curtains. If
your kitchen has suitable walls, adding
an old-fashioned stencil border is a great
finishing touch.

Pierced or Pricked Paper

This is one of the simplest crafts around and you don't need any glues, paints or special tools. You can use many types of paper, for example, writing papers, shelf trims, gift wrapping and even old greeting cards.

Before You Begin

❏ Use a firm type of paper but one that is not too rigid, as the indentations will be hard to make.

❏ This technique is also good for trimming writing paper. Large holes can sometimes be attractive in amongst a design, and these are created with the single-hole paper punch.

MATERIALS

☐ suitable paper
☐ a sharp darning needle or a noticeboard pin which has a portion of plastic at its base, for making the holes
☐ a sheet of soft particle board for resting the paper on
☐ dressmaker's pins to hold the paper and design sheet in place on the particle board
☐ a single-hole paper punch used to make the larger holes
☐ a design to use as a pattern

METHOD

1 Place the paper on to the particle board. Position the decorative pattern over the paper. Secure the two layers together by pinning through the design in several places so that the hole you make becomes part of the design.

2 Continue to pierce the paper, following the pattern. Make the indentations about 3 mm apart, and try to keep them evenly spaced.

Above: Pricked paper shelf edging
Left: A country kitchen with all the trimmings
Below: Pricking diagram for the shelf edging

Decorative Shelf Papers

Before You Begin

❏ You will need firm paper of a size which covers the shelf and allows the desired drop over the front of the shelf.

❏ You will have both raised 'bumps' and a flat surface resulting from the paper being pierced. Decide which side you wish to have as your right side. If you wish to have a combination of both you will need to flip the paper over and reposition the pattern while you work.

METHOD

1 Place the design to be pierced just in from the edge of the paper, then continue, following the general instructions for paper pricking on this page.

2 Cut the paper away to within 5-6 mm of the outside edge of the design to give the shelf paper an interesting edge.

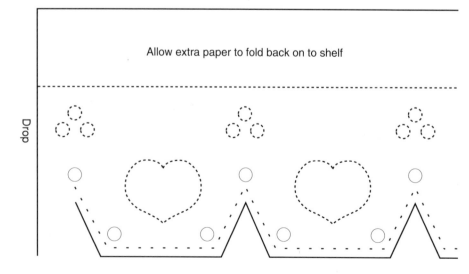

Allow extra paper to fold back on to shelf

Drop

Quilted Kitchen Set

You will see that all of these pieces use prequilted fabric, teamed with the matching unquilted material, or you can quilt your own fabric. To do this, baste a piece of polyester wadding to the wrong side of your plain fabric and stitch over it with a pattern of diagonal rows of stitches.

Pot Holder

MATERIALS

- two pieces of prequilted cotton main fabric, each 90 cm x 20 cm or plain fabric and polyester wadding in the same size
- two pieces 23 cm x 20 cm main fabric and two pieces of the same size from a contrasting cotton fabric for hand pieces
- 3 m of corded piping
- matching sewing thread

METHOD

1 cm seams allowed throughout.

1 Quilt fabric, if necessary, following the instructions on How To Quilt Fabric in the box on page 134.

2 Sew corded piping to one 20 cm edge of each main fabric hand piece, with right sides facing and raw edges matching. Pin lining hand pieces over trimmed pieces, with right sides facing and raw edges matching. Stitch the 20 cm seam following previous stitching. Turn the hand pieces right sides out and press.

3 Place the trimmed hand pieces at opposite ends of one main piece, with raw edges matching. Pin in place, then place remaining main piece on top of pinned main piece, so that raw edges are matching. Pin through all thicknesses. Using a kitchen cup as a guide, round off the corners of the pot holder. Remove untrimmed main piece.

4 Pin corded piping around all the edges on the right side of the trimmed main piece, clipping the seam allowance of the piping where needed. Overlap the ends. Pull a little cord out of the piping and cut it off to eliminate bulk. Stitch around piping.

5 Place remaining main piece over trimmed piece, with right sides facing and raw edges matching. Stitch, following the previous stitching, leaving an opening for turning. Clip seams. Turn pot holder to right side and press. Handsew opening closed.

Left: Pretty and practical, this quilted pot holder is an essential in any country kitchen. Remember to use a crisp, cotton fabric in a traditional small print and to trim it with contrasting binding

Tea Cosy

❏ Measure your teapot to be sure that our tea cosy will fit. Adjust the size if necessary.

MATERIALS

- two pieces of prequilted cotton main fabric and two pieces of lining fabric each 37 cm x 28 cm, or plain fabric and polyester wadding in the same size
- 1.80 m of corded piping
- matching sewing thread

METHOD

1 cm seams allowed throughout.

1 Quilt fabric if necessary following instructions on How To Quilt Fabric in the box on page 134.

2 Using a kitchen cup as a guide, round off the two top corners of each main and lining fabric piece. Pin corded piping around the edge of the right side of one main fabric piece with raw edges matching and right sides facing. Stitch piping in place. Clip seam allowance of piping where necessary, for ease.

3 Place remaining main fabric piece over the trimmed piece, with raw edges matching and right sides facing. Stitch, following the previous stitching.

4 Pin piping around the bottom of the right side of the main piece, with raw edges matching and ends overlapping. Pull out a little of the cord from the piping and cut it away to eliminate bulk. Stitch piping in place. Do not turn the piece to the right side.

5 With right sides facing and raw edges matching, stitch lining pieces together around the sides and top edge. Do not turn lining to the right side. Place lower edges of the main piece and the lining together, with right sides facing and raw edges matching. Be sure to align the side seams. Stitch around the lower edge, following the previous stitching, leaving an opening for turning. Turn the tea cosy to the right side through the opening. Handsew opening closed. Push the lining up into the main piece. Attach lining to the main fabric along the seamline with invisible hand stitches.

Table Napkin

MATERIALS

- [ ] one 50 cm square each of main cotton fabric and of contrasting cotton fabric
- [ ] 2.10 m of corded piping
- [ ] matching sewing thread
- [ ] 50 cm of bias binding in the same colour as the corded piping for the napkin tie

METHOD

1 Using a kitchen cup as a guide, round off the corners of the main and contrast fabric pieces.

2 Make the napkin in the same way as the place mat, omitting the quilting.

3 Fold the bias binding over double lengthways, with wrong sides facing and the folded edges matching. Stitch along folded edges. Knot the ends. Stitch the centre of the bias binding 12.5 cm down from one corner.

4 Fold the side with the tie attached in half, with wrong sides facing. Roll the opposite side of the napkin towards the end with the tie. Wrap the tie around the rolled napkin and tie into a bow.

Place Mat

MATERIALS

- [ ] one piece of pre-quilted main fabric 50 cm x 34 cm or plain fabric and polyester wadding in the same size
- [ ] one piece of backing fabric in the main fabric or a contrasting one, 50 cm x 34 cm
- [ ] 1.80 m of corded piping
- [ ] matching sewing thread

METHOD

1 Quilt fabric if necessary following instructions on How To Quilt Fabric in the box on this page.

2 Using a kitchen cup as a guide, round off the corners of the main and backing fabric pieces. With right sides facing and raw edges matching, pin piping around

Above: Carry through your country kitchen decorating scheme into this matched set of quilted tea cosy, place mat and napkin. You can choose to use the same fabric as your curtains, as we have done, or you can complement your curtains with another small print in toning colours

quilted main piece, clipping the seam allowance at curves for ease. Overlap the ends of the piping. Draw out a little cord from the piping and cut it off to eliminate bulk. Stitch piping in place.

3 Place the backing piece over the main piece, with edges matching and the right sides facing. Stitch around the edge, following the previous stitching line and leaving an opening for turning the place mat. Turn the place mat to the right side through the opening. Handsew the opening closed with small, invisible stitches. Press place mat.

HOW TO QUILT FABRIC

You can quilt your own fabric with your sewing machine, using a quilter's guide to plan the squares and spaces. The guide looks like an arm that extends from behind the sewing machine's presser foot into the centre of the machine.

The first row of stitching is made, then the quilter's guide is adjusted to sit along this stitching. Further rows of stitching are made, each one the same distance from the previous one, as measured by the quilter's guide.

It's an easy way to achieve professional-looking quilting and you can still use ornate machine stitches or twin-needle stitches for your quilting.

Wine Rack

This project is a simple storage idea which can be adapted to the space available. The wine rack shown here will hold five dozen bottles and is built using knockdown fittings which can easily be dismantled.

Above: Make this simple but effective wine rack in just a few hours
Left: Wire mesh being fitted to the prepared poles

MATERIALS

- ☐ 200 mm x 25 mm pine, one of 1.50 m, two of 1.20 m
- ☐ 100 mm x 100 mm galvanised steel reinforcing mesh, two of 600 mm x 1000 mm
- ☐ eight knockdown joint blocks
- ☐ 250 mL polyurethane
- ☐ 250 mL black self-priming epoxy paint or a black spray can

SPECIAL TOOLS NEEDED

- ☐ bolt cutters
- ☐ 8 mm drill bit

METHOD

1 Cut the steel reinforcing mesh to the dimension of 6 x 10 holes using bolt cutters. The bars are approximately 5.5 mm thick. The bottom edge can be a factory edge without projections. If the bolt cutters are held against the side of the adjacent bar, you will achieve a 5 mm projection for fixing into the timber.

2 Paint the mesh black. The job will take several hours by brush. It will be much quicker if you use a spray can, but overspray may present a problem. Make sure you protect walls with drop sheets or spray outside.

3 Cut the sides to length, allowing for the wire mesh, the bottom shelf and ground clearance. Total length is 1100 mm. The bottom shelf should be 600 mm plus 5.5 mm, say 606 mm. The top will overhang the sides slightly, and so is cut to 665 mm.

4 On the two sides, mark in two lines 20 mm from the front and the back. Down that line from the top, mark 3 mm, 103 mm, 203 mm, 303 mm and so on to allow for the ten bays. On the top piece, the rows of holes are set back by 5 mm, therefore 25 mm from the front and 15 mm from the rear.

5 Oversized 8 mm holes can now be drilled to take the steel. To protect against drilling too deeply, make a drill depth stop from a scrap of 25 mm x 25 mm timber so that you only penetrate timber to 10 mm.

6 Separate the knockdown fittings and fit the female part to the facing side of the joint, and the male part to the ends of the adjoining board. This will draw the parts together. The front blocks are fixed with the centre 50 mm from the front, and the rear ones 45 mm from the rear.

7 Assemble the unit with the bottom shelf first; insert the mesh and then the top, being careful to align all components correctly. When finished, dismantle and clean up the timber with abrasive paper. Coat with a polyurethane or similar.

8 When the unit is dry, you can re-assemble and stock it.

Decorating with Découpage

Découpage is about covering almost any flat or gently-curving surface with paper cut-outs. Traditionally it involves varnish, sandpaper – and lots of elbow grease! In our clever version, PVA (polyvinyl acetate) adhesive replaces the old materials and most of the hard work!

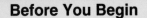

Before You Begin

❏ Gather up as much découpage material as you think you will need and have all the pieces cut out before you begin. You can add more later but you'll need a reasonable supply to begin with.

❏ Plan the design you wish to achieve before you start gluing. Experiment with colours and the distribution of motifs.

❏ If you wish to cover the item completely, use a layer of background paper pieces first. Cut these small shapes at random and overlap them to completely cover the item. Glue the decorative motifs on as the next layer.

❏ Items covered with glue, once completely dried, may be wiped clean with a damp cloth, but never immersed in water.

MATERIALS
PVA adhesive
soft brush for applying adhesive
pieces of wallpaper; wrapping paper; greeting cards; magazine clippings etc
objects to be covered, such as tins; trays; place mats; papier-mache shapes; terracotta pots etc
small sharp scissors for cutting paper

METHOD

1 Cut out motifs from paper precisely or leave a 5 mm margin around motif.

2 Begin placing motifs according to your design by coating a small area with undiluted adhesive and placing cut-out motif on to glued area. Once it is in place, coat motif with adhesive.

3 Repeat this process until design is completed. Allow to dry, then coat with adhesive again. For a deep shine repeat this last step.

Sensational
Storage

*Y*ou can add decorative
touches to functional storage
easily using fabric and paint.
Some simple recycling will
produce a padded blanket
box from an old, much loved
toy box, or you can try new
ways with fabric découpage
to transform basic wooden
boxes into instant heirlooms.

Blanket Box

This padded, chintz-covered box started life as a toy box but had become rather battered. Provided your old box is solid and has suitable timber for holding the fabric, looks don't matter!

Blanket Box before renovation

Before You Begin

❑ Decide on your fabric. Stripes are attractive, but you will have to match carefully through from front to back and over the lid. The easiest fabric to choose is one with a small print or an all-over pattern that does not require matching.

❑ Measure your own box carefully. You may find it easier to measure each panel of the box and draw these outlines and measurements on paper, then calculate fabric quantities, adding in extra for turning under and overlapping.

MATERIALS
☐ fabric – for our box we needed 4.50 m of outer fabric and 4 m of lining
☐ same quantity of medium thickness polyester wadding as total fabric
☐ narrow, ornate furnishing braid for inner trim – we needed 4.50 m for our box
☐ approximately 1.50 m strong cord or fine chain
☐ four eye-hooks
☐ staple gun
☐ craft glue
☐ decorative upholstery tacks
☐ decorative handles
☐ three hairline hinges (these are less visible than conventional hinges)
☐ strong dressmakers' pins
☐ small tack hammer

METHOD

1 Cover box completely with wadding, using a staple gun to secure edges. Cover top of box with extra wadding if padding is necessary. Make sure edges are neat and that you use enough staples to keep wadding edges flat.

2 First line box with lining fabric, covering panels with pieces cut to size plus a turn-under allowance. Glue these carefully into place. Take lining all the way up to lip of box.

3 Cover outside of box with cut-to-size (plus turn-under allowance) pieces of fabric, having sufficient fabric to come over top of box down into inside to overlap lining and down on to outside base. Hold fabric in place with dressmakers' pins, until you have secured side edges with decorative tacks. Space these tacks at about 2 cm intervals. When you have folded outside fabric to the inside, secure edge around box with staples, in an even line about 3 cm down from lip. Fold fabric neatly into corners. If necessary, sew edges together by hand to hold pieces together. Glue braid to cover line where fabrics meet, securing corners with tacks.

4 Tack outside fabric on to base, folding corners where necessary. Cover base with lining fabric and braid if desired.

5 Cover outside of lid, bringing fabric inside as for the box. Cover inside of lid with a panel of lining fabric and cover meeting line with braid. Tack corners.

6 Screw hinges to box and lid, securing lid evenly in place. Establish a suitable angle at which lid remains open, measure and fasten cords or chains to hold it at this point. Screw eye-hooks inside lid and sides of box. Tie and glue cords neatly, perhaps binding over raw edges of cord with a band of thread. Chains need to be opened with pliers and reclamped around eye-hooks.

7 Attach decorative handles to sides and centre front of box.

8 Any overlap of fabric inside box that does not sit well can also be tacked.

Left: Close-up of Blanket Box showing use of braid on the inside and hairline hinges
Right: Completed Blanket Box, covered in fabric to match bedroom decor

140

Chest of Drawers

Take an old timber chest of drawers, add some paint and a stencil or two, some smart new handles and you will have a decorative treasure that you'll be proud to have in your home.

MATERIALS
- [ ] chest of drawers
- [ ] acrylic paints for initial coat and for stencilling pattern
- [ ] fine sandpaper
- [ ] firm cardboard for cutting stencil
- [ ] sharp craft knife
- [ ] stencil brushes
- [ ] indelible felt-tipped pen for tracing stencil
- [ ] clear lacquer

METHOD
See stencil design on Pull Out Pattern Sheet at back of book.

1 Remove handles. Fill any dents and marks with filler where necessary. Sand chest and apply base coat as per manufacturer's instructions. Sand again and apply second coat of paint.

2 Cut out stencil with sharp knife and apply to chest as instructed in Down To Detail on page 114. You can purchase a suitable stencil if you would rather not make your own. Apply bands of colour in mouldings if desired.

3 Apply sealing coat of clear lacquer. Paint handles and re-attach, or fit new handles to complement the new look.

Right: Stencilling detail
Top: Chest before stencilling
Far right: Decorated Chest

Down to DETAIL

Baskets

Decorated baskets bring a warm, country look to your home. Any size basket, as long as it is solid and firmly woven, can look beautiful and can still earn its keep by serving some practical purpose.

Basket with Stiffened Fabric Trim

Before You Begin

❑ Decide on the arrangement of your trims and, if necessary, paint your basket in colours to match. You can follow our ideas or do your own thing.

❑ Estimate fabric lengths needed for stiffened bows by tying the tape measure into a bow and placing it on the basket, adjusting the length to find the correct size.

MATERIALS
- ☐ basket
- ☐ container of fabric stiffener, available from craft shops
- ☐ scissors
- ☐ trims such as fabric; lace; fabric borders used as lining or sewn into ties for bows; lengths of ribbon; artificial or handmade ribbon flowers
- ☐ PVA adhesive or glue gun
- ☐ paints and paintbrushes
- ☐ tape measure

METHOD

1 Using fingers, thoroughly cover flowers, ribbon or fabric with fabric stiffener, rubbing it well into fabric. While still wet, arrange trim on basket – either by draping, tying or pinning into place. Fabric stiffener can work as a glue, but heavier trims should be reinforced with extra glue when trim is dry and stiffened.

2 For a stiffened lace trim, glue smooth lace to line basket, using stiffener as glue. Trim edge with wet, stiffened, pregathered lace, adjusting gathers as it starts to dry. When completely dry and stiff, paint basket and trim as desired.

This basket has everything! We have trimmed a painted basket with a large, stiffened fabric bow

Basket with Fabric Découpage

MATERIALS
- ☐ fabrics which feature clear motifs suitable for cutting out, preferably cotton
- ☐ sharp scissors
- ☐ PVA adhesive
- ☐ paint in colours to match fabric
- ☐ paintbrushes

METHOD

1 Paint basket and allow to dry. Cut out motifs precisely, adding elements such as leaves or extra buds to build it up. Using a paintbrush, coat motif position on basket and back of motif with glue. Place motif on to glued area, overlapping any extra pieces needed. Coat motif with more glue. Allow to dry.

2 PVA adhesive dries shiny and clear so you can continue coating entire basket with glue to seal it and give it lustre. Baskets coated in this way can be wiped with a damp cloth but not immersed in water. Clear gloss paint can be used as a sealer to give a shinier finish, but it cannot be immersed in water either.

Fabric motifs and a large bow have transformed this old basket

Baskets with Fabric Lining

MATERIALS
- square or rectangular basket
- paint in colours to complement fabric trim
- fabric strip for side panel equal to inside depth plus 6 cm x twice inside basket circumference
- fabric strip 16 cm wide x same length as side panel
- fabric piece and polyester wadding same size as inside base
- PVA adhesive clear spray-on lacquer
- motifs from lining fabric for découpage

METHOD

1 Paint basket if desired. Allow to dry. Découpage outside of basket with

Above: Open baskets are easy to line and decorate with découpage

cut-out motifs and seal with clear spray-on lacquer or PVA adhesive.

2 When basket is dry, line with fabric as follows: Fold over 2 cm on one short end of fabric strip; press. Fold over 5 cm on one long edge; press. We pleated our strip at both edges with a pleating attachment, available for all types of standard sewing machines. If this is not available, stitch a gathering stitch 1 cm from lower raw edge and another 2 cm from top folded edge. Draw up gathers to fit inside basket, allowing folded short end to overlap raw short end at a corner. Glue panel into place, keeping folded edge at rim of basket and lower gathering at base.

3 Stitch base fabric and wadding together close to edge, glue into base, covering edge of side panel.

Above: Cut out motifs from lining fabric to use for découpage

4 Fold 4.5 cm on long edges of 16 cm wide strip inwards so that edges overlap at centre. Fold in 2 cm on one short end. Press. Stitch two parallel gathering rows along overlap. Draw up gathers

to fit base circumference of basket. Starting at one corner, glue gathered area of strip around base, covering fabric meeting line. Overlap folded end over raw end and glue into place.

Wastepaper Basket

MATERIALS
- round wastepaper basket
- fabric strip which is height of basket side plus 32 cm x one and a half times circumference of basket lip
- two lengths 1 cm wide ribbon or cord each twice circumference of basket – (this is not seen so may be any colour)

These pretty covers are easy to remove for laundering

METHOD

1 With right sides facing, stitch short sides of fabric strip together in 1 cm seam. Neaten raw edges.

2 Fold over 1 cm on one raw edge, then again 1.5 cm. Stitch, leaving opening at seam for inserting cord or ribbon. Fold 1 cm inwards on remaining raw edge; press. Fold another 9 cm. Stitch along first fold. Press 9 cm wide edge back on to right side, folding at stitching. Stitch again through all thicknesses 1.5 cm away, forming a 7.5 cm frill when gathered.

3 On inside, unpick seam between stitching rows to allow for cord insertion. Insert one cord length each into top and bottom casings. Pull fabric over basket and draw up cord around base. Draw up top cord, adjusting gathers to fit. Tie cords into bows and tuck out of sight.

146

Hat Boxes

Decorated hat boxes have made a welcome return. They are great for storing all sorts of things – including tiny hats!

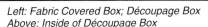

Left: Fabric Covered Box; Découpage Box
Above: Inside of Découpage Box

Above: Inside of Découpage Box

Before You Begin

❑ How much fabric and wadding you need will depend on the size of your box, whether you are covering it or just lining it. We used approximately 1.30 m each of 115 cm wide fabric and wadding for the Fabric Covered Box.

❑ Allow 1.5 cm turn-under and overlap allowances around edges of all fabric and wadding, unless instructed otherwise.

MATERIALS
- ☐ sturdy, lidded wooden box
- ☐ two pieces firm cardboard for base and lid lining
- ☐ PVA adhesive
- ☐ small paintbrush to apply glue

For Fabric Covered Box:
- ☐ fabric to cover
- ☐ medium thickness polyester wadding
- ☐ pins to secure fabric
- ☐ strip fabric 90 cm x 20 cm for bow

For Découpage Box:
- ☐ fabric motifs
- ☐ fabric and wadding for lining
- ☐ spray-on paint, clear and coloured
- ☐ strip fabric twice circumference x 16 cm for frill

Fabric Covered Box

METHOD

1 Cut four lids each from fabric and wadding, two from cardboard. Cut one strip of fabric and wadding the circumference of base x twice depth of box. Cut one strip of fabric the circumference of lid x twice depth of lid, and one of wadding with turn-under allowance only on one side.

2 Glue wadding on to lid, gluing overlap allowances on to sides. Place wadding side strip level with top of lid and glue around lid sides, taking overlap inside. Lightly handsew to top lid piece. Trim cardboard lid liner to size. Cover with wadding, turning and gluing overlap to back of cardboard. Set aside.

3 Cover box with wadding as for lid. On outside, trim away depth of lid from wadding at top. Glue edges. This is cut away to make lid fit better. Trim cardboard base liner to fit. Cover it with wadding, turning and gluing overlap to back. Cover lid cardboard piece with fabric as for base cardboard piece, taking fabric overlap to back of cardboard and gluing or stitching to secure it in place.

4 Cover lid top with fabric, stitching allowances to wadding on sides. Press under 1.5 cm along one long edge of lid side piece. Secure with small stitches or glue at pressed edge, taking raw edge to inside. Glue to base. Glue lid cardboard liner into place. Repeat process for box, covering base, sides and inner sides with fabric. Glue cardboard liner into position.

5 Fold bow fabric over double, lengthways, with right sides facing. Trim ends to an angle. Stitch around raw edges, leaving opening for turning. Trim corners, turn and press. Tie bow and stitch on lid.

6 Glue braid around inside of box and lid to cover joins, if desired.

Découpage Box

METHOD

1 Cover both pieces of cardboard with wadding and fabric, following method for Fabric Covered Box. Set aside.

2 Paint box inside and out, except for inner bases of lid and box. Set aside to dry. Spray box with clear lacquer, inside and out, to seal.

3 Fold in 1 cm on one short end of fabric strip and 4.5 cm on each long side. Press. Stitch a gathering thread along centre, through all thicknesses. Draw up gathering to fit around inside base. Glue covered cardboard pieces in place inside box and lid. Glue ruffle in place inside box, overlapping raw edge with folded end.

4 Découpage box using method for Baskets with Fabric Découpage on page 145. Seal outside with clear paint.

New Looks for Old
FEATURE

Many storage-type items around the house lend themselves to renovation and will go on giving good service, so why not trade new looks for old?

When you're considering the possibilities, don't make the mistake of thinking the only way to improve the situation is to start again. Firstly, it is not always the most practical solution; secondly, the constraints of your decorating budget usually won't allow such luxury; and thirdly, in the interests of the planet, recycling should always be a priority.

Many items have exciting potential. Take that battered tin trunk in the garage, or that storage chest that has seen better days. On the following pages, you will see how they can be transformed in ways that not only add an attractive focus to your home, but also increase storage space.

In fact, once you start looking at old pieces of furniture, you will agree that they simply don't make them like that anymore! The high cost of materials and labour has led to shortcuts and, despite the greater variety available today, it has also led to the demise (in all but the most finely crafted) of the cupboard that closes perfectly and the drawer that glides shut.

Talking timber

Timber is a rapidly diminishing resource. We should all aim to protect the world's diminishing forests by retaining and restoring old wooden pieces.

There are two ways to tackle the task of renovating timber storage pieces:

❑ Restoration – whereby the style of the piece is retained and the original finish restored.
❑ Revamping – whereby the original form of the item is retained but its finish and character is completely altered.

Workbench from Country Form

Tin from Country Form

The other method of cleaning up the surface is by sanding, beginning with a coarse grade of sandpaper and gradually using finer and finer grades. It is hard work but very rewarding.

Revamping

A smooth timber surface provides you with a clean canvas for a whole range of finishes which can totally transform the piece. Painted finishes are ideal for lower quality timbers and timber veneers. The feature, *Paint Finishes* on page 52, will tell you all you need to know to get started. Don't forget that you don't need to give an all-over finish for it to be effective – explore the possibilities of stencilling and outlining as well.

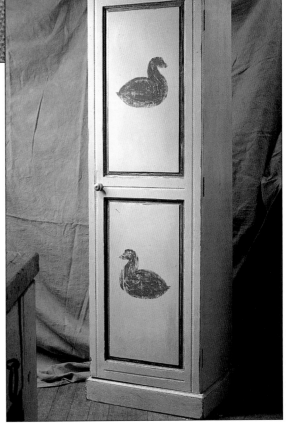

Cupboard from Country Form

Restoration

There is a great revival of interest in old-style, antique or rustic furniture and reasonably priced pieces are becoming hard to find. All the more reason to 'rescue' one you come across, tucked away in a second-hand store (or your garage!).

Generally, the first step to restoration is the stripping of the existing surface. If you want to get right back to raw timber, you may need to use a professional stripping service. If it is quite a small piece, you can strip it using one of the many commercial products available. Always test a small, hidden area first.

Far left: An industrial work bench makes an interesting display feature
Left: An old galvanised tin has been painted and stencilled to give it a new lease of life
Above: Second-hand shop bargains, stripped and stained like this cabinet, greatly increase their value
Right: A simple wooden cupboard has been stencilled and 'lined' to give it a new character

Bathroom
beauties

With *a frill here, a stencil there and a few metres of pretty fabric, you can give your existing bathroom a bright new look – and it won't break the bank.*

Begin with a drawn plan and some idea of a new colour scheme – though you may have to accept the limitations of the existing colours of the tiles and other fittings. The soft pink and white colour scheme of this bathroom is carried through in the shower curtain, festoon blind, basin skirting and wall stencilling. Avoid the introduction of too many colours, so as not to add clutter to a less-than-generously proportioned bathroom. Remember, the fabric and trimmings you choose will have to withstand the damp environment of the bathroom. Check with your supplier before you buy to avoid disappointment later.

Festoon Blind

For a soft, romantic look, nothing beats festoon blinds. The fabric you choose will set the style for your blind, from the soft and feminine look of sheer lace to the charm of this crisp cotton.

Before You Begin

❏ To calculate how much fabric you need, measure the width and length of the window and multiply each measurement by two. If you need to join two pieces of fabric to achieve the right width, do so with small flat seams.

❏ If you are going to trim your blind with a frill, you will need twice the distance to be covered by the frill, a length of purchased piping (or make your own) equal to that distance and bias binding as long as the frill.

MATERIALS
☐ sufficient fabric for the blind and the frill (see *Before You Begin*)
☐ sufficient matching bias binding
☐ sufficient matching piping
☐ length of pencil pleating tape, which draws up to the width of your window
☐ ring tape, four times the length of your blind
☐ curtain track, the width of your window
☐ curtain rod, the width of your window
☐ brackets for the rod

METHOD
See page 27 for the cord threading diagram.

1 Cut a strip of fabric 18 cm x the length required for your blind, for the frill.

Bind one long edge of the strip with bias binding. Gather the other edge to the length required to fit around the sides and lower edge of the blind.

2 Baste the piping around the side and lower edges of the right side of the fabric piece (or joined pieces) with raw edges matching. Pin the frill to the edge, over the top of the piping, with raw edges matching and right sides facing. Stitch through all thicknesses. Press the seam allowances towards the blind. Stitch again in the gutter of the piping, securing the seam allowance.

3 Turn in 2.5 cm on the top edge of the blind and the frill. Press.Unravel the draw cords of the first 5 cm of the pencil pleating tape. Pin the upper edge of the tape to the top of your blind, 1.5 cm from the edge. Stitch down all edges of the tape, stitching the top hem as you go. Do not draw up the cords.

4 Stitch the ring tape down the sides of the blind, just inside the frill, and at two equally spaced points across the blind from top to bottom hems. Leave an extra 6 cm of tape at the bottom of each length. See the cord-threading diagram for the location of the cords.

5 Loop this tape back on itself so that the end is just above the hem. Stitch. These loops are to hold the bottom rod.

6 Gather the pencil pleating cord, until the blind gathers to the width of the curtain track.

7 Attach the eyelets to the window frame, just below the track, to correspond with the top of each strip of ring tape, and another, just below one curtain track bracket, through which you will thread the blind cords.

8 Cut a cord for each strip of ring tape, long enough to reach from the bottom rod, up the blind, through the eyelets, across the top and down to the side where the extra eyelet is, leaving sufficient length for knotting them below the eyelet.

9 Loop the rings together as you go to form a permanent blousing effect. Attach the blind to the curtain track with the hooks. Insert the rod through the tape loops at the lower edge of the blind.

Basin Skirting

These simple-to-make panels of fabric can hide unsightly plumbing and even create new storage space, as the space they conceal can contain shelving. As there are countless shapes and sizes for bathroom basins/ units there is no precise pattern for making it – rather we give a method for making the frill, with several variations for fixing it in place.

Before You Begin

❏ First measure the depth and width of the frill. If you plan to gather the fabric, allow double the width needed. If you take advantage of a pattern in the fabric, such as these stripes, to form pleats, work out the width of pleated fabric required. The striped panel holds the pleats in place.

❏ Don't forget to make a split in a suitable place for access to the storage space behind. You can achieve this by making your frill in two sections so that each can be drawn back as needed.

❏ Consider using the same fabric to make shower curtains and frilled blinds. A truly coordinated look can work wonders in an otherwise basic bathroom!

MATERIALS
☐ sufficient fabric
☐ elastic
☐ cup hooks
☐ small rings

METHOD

1 Establish how you are going to secure the frill, as this will have a bearing on the style. Rounded basins on a pedestal can have a frill with a casing, allowing strong elastic to be threaded through it. The ends of the elastic are hooked over two cup hooks fixed to the wall on either

side of the basin at the height of the casing. The frill will naturally gather on to the elastic.

2 Pleats work well with basin units, where there are angles like this one. Screw cup hooks into the wall at the height of the striped panel, and again in the concave angle. Add more hooks elsewhere if it seems appropriate. Pleat the fabric to fit exactly. Attach small rings by hand at the back of the stitched panel to coincide with the hooks.

Shower Cap

MATERIALS
- ☐ 60 cm of 115 cm wide cotton fabric
- ☐ 60 cm of 115 cm wide plastic sheeting
- ☐ 2 lengths of bias binding, each 2 m long (one could be self fabric)
- ☐ 1 cm wide elastic

METHOD

1 Cut two circles 60 cm in diameter, one from the cotton fabric and one from the plastic sheeting.

2 Place the plastic circle against the wrong side of the cotton fabric. Stitch around the outside edge. Trim both fabric and plastic close to the stitching.

3 Bind the joined edges of the circles with self-fabric bias binding, turning in the raw ends where they meet.

4 Stitch the second length of bias binding 6 cm from the edge, on the plastic side, to form the casing for the elastic.

5 Thread the elastic through the casing. Check the fit before joining the ends of the elastic.

Toilet Roll Holder

MATERIALS
- ☐ two strips of cotton fabric, each 90 cm x 14 cm
- ☐ iron-on interfacing, 90 cm x 14 cm
- ☐ strip of fabric, 12 cm x 3 cm for the loop
- ☐ 3.20 m of 1.5 cm wide lace edging
- ☐ 1.30 m of 3 mm wide satin ribbon
- ☐ small wooden curtain ring
- ☐ craft glue

METHOD

1 Iron the interfacing on to the wrong side of one fabric strip. Trim both strips of fabric to a point at one end.

2 Stitch two rows of lace down the centre of the interfaced strip so that the straight edges of the lace meet in the middle. Stitch a length of ribbon over the line where the laces join.

3 With right sides together and raw edges matching, stitch lace all around the lace-trimmed piece, pleating the lace at the point and the corners for ease.

4 Place both fabric pieces together with right sides facing and raw edges matching. Stitch, following the previous stitching line and leaving the straight end open. Trim the fabric at the points and corners. Turn to the right side and press.

5 Turn under 1 cm at the open end, fold this end to the back and slipstitch to the back of the holder with the corners matching.

6 Fold the strip for the loop over lengthways with right sides together. Stitch along the long side. Turn and press. Topstitch along the length with four rows of stitching.

7 Wind the ribbon around the curtain ring to cover it, gluing the ends to secure them. Fold the strip for the loop

Toiletry bag, toilet roll holder and shower cap

Left: The bathroom showing the shower curtain, festoon bind and trimmed towels
Below: Detail of the wooden bathmat showing the cord threaded through plastic tubing

Shower Curtain

This shower curtain is totally decorative, covering a purely functional, plastic shower curtain already in place.

MATERIALS

☐ sufficient fabric to cover the existing curtain. Plastic curtains are not hemmed at sides and lower edge, so be sure to allow extra fabric for 5 cm deep side and lower hems, and the 10 cm turnover at the top. If necessary, join fabric lengths together with flat seams to achieve the desired size.
☐ matching sewing thread

METHOD

1 Fold in 1 cm on the sides, then fold another 4 cm. Press and stitch. Fold up the lower hem and stitch in the same way. Fold over 5 cm at the top then fold another 5 cm. Stitch along the first fold.

2 Make buttonholes for the curtain rings at the same intervals as they are on the plastic shower curtain. Hang the fabric curtain on the outside of the plastic one by pushing the hooks through the buttonholes of both curtains at once.

3 If you wish to hook the fabric curtain out of the way or tie it to one side, you can purchase a suitable water-resistant cord and tassel and attach a hook to the wall at the appropriate height.

Trimmed Towels

Across the ends of most towels is a flat, woven band. This is the ideal place to stitch rows of ribbon or braid. You can also stitch lace or scalloped trims under the edge of a length of ribbon or fabric.

Remember to trim your face cloths, bathmats and hand towels for a truly coordinated look in your bathroom.

around the ring over the ribbon ends. Glue the ends of the loop. Slipstitch the loop to the point on the wrong side of the holder. Tie a small bow and attach it as shown.

8 Stitch across the holder, halfway between the handsewing and the lower folded edge, dividing it into two compartments.

Toiletry Bag

MATERIALS

☐ 60 cm x 28 cm cotton fabric
☐ 60 cm x 28 cm plastic sheeting
☐ 1.60 m of 12 mm wide satin ribbon

METHOD

1 Fold the fabric over lengthways with right sides together. Stitch the sides. Do the same with the plastic.

2 Turn the fabric bag right side out. Trim 5 cm from the top edge of the plastic bag. Slip the plastic bag inside the fabric bag.

3 Turn in 6 mm at the top edge of the fabric bag. Turn under another 5 cm to cover the top edge of the plastic bag. Stitch through all thicknesses at the fold and again 1.5 cm away to form the casing.

4 Open the stitching of the side seams between the casing lines. Cut the length of ribbon in half. Thread one half in one opening, through the casing and out the same opening. Repeat with the other half of the ribbon at the other opening. Knot the ribbon ends together.

Bath Mat

This is a terrific solution to the perennial problem of soggy bath mats. An occasional scrub-down and an airing are all that are needed to keep it looking like new.

Before You Begin

❑ Decide what size mat you can accommodate in your bathroom before purchasing materials. Our mat measures 45 cm x 58 cm. Remember when you are deciding, that plastic tubing creates a 2 cm gap between each piece of timber.

MATERIALS
❑ ten lengths of dressed (planed) pine (PAR/DAR) 4 cm wide x 2 cm deep x 45 cm long
❑ 1 m of 14 mm diameter non-perishing plastic tube
❑ 2 m of 12 mm diameter nylon rope
❑ electric drill with 16 mm and 13 mm diameter drill bits

METHOD

1 Cut timber to size. Line up lengths side by side on their sides and rule a line 10 cm in from each end across all timber sides. Turn timber lengths over and repeat lines on other side for accurate drill positions. Find centre of each side of timber pieces and mark this across ruled lines.

2 Drill right through both sides of each timber piece at centre marking using small bit first, then drill through same hole with larger bit only to a depth of 1.5 cm.

3 Cut plastic tubing into 5 cm lengths. These are used to separate timbers. Thread rope through timber and plastic tubes, starting at one end and working down one row of holes, out opposite end and back through remaining row of holes to other side. Knot ends securely. Hold knots over a lighted match to fuse ends.

Plastic tubing linking boards

Bedtime
stories

In days past, bedrooms were often the forgotten rooms in the house, at least as far as decorating was concerned – but no more! These days the decor of most bedrooms revolves around the wonderful array of bed linens available. You can dress up the most uninspiring room with clever use of fabric for sheets, pillowcases and quilt. And don't forget to carry the theme through into curtains or blinds to match.

Making your own bed linen is easy, lets you create your own decorating scheme and can save you money too! Remember to measure the bed carefully – small differences won't matter for flat sheets, but accuracy is important for ruffles or valances.

Embroidered Accessories

Delicate pansies in simple cross stitch give real charm to pillow-cases and tie-backs, adding gentleness to your private retreat.

MATERIALS

- [ ] paper
- [ ] pencil
- [ ] 46.5 cm of 12.5 cm wide 14 count white Aida for pillowcases and 54 cm x 23 cm for each Tie-back
- [ ] one pair plain white, frilled pillowcases
- [ ] 80 cm of white cotton fabric for Tie-back backing
- [ ] narrow white satin ribbon
- [ ] DMC Stranded Cotton, 1 skein each: Dark Green 936; Medium Green 3347; Light Blue 800; Dark Blue 311; Pale Blue 775; Medium Blue 334
- [ ] 2 cm wide white lace edging

Pillowsham

METHOD

See page 160 for embroidery graph and key.

1 To prepare Aida, count five squares down from top, seven squares up from bottom and fourteen squares in from both sides and baste along these rows with contrasting coloured thread as a guide for hemming.

2 To commence sewing, find and mark centre of Aida by folding widthways and lengthways. Count fifteen squares down from basted line and work your cross stitch following design graph and key.

3 Keep repeating pattern along length of Aida by counting down five squares from bottom stitch of completed design. Leave five squares between each pattern.

4 When pattern is completed, back stitch around flowers, using a single strand of 311 and, where indicated by a half cross, back stitches of 936.

5 When stitching is finished, fold Aida along basted lines to mark hems. Pin lace edging under folded edges and stitch in place.

6 Pin Aida on to pillowcase and sew into place by hand or machine.

Tie-back

METHOD

1 Draw the shape of the Tie-back on to a sheet of paper. Using this as your pattern, cut two Tie-backs from Aida. Fold Aida fabric widthways and lengthways to find and mark centre. Centre first motif over this point.

2 Because of Tie-back shape, the two outer designs must be stepped. For left-hand motif, count up ten squares from green at bottom of centre design. Count one square up for right-hand design.

3 Sew lace edging around right side of each Tie-back with right sides facing and raw edges even.

4 Cut out two backing pieces, using your pattern. Place backing and embroidered pieces together with right sides facing. Stitch around outside edge, leaving an opening for turning. Turn to right side and press. Sew ribbon to ends of Tie-back to secure it to a wall hook.

By Sherril MacLean, Photographed by Murray Cumming/Cumming Enterprises

Embroidered curtain Tie-back and Pillowsham add old-world charm to a bedroom

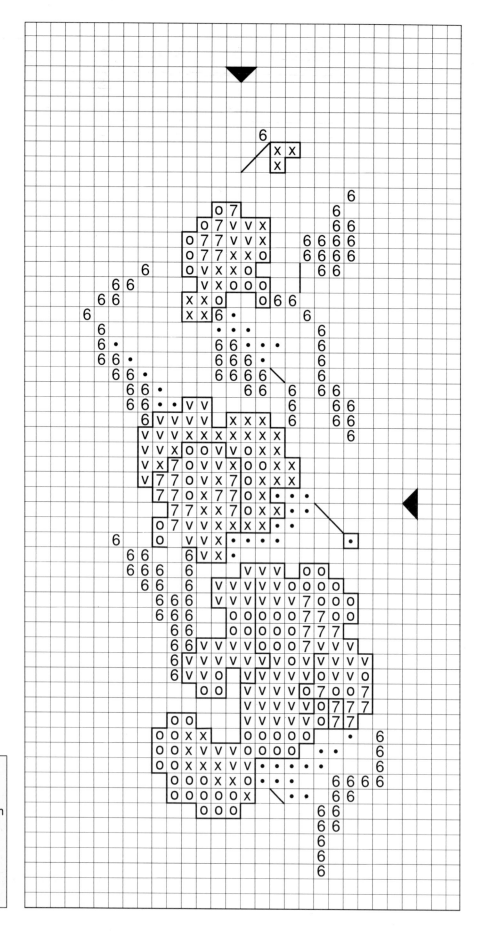

KEY

	DMC	Colour
6	936	Dark Green
•	3347	Medium Green
X	800	Light Blue
7	311	Dark Blue
V	775	Pale Blue
O	334	Medium Blue
Cross stitch	2 strands	
Back stitch	1 strand	

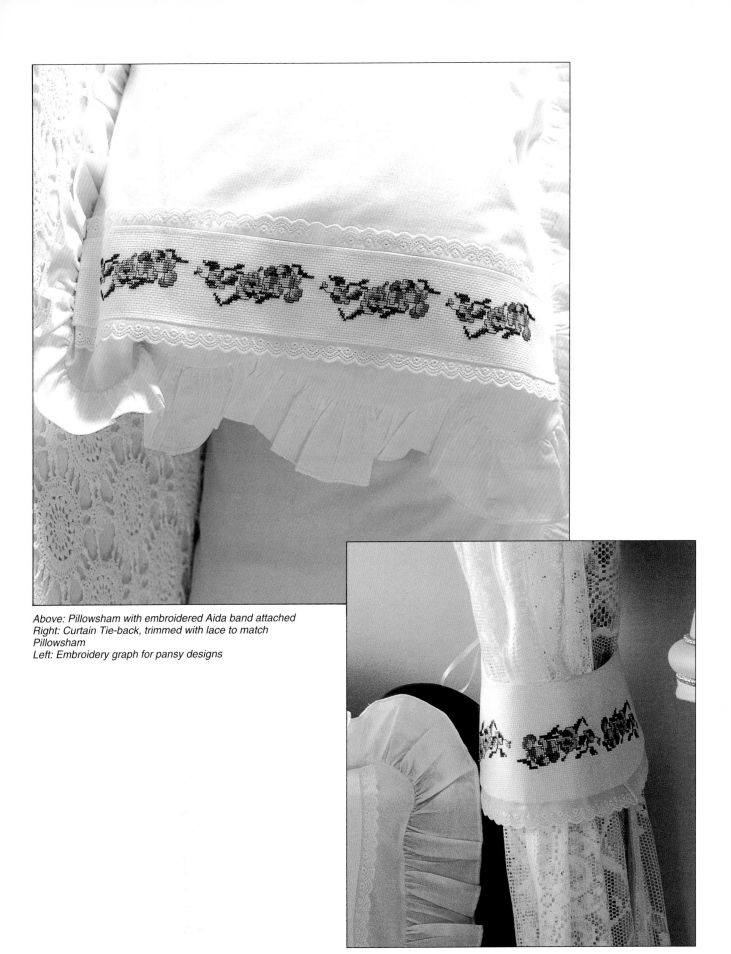

Above: Pillowsham with embroidered Aida band attached
Right: Curtain Tie-back, trimmed with lace to match Pillowsham
Left: Embroidery graph for pansy designs

161

Bedroom Set

Filling your bedroom with the dazzling beauty and romance of English roses, these coordinates are just what decorating dreams are made of.

The Bedspread and Lampshade adapt a 17th and 18th century technique called broderie perse, a type of appliqué in which motifs are cut from a piece of print fabric and then applied to a larger piece of material. At about this time, printed chintz, imported from India, was very popular in Britain – so popular, in fact, that imports of chintz were banned for a while, in order to protect the local industry. Broderie perse was a means of making a small amount of precious material go a long way.

Bedspread

Before You Begin

❏ The Bedspread was made to fit a standard double bed but can quite easily be adjusted to fit a larger sized bed by altering the size of the central panel. The best way to ensure a good fit is to draw a diagram for your own bed like the one shown here, marking your own measurements. Following your diagram, calculate the amount of fabric you will need.

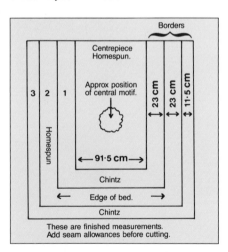

These are finished measurements. Add seam allowances before cutting.

❏ The borders of printed fabric were cut across the width of the fabric and joined to give the correct length. If your fabric has a one-way pattern, mark the top edge of each piece as you cut it and place that edge towards the centre panel.

❏ Traditionally, these bedspreads were not quilted. You can quilt yours, if you prefer, by cutting a piece of wadding to the size of the complete Bedspread and basting it to the wrong side of the Bedspread before you begin quilting around the motifs. Use a sheet for the backing and bind the edges with a complementary fabric or the plain homespun.

MATERIALS
❏ sufficient print fabric and plain homespun. (We used 3.50 m of print fabric and 3.75 m of plain homespun.)
❏ double-sided fusible webbing
❏ matching sewing thread

METHOD

1 Draw a diagram for your Bedspread like this one, using your own measurements. Cut out centre panel, print and plain panels, following your diagram.

2 After experimenting with possible arrangements, roughly cut out motifs for your appliqué from remaining print fabric. Fuse webbing to wrong side of motifs and cut out carefully, very close to edge of motifs.

3 Peel off paper backing from motifs for centre panel and fuse them into place.

4 Sew on first print border, mitring corners for a neat finish.

5 Sew on first plain border, mitring corners. Prepare and apply appliqué motifs in same way as for centre panel.

6 Sew on outer print border, mitring corners. Hem around outside edge.

By Morag Robinson. Photographed by Murray Cumming/Cumming Enterprises

Boomerang Pillowcase

❑ If the front is to be quilted, the front pieces must be cut out at least 5-6 cm larger all around to allow for shrinkage during the quilting process.

MATERIALS

☐ 1.10 m fabric for front and frill
☐ 85 cm toning fabric for back
☐ 90 cm square wadding (if quilting)
☐ 90 cm square lawn or calico for lining (if quilting)

METHOD

See Pull Out Pattern Sheet at back of book.

Pattern Outline: ━━━━━━━━

1 From main fabric, cut one front, three 7.5 cm wide strips for frill, one back and one flap. If you are quilting front, cut out one front in wadding and one in lining as well.

2 Smooth lining on a table, face down. Place wadding on top, then main front piece face upwards. Make sure there are no puckers or wrinkles. Pin through all thicknesses using safety pins, or baste layers together. Quilt around motifs by hand or machine. When quilting is completed, recut front to correct size.

3 Join strips for frill. Make a narrow hem or overlock along one long edge. Selvages will act as finish on two short ends. Run a row of gathering stitches along other long edge. Gather fabric until it measures approximately 2.16 m.

4 Pin frill to front with right sides facing and raw edges even, easing in a little extra width on corners A and B. Pin or baste finished edge of frill to front, taking care to catch in corners. This will stop frill from folding or dropping out of place and from being caught in seams. Take special care at corners C and D to fold end of frill back out of way of seamline, as this end of frill is not stitched down (Fig. 1).

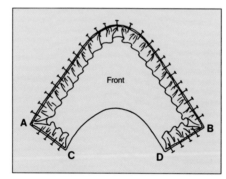

Fig. 1

5 Sew frill in place, leaving finished edge pinned or basted until all work is complete.

6 With right sides facing, pin flap to right side of front at one end. This will be open end of pillowcase. Sew only across end, then open out flap to hang from end as shown by dotted line (Fig. 2).

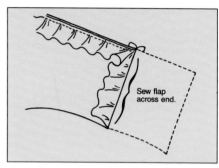

Fig. 2

7 Finish matching end of back with a small hem. Pin back to front with right sides together and pinning all around except where there is a hem.

8 Fold open end of flap back over end of pillow and pin side seams (Fig. 3).

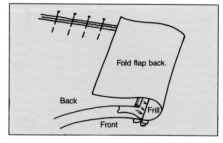

Fig. 3

9 Sew around pillowcase, except across end where flap is folded back. Turn whole cover right side out and remove pins or basting. Press well.

Boomerang Pillowcase showing quilting detail

Lampshade

❑ Our frame has a base 112 cm in diameter and is 23 cm deep; the top is 99 cm in diameter. Adjust the measurements to fit your shade.

MATERIALS
- ☐ 114.5 cm x 31 cm wide rectangle of fabric
- ☐ 2 m pregathered lace
- ☐ 2 m braid
- ☐ small amount of contrasting ribbon for bow
- ☐ PVA adhesive
- ☐ elastic
- ☐ fusible webbing

METHOD

1 Cut out appliqué motif from fabric, apply fusible webbing to back and position appliqué in centre of fabric rectangle. Satin stitch around motif.

2 Join fabric short ends with a tapered seam, with piece starting at 112 cm wide and decreasing to 99 cm.

3 Make an elastic casing at top and bottom. Thread elastic through casing after placing cover over frame. Draw up elastic until cover sits firmly on frame.

4 Glue lace and braid around top and bottom of Lampshade. Glue a small bow in centre at bottom of appliqué.

Valance

❑ Check the depth of the frill required for your own bed, remembering to add about 2.5 cm for seam allowances. On the illustrated valance, the finished depth of the frill is 35 cm. The cut depth before sewing is approximately 37.5 cm. This depth of frill allows three lengths to be cut from one width of fabric. Measure around the bed, two sides and one end. Double this measurement. This will give the total length of the frill. Since you will be able to cut three lengths from the width, divide the total length of the frill by three. Add enough for the seam allowance for two joins and the hems for two ends. This will give the amount of fabric required. Our version needed almost 2 m of fabric for the frill.

MATERIALS
- ☐ sufficient fabric for Valance
- ☐ sufficient sheeting or homespun for base rectangle
- ☐ matching sewing thread

METHOD

1 Measure top of bed base and, using calico or sheeting, cut a rectangle to fit this part.

2 Join sections of frill to make one long piece. Hem short ends and make a very narrow hem along one long side.

3 Run two rows of gathering stitches along other long side, preferably in quarters or even eighths, for ease of working. Pull up gathers evenly to correct length for going around calico or sheeting rectangle.

4 Sew to edge of calico rectangle on three sides. Press well.

By Morag Robinson. Photographed by Murray Cumming/Cumming Enterprises

Lampshade with appliqué trim

Down to DETAIL

Log Cabin Quilt

Log cabin is perhaps the most popular of the traditional quilting patterns. The design depends on the contrast between the light and dark fabrics used in each of the quilt blocks. The placement of the light and dark halves of the blocks determines the particular log cabin design.

Before You Begin

❏ In this quilt, the blocks are arranged in the 'straight furrow' pattern, where the dark halves are set adjacent to one another in a diagonal line across the quilt.

❏ Traditionally, the log cabin design is a great way of using material scraps left over from other projects. Making a scrap quilt can be quite a challenge but it is also very satisfying. For this quilt, three or four pieces of fabric were purchased to supplement the forty or fifty different scrap fabrics. Some scrap fabrics which did not quite suit the rustic colour scheme were dyed in tea to give the right tones. Continuity is maintained by using the same colour for the centre square of each block. This centre square is usually red or yellow, representing the warm fireplace at the centre of the cabin.

❏ You can also mix different weights of fabric in a log cabin quilt but, if you intend to wash it, it is best that you use cottons or polycottons. If you are prepared to have it dry-cleaned, you can use velvets, silks and other textured fabrics.

❏ The size of the quilt can be varied by adding or subtracting blocks, by making the centre of each block rectangular instead of square or by adding more strips to each block.

❏ Quantities given for fabrics can only be approximate, as the actual amounts needed will depend on the size of your scraps.

❏ Always collect more scrap pieces than you think you will need to give you the greatest scope in arranging the colours. In this quilt, there are no two blocks which are identical and no fabric is repeated in the same block.

❏ When joining your blocks and rows, it is important to keep the seam allowances constant, the seams aligned and all the angles square. If you fail to do this, the blocks will be distorted and your quilt will not come together neatly.

Size: 140 cm x 160 cm approximately
Total number of blocks: 42, set 6 x 7

MATERIALS
☐ approximately 1.25 m light fabrics
☐ approximately 1.75 m dark fabrics
☐ 25 cm red or yellow fabric for centres
☐ 1 m total of scraps or one fabric for borders
☐ 140 cm x 160 cm wadding
☐ 140 cm x 160 cm backing fabric
☐ Olfa cutter and mat
☐ pins
☐ matching sewing thread

METHOD
6 mm seams allowed.

To piece quilt top
1 Cut all fabrics into strips approximately 4 cm wide. Using an Olfa cutter, you can cut many layers at same time. Cut 6 cm wide strips, then cut into 6 cm squares for centre of each block.

2 Group all fabrics into three piles – one light, one dark and all centre squares.

3 Take a pile of centre squares and chainsew them, right sides together, to edge of a light strip. Cut squares apart, even with edge of centre square. Press seams away from centre square.

4 Sew a light strip at right angles to strip just sewn. Cut and press. One light round is now complete.

5 Sew a dark strip to edge of centre square, placing it at right angles to strip just attached. Cut and press.

6 Attach another dark strip to fourth side of centre square in same way. Cut and press. One whole round is now complete.

7 Continue attaching strips, light on one side, dark on the other, for three rounds. Make forty-two blocks in same way.

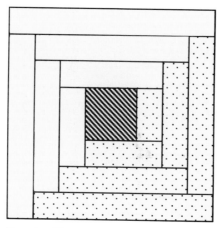

Complete Block

To assemble

1 The best way to assemble your quilt top is to lay all blocks on a flat surface (your floor is ideal) in 'straight furrow' style (Fig. 1).

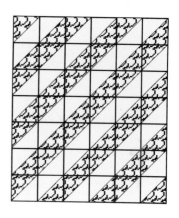

Fig. 1

2 Join blocks together horizontally in seven rows of six blocks (Fig. 2).

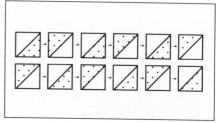

Fig. 2

3 Join rows together to form quilt top (Fig. 3).

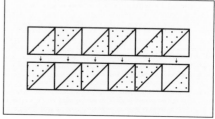

Fig. 3

4 If you want to add borders, you can make them by sewing remaining scrap strips together or by cutting appropriate lengths from a toning fabric. To calculate length of side borders, measure length of quilt top. Always measure through quilt centre, not down sides. Cut two borders to this length and 10 cm wide. Join borders to sides of quilt top with right sides together.

5 For top and bottom borders, measure width of quilt top, including side borders, measuring through centre. Cut top and bottom borders to this length and 10 cm wide. Sew them in place. Press quilt top well.

By Morag Robinson, Photographed by Murray Cumming/Cumming Enterprises

To quilt

1 Place complete quilt top face down on a flat surface. Place wadding on top and backing fabric on top of that, facing upwards. Secure three layers together with safety pins or by basting.

2 On right side, quilt by stitching in squares as shown or in a pattern of your own. If you prefer, you can tie your quilt with strong cotton at intersection of blocks and in centres of blocks.

3 Cut strips of fabric 10 cm wide for binding. Measure lengths required in same way as for borders. Fold binding strips over double with wrong sides together. Pin bindings to right side of quilt, first sides and then top and bottom, with raw edges even. Stitch. Turn folded edge to wrong side of quilt and slipstitch in place. Sign and date your quilt.

Choose light and dark fabrics for your log cabin quilt

LOG CABIN QUILTS

Log cabin quilts are ideal for beginners and the pattern can be easily adapted to smaller projects such as cushions, pot holders and placemats. This quilt is a log cabin quilt in the 'barn raising' style, one of the most popular patterns. It can be a true scrapbag quilt, utilising quite small pieces of fabric where the only governing factor is the contrast between light and dark colours.

Like all log cabin quilts, it is based on a pattern of light and dark rectangles, pieced around a centre square. The rectangles are laid in such a way as to represent the logs used by the early American settlers to build their cabins. Some early quilts even had a little chimney sewn in to further underline the theme. The centre square of the block is often red, to denote the fireplace, or yellow, to represent the lighted window or warm hearth.

These days, most log cabin quilts are made from light and dark printed, dress-weight cottons but, in the past, quilters often used wool as well. Mixing silks, velvets, and other 'luxury' fabrics produces a lovely quilt with quite a different feeling about it. Traditional log cabin quilts were made without a border, but this is not a hard-and-fast rule and these days quilters often add a plain or print border.

While the basic ingredients of a log cabin block remain the same – half in light and half in dark – changing the way in which the rectangles are placed or the blocks are joined will give you quite a different-looking quilt. Joining the blocks so that the dark halves are adjacent to one another and the light halves are adjacent to one another, gives a design of alternating light and dark diamonds. Piecing the blocks and joining them so that the dark and light halves form alternating diagonals, reminiscent of a roof line, make this design known as 'barn raising'. Placing the blocks so that the dark and light halves travel diagonally across the quilt creates the pattern known as 'straight furrow'.

Making a block so that the light and dark quarters are opposite their mates and joining the blocks side by side across the row, makes yet another pattern called 'courthouse steps'.

Above: A log cabin quilt
Right: A log cabin place mat in the 'barn raising' style

169

18 m of twill tape. Length of tape required is equal to number of rows of tape x length of quilt cover. Decide on the width of channels best for your fabric.

❏ A feather quilt is, theoretically, washable – but the bulk is daunting when hanging it out to dry. Dry cleaning is effective. Hanging your quilt out regularly to air in the sun will keep it smelling clean and fresh.

❏ Those experienced with feathers and down say that one should only work in the bathroom with the door shut! When filling your quilt, place the open bag of feathers in the bath. This helps to confine the fly-away feathers to a relatively draught-free area with little for them to stick to.

❏ Pegging the quilt (at each channel) to a line strung above the bath may help you to fill channels evenly.

MATERIALS
☐ sufficient fabric to cut a front and a back of desired size and allow 10 cm for turning, all around
☐ sufficient filling of your choice (see Before You Begin)
☐ sufficient 5 cm wide cotton twill tape (see Before You Begin)

METHOD

1 Press in 10 cm all around each quilt piece to mark foldline for hems. Fold quilt and press along tape lines at decided distances apart. This step is not necessary if you have striped fabric that indicates the channel widths.

2 Stitch one edge of tape along one stripe/crease on the wrong side of one quilt piece. Then stitch other side of tape to same stripe/crease on wrong side of other quilt piece. Be sure to stitch very close to tape edges. Continue to stitch tape along both pieces until all channels are formed.

3 Turn in 5 cm on sides and lower edge. Turn in another 5 cm and stitch down. Fill channels evenly, smoothing the filling right down the channels. When satisfied with quantity of filling, fold over top edge and sew in same way as sides.

4 You can attach two 1 m ties to the end of your quilt to attach it to your bed or to tie it into a bundle for storage for times when it's not in use.

Continental Quilt

These feather or down-filled quilts, also called duvets or doonas, are the ideal solution for cold winter nights. They provide the warmth of several blankets without the weight.

Before You Begin

❏ The size of your quilt is entirely up to you. Generally a double bed quilt should be approximately 2 m x 2 m and a single bed quilt 2 m x 1.60 m.

❏ Use a very closely woven fabric, like japara (not always easy to find), downproof cambric or a very closely woven furnishing chintz or cotton. Don't use sheets – feathers like to work their way through the threads of the fabric and escape!

❏ If joining lengths of fabric to make a single piece, use edge-concealing seams such as run-and-fell or French seams.

❏ The choice of filling is up to you. Down is more expensive than feathers, but is warmer, lighter and bulkier. A combination of feathers and down is a good compromise. Polyester fibre is suitable for anyone allergic to feathers.

❏ Generally, filling comes in packs by weight. Approximately 1.5 kg of feather and down combination filling was needed for our double bed quilt. Polyester fibre weighs more than feathers. Experiment until you are happy with the weight and feel of your own quilt.

❏ Tape is used to create channels for the filling. Choose firm cotton twill tape. Bias binding is unsuitable. Quantity of tape will depend on how many channels you make in your quilt. For our double bed quilt, 20 cm wide channels suited the fabric pattern. This meant that we had nine rows of tape (giving us ten channels), so we

These soft surprises will delight you. Cushions on beds, sofas and chairs add luxury and comfort, and can bring a fresh new look to any setting. You'll also find out how to make a traditional feather-filled bed quilt.

Cushions

Nothing adds instant decorating impact like beautiful cushions. They are easy to make, take little fabric and come in so many shapes and styles that you'll find it difficult to decide which ones to make.

Note: 1 cm seams allowed.

Frilled Piped cushion

MATERIALS
- ☐ 40 cm square for front, and two backs, each 40 cm x 22 cm
- ☐ 1.70 m piping (optional)
- ☐ 30 cm zipper
- ☐ 3.20 m of frill in desired style
- ☐ 40 cm square cushion insert

METHOD

1 Make two-colour frill as instructed in Down To Detail on page 174.

2 With right sides facing and raw edges matching, sew piping (if desired) and then frill around edge of cushion front as instructed in Down To Detail on page 174. If attaching frill after piping, sew over stitching line for piping. Insert zipper in back following instructions in Down To Detail on page 174.

3 Place back and front together with right sides facing. Sew around outside edge following stitching line of piping. Clip away bulk at corners. Turn and press.

Striped Cushion

MATERIALS
- ☐ four matching triangles each 58 cm x 42 cm x 42 cm for front, and two backs each 58 cm x 31 cm
- ☐ 58 cm square thin polyester wadding
- ☐ 30 cm zipper
- ☐ 40 cm square cushion insert

METHOD

1 Carefully join two triangles along one 42 cm seam and press seam open. Repeat for other two triangles. Carefully matching stripes, sew two halves of cushion front together. Press seam open.

2 Baste wadding to wrong side of cushion front.

3 Insert zipper in cushion back as instructed in Down To Detail on page 174. Open zipper. Place front and back together with right sides facing and stitch around outside edge. Trim excess bulk from corners and seams. Turn to right side and press.

5 Carefully pin through all thicknesses 9 cm from edge to form flange. Stitch along pin line.

Appliquéd Piped Cushion

METHOD

1 Cut appliqué from fabric and attach motif on to cushion front as for the easy Appliqué Cushion on page 203, having the stitching on the edge of the motif, rather than 1 cm away. Choose sewing thread to harmonise with background fabric and motif.

2 Make piping and cushion in exactly the same way as the Frilled Piped Cushion, omitting frill.

Piped Cushion with Contrast Band

MATERIALS
- ☐ 40 cm square for front, and two backs, each 40 cm x 22 cm
- ☐ four strips border fabric, each 32 cm x 9 cm
- ☐ 1.7 m contrast piping (see page 174 for making instructions)
- ☐ 30 cm zipper
- ☐ 40 cm square cushion insert

METHOD

1 Trim short ends of strips to perfect diagonals. Join strips to form mitred square which fits cushion 4 cm from outside edge. Clip 1 cm in on corner seam. Press seams open. Press under 1 cm on inside and outside edges of square. Pin square on to cushion front and edgestitch into place.

2 Attach piping and insert zipper as instructed in Down To Detail on page 174. Open zipper. Place front and back together with right sides facing. Stitch around outside edge. Trim excess bulk from corners and seams. Turn and press.

Frilled Cushion with Contrast Band

MATERIALS
- ☐ 40 cm square for front, and two backs, each 40 cm x 22 cm
- ☐ four strips of border fabric, each 40 cm x 9 cm
- ☐ 3.2 m of pre-sewn frill
- ☐ 30 cm zipper
- ☐ 40 cm square cushion insert

METHOD
1 Trim short ends of border strips to perfect diagonals. Join strips together to form mitred square. Clip 1 cm in on corner seams. Press seams open. Press under 1 cm on inside edge of border.

2 Pin border to cushion front, matching outside edges. Edgestitch inside edge of border on to front. Attach frill as instructed in Down To Detail on page 174.

3 Insert zipper as instructed in Down To Detail on page 174. Open zipper. Place front and back together with right sides facing. Stitch around outside edge in previous stitching line. Trim excess bulk at corners and seams. Turn and press.

Cushion with Padded Edge and Contrast Band

MATERIALS
- ☐ 56 cm square for front, and two backs, each 56 cm x 30 cm
- ☐ four strips border fabric, each 40 cm x 9 cm
- ☐ 56 cm square thin polyester wadding
- ☐ 30 cm zipper
- ☐ 40 cm square cushion insert

METHOD
1 Trim short ends of border strips to perfect diagonals. Join strips to form mitred square which fits on cushion front 8 cm from edge. Clip 1 cm in on corner seams. Press seams open. Press under 1 cm on inside and outside edges of border square. Pin square on to cushion front and edgestitch into place. Baste wadding to wrong side of trimmed cushion front.

2 Insert zipper as instructed in Down To Detail on page 174. Open zipper. Place cushion front and back together with right sides facing. Stitch around outside edge. Trim excess bulk from corners and seams. Turn and press.

3 Carefully pin through all thicknesses along outside edge of border to form 8 cm flange. Stitch down along previous stitching line.

Floral Cushion with Contrast Edge

MATERIALS
- ☐ 40 cm square for front, and two backs, each 40 cm x 22 cm
- ☐ eight strips for flange, each 56 cm x 9 cm
- ☐ four strips thin polyester wadding, each 56 cm x 9 cm
- ☐ 30 cm zipper
- ☐ 40 cm square cushion insert

METHOD
1 Baste wadding strips to wrong side of four flange strips. Trim short ends to perfect diagonals and join strips to form mitred square. Trim excess wadding from seams. Turn and press. Join other four strips in same way, omitting wadding.

2 Place two flange squares together with right sides facing and stitch around outside edge. Trim excess bulk at corners and seams. Turn and press. Baste inside edges together.

3 With right sides facing, pin cushion front to inside edge of flange, matching raw edges and corners. Stitch through all thicknesses.

4 Insert zipper as instructed in Down To Detail on page 174. Open zipper. Place front and back together with right sides facing, tucking flange out of the way and sewing around outside edge in previous stitching line. Trim excess bulk at corners and seams. Turn to right side through zipper opening and press.

Down to DETAIL

Cushions

To make continuous corded piping

1 Cut a piece of fabric as shown in Fig. 1. Mark bias strips as shown.

2 Fold fabric with right sides together, so that points A and B are matching. Note that one strip width extends at each side. Join AA to BB with a 6 mm seam. Press seam open (Fig. 2).

3 Cut along bias strip marked lines, giving you one continuous strip of bias fabric. Fold this strip in half over piping cord. Secure cord inside fabric by stitching close to cord, through all thicknesses using the zipper foot of your machine. Match sewing thread to fabric.

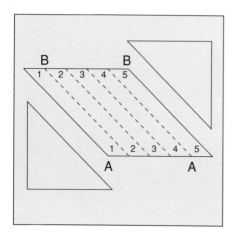

Fig. 1

To attach piping

1 With right sides facing and raw edges matching, pin piping around edge of cushion front, clipping piping seam allowances at corners. Cut 2 cm of cord out of one end of piping to lessen bulk at overlap. Overlap piping ends.

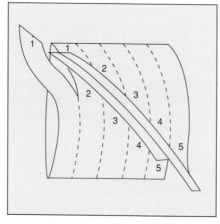

Fig. 2

2 Sew on piping using the zipper foot of your machine.

To insert a zipper

1 Cut two cushion backs. With right sides facing, match two long sides of cushion backs. Stitch both ends closed in a 2 cm seam, leaving an opening the length of your zipper, at the centre. Press seams open.

2 Insert zipper into opening. Open zipper before joining cushion back and front in order to turn cushion through zipper opening (see picture below).

To make a one-colour frill

1 Cut frill 22 cm wide and twice the circumference of your cushion in length. For a 40 cm cushion your frill strip will measure 3.20 m x 22 cm. If necessary, join strips to make required length. Join short ends of frill to form a circle.

2 Fold over double, lengthways, with wrong sides together and raw edges matching. Gather frill 1 cm in from raw edge. Pull up gathering to fit cushion front (see picture above).

To make a two-colour frill

1 Cut two frills, one 14 cm wide and another in contrasting fabric 11 cm wide and twice the circumference of your cushion in length.

2 With right sides facing match one long raw edge of each strip and stitch 1 cm from edge. Press seam to one side. Join short ends of frill to make a circle.

3 Fold fabric over double, lengthways, with wrong sides together and raw edges matching. Press. Gather frill 1 cm in from raw edge. Draw up gathering to fit outside edge of cushion front.

4 This technique gives a frill with the appearance of a contrast fabric binding at the outer edge (see picture above).

Bed Linen

Making your own bed linen is easy, lets you create your own decorating scheme and can save you money too! Remember to measure the bed carefully – small differences won't matter for flat sheets, but accuracy is important for ruffles or valances.

FABRIC REQUIRED FOR SHEETS AND QUILT COVER

	Queen Size	Double Bed Size	Single Bed Size
Flat Sheet	2.80 m	2.30 m	1.60 m
Fitted Sheet	2.70 m	2.20 m	1.50 m
Quilt Cover	4.20 m to finish at 2.10 m x width of sheeting	3.60 m to finish at 1.80 m x width of sheeting	2.80 m to finish at 1.40 m x width of sheeting

FABRIC REQUIRED FOR PILLOWCASES

Plain Pillowcase	50 cm
Ruffled Pillowcase	70 cm
Buttoned Pillowcase	50 cm main fabric; 50 cm x 14 cm (or width desired) contrast
Flanged Pillowcase	70 cm

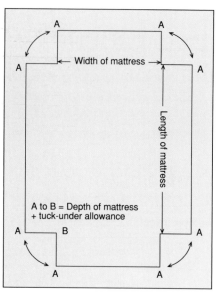

METHOD
Cutting and sewing methods apply to all sizes. Use 1.5 cm seams and neaten all raw edges.

Fitted Sheets

1 Cut squares from each corner (see diagram). Join points 'A'. Sew from outside edge to inner corner, forming an angle at each corner of sheet.

2 Hem around outside edge. Sew 1 cm wide elastic to seam allowance of each corner seam, using zigzag stitch and stretching elastic as you sew.

3 Sew elastic around hem at corners, starting and finishing 40 cm either side of corner seam, stretching elastic as you sew.

Flat Sheets

1 Turn under 5 mm along raw side edges. Turn under 1 cm for hem. Press and stitch down.

2 Turn over top and trim as desired with contrast fabric, lace, ribbon or a stencilled pattern.

Quilt Cover

1 If using sheeting, place selvages at top and lower edges. If using cotton or polycotton dress fabric, join lengths to achieve overall size.

2 If using a zipper to close quilt cover, join ends of one short side, using a 1.5 cm seam leaving correct opening for zipper. Press open seam allowance. Insert zipper. Open zipper. Turn quilt cover so that right sides are facing. Sew front to back right around, using a 1.5 cm seam allowance. Turn quilt cover to right side through zipper opening.

3 If using Velcro or small buttons, place front and back together with right sides facing. Sew all around with 1.5 cm seam allowance and leaving a 1 m opening at one narrow end. Stitch down seam allowances at opening, then sew on closures of your choice.

4 You may like to sew ties of cotton tape inside cover at each corner and on each corner of quilt. Tie these to keep quilt in place within cover.

Bed Ruffle/Valance

It is difficult to give exact measurements and fabric quantities as beds are different heights. The base is same size as mattress top plus seam allowances. Ruffle is same depth as height of bed base from floor plus hems, and length of ruffle should be twice bed length plus bed width x 2.

1 For beds with no bed posts or board at foot, simply hem bedhead end of base. Join ruffle into one continuous strip. Hem short ends and one long edge. Gather remaining raw edge. Stitch ruffle around raw edges of ruffle base.

2 For beds with bedstead posts, hem head end as above. Finish ruffle on either side of posts, with short edges hemmed and butted together at corners. Hem one long side, gather the other and attach to base as above.

3 You can sew ties on either side at top to tie around bed posts or base legs if you wish. Sew 10 cm of elastic to one end of each tie and other end of elastic to ruffle/valance corner. Elastic will take strain off ties and prevent stitching from snapping.

Down to DETAIL

Pillowcases

Plain Pillowcase

1 Cut fabric 50 cm x 1.60 m. Turn in raw edges on both short ends. Stitch 1 cm seam on one end and 5 cm seam on other. Trim on 5 cm seam end as desired.

2 Fold fabric as shown in diagram. Stitch down sides, turn and press.

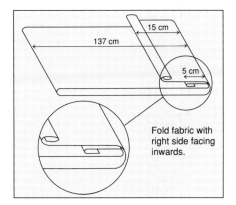

15 cm

137 cm

5 cm

Fold fabric with right side facing inwards.

Ruffled Pillowcase

1 Cut a front piece 78 cm x 50 cm. Cut two backing pieces, one 70 cm x 50 cm and another 22 cm x 50 cm. Cut piece for ruffle 5.20 m x 20 cm.

2 Join short ends of ruffle strip. Fold over double with raw edges matching. Gather raw edges.

3 Stitch ruffle around all edges of front piece, with right sides facing and raw edges matching.

4 Narrow hem one 50 cm edge of each backing piece. Place both back pieces on right side of front piece with right sides facing, overlapping hemmed edges and having outside edges matching. Stitch around outside edge through all thicknesses. Turn and press.

Buttoned Pillowcase

1 Cut a piece 1.52 m x 50 cm. Cut another piece 50 cm x 14 cm.

2 With right side of small piece facing wrong side of larger piece, stitch together across one short end. Press small piece to right side of larger piece.

3 Press under 1 cm on other 50 cm raw edge of small piece. Tuck contrast piping under this pressed edge and stitch through all thicknesses. Press under 1 cm on other 50 cm raw edge of larger piece then press under 5 cm. Stitch. Fold pillowcase with right sides together and short ends matching, securing stitching firmly at opening edge. Turn and press.

4 Make five evenly spaced buttonholes across front 4 cm down from opening. Sew corresponding buttons to inside of back opening. Bind opening edges to match contrast panel if desired.

Flanged Pillowcase

1 Cut one front piece 70 cm x 96 cm. Cut two back pieces, one 80 cm x 70 cm and another 35 cm x 70 cm.

2 Narrow hem one 70 cm end of each back piece. Place back pieces on front piece with right sides facing, hemmed edges of back pieces overlapping and all raw edges matching. Stitch around outside edge. Trim corners of bulk. Turn to right side and press.

3 Stitch all around pillowcase 8 cm in from stitched edge to form flange. To trim, add lace or trimmings at this stitching line and insert 3 mm wide satin ribbon through lace. Tie ends of ribbons into bows at corners.

Down to DETAIL

Stencilled Bedhead, Cushions and Quilt

You don't need to be rich or an artist to own this original work of art! Add a little ingenuity and some stylish paintwork and you can make this bedhead yourself! The bedhead is actually an old picture frame, surrounding a stencilled fabric panel which matches the stencilled quilt. These long narrow frames were commonly available during the 1920s and are usually solidly constructed of lightly carved wood. You could make a similar frame for yourself. The moulded timber pieces are usually available at specialist timber shops, or perhaps a professional picture framer could advise you.

As to which design you stencil, that's entirely up to you. There are a number of designs on the Pull Out Pattern Sheet at the back of this book or a variety of prepared stencils can be purchased or make your own from any design or pattern that pleases you.

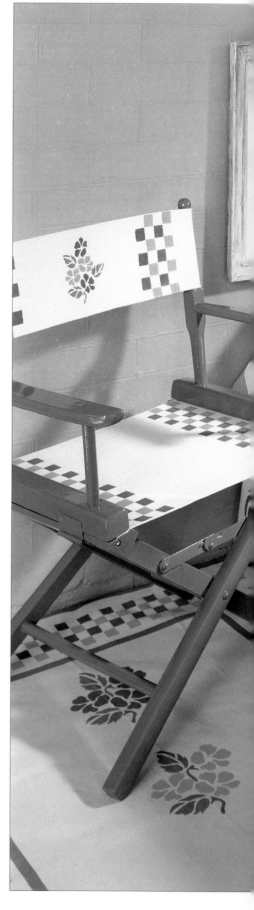

Bedhead

MATERIALS

- ☐ one large rectangular, wooden frame in good condition
- ☐ sufficient cotton fabric to fit into the frame, allowing approximately 10 cm around all the edges for fastening to the frame
- ☐ manila card for the stencil
- ☐ turps (white spirit)
- ☐ linseed oil
- ☐ coloured pencils
- ☐ sharp craft knife
- ☐ board for cutting stencil on
- ☐ stencilling paints and brushes
- ☐ a staple gun or strong sewing needle and thread
- ☐ piece of firm backing board and thick polyester wadding, each the size of the inside measurement of the frame
- ☐ 3 cm wide masking tape
- ☐ wide, thick brown paper
- ☐ two eye hooks and wire for hanging the frame
- ☐ small tacks and a hammer

METHOD

See Page 181 for the large stencil and the Pull Out Pattern Sheet at the back of the book for the small one.

For the stencilled fabric:
Following directions on page 179, stencil the design on to the fabric so that the motifs sit evenly within the frame. Allow it to dry thoroughly. Press on the wrong side.

For making the frame:

1 Press in and sew a 1 cm hem all around fabric.

2 Place the wadding over the backing board. You may need to tape it into place temporarily. Place the stencilled fabric over wadding, positioning it so that the design is in its right position. Tape the fabric edges to the wrong side of the board, checking that you have not distorted the fabric. Staple the fabric edges to the backing board, or stitch the edges together from top to bottom and then from side to side, using a handsewing needle and strong thread. Pull the thread firmly to keep the fabric in place.

3 Place the covered board into the frame, hammering in small tacks on the back around the frame's inner edge to keep the covered board in place.

4 Cover the back of the board with brown paper, folded or cut to size. Cover the edges of the paper with masking tape, taking the tape on to the back of the frame as well. Insert the eye hooks into each side of the frame at the back. Check the required length for the hanging wire. Wind the ends of the wire securely around the eye hooks. Hang the frame at a suitable height above the bed.

Quilt Cover

Before You Begin

❏ This quilt cover is designed for a single bed. The same method can be used to make a larger cover simply by increasing the number of stencilled panels used.

MATERIALS

For the quilt cover:
☐ 7.50 m of 90 cm wide calico or 4 m of 137 cm wide calico
☐ 5.50 m of 112 cm wide homespun cotton in a contrasting colour to match or complement your chosen stencil colour.
☐ 60 cm of continuous zipper or two 30 cm dress zippers
☐ manila card for making the stencil
☐ craft knife or sharp, pointed blade
☐ stencil brushes or sponges, one for each colour
☐ cutting board for cutting stencil on
☐ linseed oil
☐ mineral turpentine (white spirit)
☐ stencilling paints

METHOD

See Pull Out Pattern Sheet at the back of the book for the floral stencil design.

For the stencilling:

1 Coat the manila card with a 50:50 mixture of mineral turpentine (white spirit) and linseed oil. Allow it to dry.

2 Trace the design on to the card and cut it out with the sharp knife. You can cut both leaf and flower designs on the one card.

3 Cut the main fabric into twelve squares each 49 cm x 49 cm. Fold each square

in half, then in half again. Mark the fold point – this is the centre of your square.

4 Place a fabric square on a flat surface, suitable for painting on. Hold it in place with pins or tape. Position your stencil on the fabric square. Paint one colour version of the design on to six squares and the other six squares with the second colour. Allow them to dry, then iron on the wrong side with a medium to hot, dry iron, to set the paint.

For the sewing:
1 cm seams allowed throughout and all pieces of the quilt are joined with right sides facing and raw edges even.

Note: Fabric strips A,B and C have been specified approximately 10 cm longer to allow for fabric movement during sewing. You may prefer to add a little more. The back of the quilt is cut out once the front is finished and can be measured accurately.

1 Cut the contrasting homespun fabric into the following strips: two pieces each 7 cm x 2.15 m for A, two pieces each 7 cm x 1.60 m for B, two pieces each 7 cm x 2.10 m for C, 9 pieces 7 cm x 49 cm for D.

2 Lay out the printed squares in three rows of four in alternating colours. Position the squares so that the stems of one colour hang 'down' the quilt and the stems of the other colour point 'up' the quilt. Starting with the first vertical row of four squares, and using three of the D strips, join the squares into a long panel,

with a D strip separating each one. Keep the layout of the squares in mind when joining the strips to the squares. Press all seams towards the strips. Repeat this procedure with the other two rows of four squares, again checking that your squares have remained according to your layout.

3 Connect the first complete long panel to the second one with one of the C strips, and then the second to the third with the other C strip.

4 Sew the B strips along the top and bottom of the quilt, then sew the A strips along both sides.

5 If necessary, recut the edges of your quilt front to make them straight. Measure the quilt front, and cut the backing piece to the same width as the front but 3 cm longer.

6 Cut across the backing strip 12 cm up from the lower edge. Rejoin these pieces in a 1.5 cm seam, leaving a 60 cm opening in the middle for the zipper or zippers. Press the seam open. Insert the zipper. If you are using two dress zippers, sew them so that the pull tabs are in the centre of the opening. When they are both pulled back, the opening will be of sufficient size to insert the quilt.

7 Place the back and front together, with right sides facing and stitch around the edges. Turn the quilt cover to the right side through the zipper opening.

Stencilled Cushion

MATERIALS

☐ one 40 cm square of main fabric to be stencilled for the front, two pieces 22 cm x 40 cm for the cushion back
☐ 30 cm zipper
☐ contrast fabric strip 1.60 m x 8 cm for the border
☐ contrast fabric strip 3.20 m x 22 cm for the ruffle
☐ 40 cm cushion insert

METHOD

1 cm seams allowed throughout.

1 Stencil the same floral motif as on the quilt on to the cushion front, following the stencilling instructions on page 179.

2 Cut the 8 cm wide contrast strip into four 40 cm lengths, then cut each end of each strip at a perfect diagonal. Join the four strips into an open square by seaming the corners together, stopping the stitching on each corner 1 cm from the inner edge. Turn in 1 cm on the inner edges of the square, press.

3 Place the border square on to the stencilled front, with the wrong side of the square facing the right side of the cushion front, raw edges even. Baste along inner edges of the border square, then stitch through all thicknesses.

4 Join short ends of 22 cm wide strip to form a circle. Fold the strip in half lengthways, with wrong sides together. Divide the strip into quarters and mark with pins, having the seam as one quarter point. Gather along the raw edges. Draw up the gathering. Pin the ruffle to the right side of the front, with a quarter point at each corner, right sides facing and raw edges matching. Stitch through all thicknesses just inside the gathering.

5 Join back pieces along 40 cm edge, using a 2 cm seam allowance and leaving a 30 cm opening for the zipper in the middle. Press seams open. Insert the zipper into the opening. Open the zipper.

6 Pin the back to the front with right sides facing, keeping the ruffle out of the way. Stitch around the edge. Trim the corners. Turn the cushion cover right side out through the zipper opening. Place cushion insert inside cover.

This is the larger stencil outline for the pillows, bedhead and the floorcloth. See the Pull Out
Pattern at the back of the book for the quilt stencil and the smaller floral stencil

181

Baby's Room

*Decorating a room for a new baby is a true labour of love.
Ideally your decor should 'grow' with the baby and still be fresh
in a couple of years time. This means avoiding tiny baby motifs
in fabric and looking for something a little more timeless.
To make the cuddly lamb toy, use the large outline on the Pull
Out Pattern Sheet, enlarged to twice the size and cut two shapes
from brushed fabric. Stitch around the edge with right sides
facing, leaving an opening for stuffing with polyester wadding.
Using embroidery stitches outline the features as indicated .The
large, square net is edged with purchased satin blanket binding
that has been stencilled to match the sheets.*

*Baby's room in a cheerful combination of
sunny yellow and crisp blue, showing the tie
backs, curtains, bassinet quilt, sheets, toy
and trimmed net.*

Trimmed Curtains

Before You Begin

❏ See the Pull Out Pattern Sheet at the
back of the book for how to measure your
window and estimate fabric quantities.
Quantities for trimmings will depend on
the size of your curtains.

❏ Decide whether you wish to have two curtains that open in the middle and are pulled to each side, or a single curtain. If two curtains are your choice, halve the width prescribed and add an extra 5 cm to each curtain for the centre hem allowances. Sewing instructions are given for one curtain, simply make two using the same method.

MATERIALS

☐ sufficient main curtain fabric (see diagram for measuring on the Pull Out Pattern Sheet at the back of the book)
☐ three strips of contrast fabric 15 cm wide x the length of your curtains for the side panels; another piece of contrast fabric 15 cm wide x width of your main curtain plus side borders for the lower panel
☐ two strips of contrast fabric, each 15 cm x 55 cm for tie backs, one for stencilling, one for lining
☐ a piece of fusible interfacing 15 cm x 55 cm
☐ 20 cm bias binding or 3 cm wide fabric strips
☐ 2 cm diameter dowelling or a curtain pole to suit your window
☐ two support brackets and screws
☐ curtain tie back hook
☐ manila card for the stencil
☐ linseed oil
☐ mineral turpentine (white spirit)
☐ pencil
☐ sharp craft knife
☐ stencil brushes and paints
☐ cutting board

METHOD

See Pull Out Pattern Sheet at the back of the book for the lamb stencil design. 1 cm seams allowed throughout.

1 Place the two side panel pieces together with right sides facing. With a pencil, mark a perfect diagonal at one end. Cut off fabric along this line on both panels. Also mark and cut off perfect diagonals at both ends of the bottom contrast panel. Sew the contrast panels together at the diagonal seams, with right sides together and stopping the stitching 1 cm from the inner edge, to form a U shape. Press in 1 cm all around inner edge.

2 Place the contrast panels on the curtain so that the right side of the contrast panels faces the wrong side of the curtain and raw edges are matching. Pin and baste. Stitch around the outside edge.

3 Press the seam and the contrast panel to the right side of the curtain. Stitch the pressed inner edge to the curtain through all thicknesses. Press. Stencil the border now if desired.

4 Turn in 1 cm at the top, then turn another 7 cm. Press. Stitch. Stitch again 3.5 cm from the top. This row of stitching forms the pocket for inserting a rod and will have a frilled effect when the curtain is in position.

5 Install the brackets. Slide the curtain on to the pole, adjusting the gathers to fit. Hang the curtain.

Stencil the curtain tie back with a lamb to match the sheets. Its features can be stencilled or embroidered and you can sew on a tiny bow as we have done

For the tie back:

1 Stencil the tie back piece following the instructions on page 179. Interface the stencilled tie back. Open out the bias binding and press flat. Fold the fabric strip or bias over double, with right sides facing and raw edges matching. Stitch the long side. Turn and press. Cut into two 10 cm pieces. Pin both ends of one length to one end of the stencilled tie back, with right sides facing and raw edges matching. Repeat for the other end with the remaining length. Place the tie back lining over the stencilled tie back. Stitch around the edges leaving an opening for turning. Turn. Press neatly.

2 Install the hook at the appropriate height. Place the tie back around the curtain and secure by hooking the loops over the hook.

Bassinet Quilt

This pretty cover is one of the simplest ways of constructing a quilt that we know of! With the same technique you can make quilts of any size.

Before You Begin

❏ You will need to work out how many and what size squares will make up a quilt to fit your bassinet. The cover shown is five squares wide x six squares long, where each square is 12 cm x 12 cm. Each 'pillow' of the quilt has a front and a back so for a quilt like this one you will need about 50 cm each of two main fabrics that are 115 cm wide.

❏ As the quilt will need to be washable, pre-shrink all fabric before sewing.

MATERIALS

☐ sufficient cotton or polycotton fabric
☐ polyester fibre for stuffing
☐ self-fabric rouleaux or contrasting ribbon

METHOD

1 cm seams allowed throughout.

1 Cut out the required number of squares from each fabric. Pair up one square from each fabric with right sides facing. Stitch around three sides leaving the remaining side open for inserting the stuffing. Clip the corners and turn the pillow right side out, making sure to push the corners out carefully. Press, turning under 1 cm on open edges.

A close up of the bassinet quilt showing how the 'pillows' are joined

Baby's bassinet with stencilled pillow shape, stencilled and trimmed sheet and pillow quilt. Make the fluffy lamb toy for baby to cuddle

2 Place the pillows in rows as determined by your quilt size, butting the edges together accurately. Sew butted edges of adjoining pillows together, using a zigzag or similar stitch.

3 Stuff pillows, taking care not to place too much stuffing in each square as it will be difficult to hold the edges together while sewing. Place open edges of one row of pillows butted to the stitched edge of the next row. Stitch together, using zigzag stitch or similar stitching. Continue joining rows in this way until desired quilt size is reached.

4 Knot the ends of 25 cm lengths of rouleaux or ribbon and stitch the centre of each length securely to the points where the pillows meet. Tie rouleaux or ribbon into bows.

Sheets

These pretty sheets are trimmed with gingham and have a stencilled pattern to match the one on the curtains.

MATERIALS

For each sheet:
- ☐ 90 cm of 115 cm wide fabric
- ☐ an additional strip, of either contrast or of main fabric, 90 cm x 15 cm for the trimmed band
- ☐ 90 cm x 5 cm strip of gingham fabric
- ☐ matching sewing thread
- ☐ stencilling equipment as for the nursery curtains

METHOD
1 cm seams allowed throughout.

1 Mark the positions for the stencilled lambs across the 15 cm wide band. Stencil the band following the stencilling instructions on page 179.

2 Press under 1 cm on the lower edge of the stencilled band. Place the stencilled band on the top of the sheet so the right side of the band faces the wrong side of the sheet, having the lamb's feet closest to the edge to be stitched. Stitch along the top and side edges of the band and sheet. Turn the band to the right side. Press.

3 Fold fabric strip over double with wrong sides facing and pin under the pressed edge of the band. Stitch down through all thicknesses. Hem all remaining edges of the sheet to finish. Press.

Pillow Shape

MATERIALS

- ☐ 30 cm of 115 cm wide fabric to match the sheets
- ☐ a piece of quilter's polyester wadding the size of your pillow shape (see below)
- ☐ sewing thread

METHOD
1 cm seams allowed throughout.

1 Make a pattern for pillow shape by tracing the curved outline of the top of your bassinet mattress and have it measure about 30 cm long. It will look a little like a half-circle. Cut two pillow shapes from the main fabric and one from the wadding.

2 Stencil a lamb on one fabric piece, using the same method as for the sheet band and curtain tie back.

3 Place wadding against wrong side of the stencilled fabric. Baste together.

4 Place remaining piece over trimmed piece, right sides facing and raw edges matching. Stitch around edge, with an opening for turning at one side. Turn shape to right side. Press. Hand sew closed.

Down to DETAIL

Fabric Shelves

These fabric shelves are ideal storage for a room where floor space is at a premium. You can store a wide variety of things, such as toys, hats or bags and, by adjusting the size of the shelves, you can store much more.

MATERIALS

☐ 2 m of 115 cm wide large check print fabric

☐ 2.20 m of 115 cm wide stripe print fabric

☐ 1.50 m of 115 cm wide small check print fabric

☐ 5 rectangles of hardboard, each 39 cm x 29 cm

METHOD

1 cm seams allowed throughout

1 Cut two rectangles of the large check print fabric for the outside panels, each 152 cm x 32 cm. Cut two rectangles of stripe print fabric for the shelves and back, each 212 cm x 42 cm. Cut eight squares of small check print for the inside panels, each 32 cm x 32 cm, and one rectangle of small check print for the inside top, 62 cm x 32 cm.

2 With right sides facing, stitch stripe print pieces together along the short edges to form one long strip. Press the seam open. Press under 1 cm at remaining short edges, topstitch and edgestitch to finish.

3 Fold strip every 30 cm to form five double-thickness open-backed shelves, with four single-thickness backs in between. Press.

4 With right sides facing, pin one small check print square to the top, back and lower edges of one shelf side. 1 cm seam allowance at front edge of square will extend past finished shelf front. Clipping into corners, stitch around top, back and lower edges to form the shelf side. Press. Repeat for other seven squares to form the entire shelf unit.

5 With right sides facing, pin one large check print piece to side of shelf unit around front, back and lower edges. Large check print piece will extend 31 cm above top of shelf unit to form top hanging section. Clipping into corners, stitch around front, back and lower edges to enclose all seam allowances. Trim seams and turn to right side. Press. Repeat for the other side.

6 With right sides facing, stitch top edges of large check print pieces together to form top hanging section. Press seam open.

7 With right sides facing, stitch small check print rectangle to top hanging section along front edge. Clipping into corners, stitch side edges of rectangle to side edges of top shelf, enclosing all seam allowances. Trim seams, turn to right side. Press.

8 Press under 1 cm along back edges of top hanging section to enclose remaining seam allowances. Slipstitch together to finish.

9 Insert five rectangles of hardboard into open backs of shelves to complete shelf unit. Top hanging section should then be suspended from an appropriate wall bracket.

Above: Fabric shelves

Fabric Fantasy

Fabrics set the decorating scheme, and the choice is endless. Colour, texture and pattern are the integral elements to watch for, but the hardest part is deciding which one to choose.

Borders and Trims

Introduce the personal touch to soft furnishings with wonderful braids and trims. Today's furnishings are increasingly ornate and generous in proportion. There is a pronounced trend towards softness and fullness in design, whether it's in the lines of well-padded sofas and soft feather-filled cushions or generous metres of fabric, draped across curtains to form swagged pelmets or gathered into festoon blinds.

Interior designers have always valued the extra 'something' given to a piece of furniture or accessory by the addition of well-chosen trims. Most stockists of furnishing fabrics have a good range of trims to choose from, and many are surprisingly inexpensive. While cost is a most important consideration, if only because it is possible to over-trim an inexpensive fabric, there are several other considerations to bear in mind when selecting your borders and trims.

Matching of styles is important. Common sense is the key here, and while creativity frequently challenges rules of colour and suitability, your 'eye' will tell you if a trim matches a fabric. Fabrics that are generally dull rather than lustrous tend to look casual – while shimmery fabrics will always have a more formal look. You need to look at trims in the same way. Simple rickrack braid will look smart but informal, and so too will bias binding, twill braids, checked ribbons and cotton laces. Lustrous formal looks are enhanced by adding twisted silk cords and tassels, brocaded braids, metallic bindings and moiré taffeta and silk ribbons. Some decorators manage to achieve wonderful 'surprises' by the unusual marriage of trims and fabric. It takes considerable skill to pull this off successfully, so take care.

Too much of a contrasting trim will become the focal point. If this is not your intention, be conscious of the impact of the trim you are adding. This is not a problem if the trim is in the same colour as your fabric. In this case it will not compete with the fabric, rather it will add interesting textured effects.

Will the braid be as long-wearing as the fabric? Be mindful of where you use the trim; hand and headrests are more prone to wearing than the back of a sofa. It is sometimes a good idea to purchase more braid than you need right at the beginning to allow for replacement of worn areas.

Is the braid washable? Will the colour run in water? If you are planning to wash the trimmed item, you should wash the trim and the fabric first. This also applies if you are trimming an existing item . Sometimes a handful of household cooking salt thrown into cold rinsing water will help to 'set' dyes in trims, but it is always wise to be sure.

New Looks for Old

One of the best low-cost decorating tricks around is to conceal shabby items with generous amounts of inexpensive fabric. It's easy to do, takes a little time and patience, but the results are wonderful and well worth the effort. Try some of these ideas for yourself and soon you'll be wanting to cover everything in sight!

Fabric-covered Chair

METHOD

You don't need a pattern to cover that old director's chair with fabric. It's a breeze if you follow these simple instructions.

1 Join lengths of your chosen fabric to make a large square. Practise on a double bed sheet to see what size square you will need. You may have to join fabric at selvages to achieve the correct area of fabric. Press seams open.

2 Open out square and place it over chair, pressing it into corners and bundling it up around bases of arms and into seat area. Pin to secure while this fitting process is carried out. Once you are satisfied with fit and drape, mark positions of eight buttonholes, one either side of arm bases, at front, and again at back.

Top right: Detail of bow
Right: Give new life to some well-loved, old pieces for a cheap redecorating idea
Below: Chair before covering

190

3 Remove fabric and make 3 cm long buttonholes as marked. Replace fabric on chair. Tie string through buttonholes to secure. Trim around base at floor level, to create even length. Remove fabric from chair and hem lower edge as marked or fold edge over piping cord and stitch down with zipper foot of your machine.

4 Make ties from scrap fabric, cut away from hem, or face them with a pretty, contrasting fabric as we have done. Cut strips about 1 m x 22 cm. Fold double, lengthways, with right sides facing. Sew around all edges leaving an opening for turning. Turn and press. Insert ties through buttonholes and tie into bows at base of arms and back of chair.

5 Make a frilled cushion for comfort as well as good looks! Cut out two pieces of contrast fabric, the same size as chair seat plus seam allowances, and sufficient frill plus seam allowances. Make cover in same way as Frilled piped cushion on page 172. Instead of a cushion insert, baste several layers of wadding together around edges and place inside cover.

Above: Trimming hem of chair cover
Below: Fabric Covered Boxes

Boxes

METHOD
These sturdy storage boxes are recycled cardboard cartons cut to a new size and shape and covered with decorative fabric.

1 Use spray-on glue, PVA adhesive, or a glue gun to cover the boxes. Remember to allow sufficient fabric at edges to tuck under and glue securely.

2 Cover cardboard completely with fabric for a professional result.

Footstool

Footstool

METHOD
You'll never believe this but under this glamorous footstool is an orange crate from the fruit shop!

1 Cut a foam-rubber base for the top and cover with fabric, pulling it down tightly at corners and edges. Secure with a staple gun or small tacks. Cut away excess fabric below staples.

2 Use selvage of fabric as bottom hem. Form a deep box pleat at each corner, staple fabric around box, placing staples beside first row, securing top cover. Trim away excess fabric close to staples.

3 Cover staple rows with a band of fabric, leaving tails at each corner.

4 Tie tails into bows. You need not sew these ties. Simply press in raw edges and fold tie over double lengthways to hide all raw edges.

Notice Board

METHOD
An old frame that has been covered with fabric makes a super notice board.

1 Cover a piece of cork with fabric. Glue a contrasting fabric all over an old wooden picture frame.

2 Insert cork into frame. Secure it with tacks as you would a picture. Attach a wire or hook for hanging.

Storage Tins

METHOD
These are useful for storing kitchen utensils, pencils on desks or even flowers.

1 Cut a strip of fabric long enough to go around the tin plus 2 cm for over and underlap x height of tin plus 5 cm to fold over the rim to the inside. You can finish your fabric under the rim if you prefer.

2 Cover empty, clean food tins with craft glue. Glue strip around tin.

Above: Notice Board
Below: Storage Tins

Say it with
Flowers

*B*ring flowers into your home with these beautiful fabric and painted blooms. This crafty collection also includes an easily constructed container for growing the real thing, and some beautiful bunches to shape a year-round fireplace screen.

Down to DETAIL

Year Round Wreaths

Wreaths bring a welcome to any front door at any time of the year. They also look charming above a fireplace or dresser. If you use scented dried flowers, wreaths are a delightful addition to bathroom and bedroom.

Before You Begin

❏ Wreath bases can be made of many things including loops of garden vines; twisted straw bound with string; polystyrene florists' rings; fabric tubes stuffed with polyester fibre; long strands of willow twisted together (the leaves will dry on strands) and thin strips of growing bamboo (again the leaves will dry on stems). What you choose will depend on your personal preference and the availability of raw materials. You can paint your base or leave it in its natural state – again this is a matter of personal preference. If you do decide to paint, spray paint is ideal.

❏ Add a loop of wire, ribbon or cord at the back for hanging your wreath.

❏ Just about anything pretty or unusual can be used to trim a wreath. Try using small and large dried flowers; dried pods; leaves; nuts; shells; purchased baubles; ribbons or fabric bows. Plastic fruit is also worth considering, especially if you paint it. It is a good idea to have all your trimmings assembled and ready for use (painted, trimmed etc) before starting. Wire the trimmings into small bunches before attaching them to the base (as above). Other trimmings may be handled singly.

❏ Have a clear plan for your wreath before you begin constructing it. Take some time to experiment with colours, shapes and the distribution of the trimming. Concentrating the decorations at the lower end and adding some trailing ribbons can be very attractive.

❏ Make wreaths for Christmas, Easter and special birthdays – even make a wreath for a bride by drying her bouquet and fashioning a small wreath from it to preserve the memory forever.

MATERIALS
☐ materials for making base
☐ assorted trimmings
☐ glue gun
☐ lightweight florists' wire
☐ optional spray paint

METHOD

1 Make base by twisting numerous strands or vines (or whatever you have chosen) around one another to form a pleasing shape. You can tuck in any loose ends or leave them to protrude.

2 Following your design, glue trimming around base with a glue gun.

3 Add ribbon bows, nuts, shells or any other suitable trimmings between decorations. Wire in hook for hanging.

Above: Wiring trimming into bunches
Left: Grape vine prunings twisted together to make rustic wreaths

Preserved Flowers

*Preserved flowers and leaves present many
charming opportunities for decorating.*

Before You Begin

❏ Always pick perfect speci-
mens for preserving. They are
at their best in the mornings,
just after the dew has dried. Be
sure they are completely dry
before beginning to treat them.

Drying Flowers with Borax

MATERIALS
❏ large, lidded plastic container
❏ quantity of borax
❏ small paintbrush
❏ sticky-tape
❏ spray-on clear lacquer

METHOD

1 Pour a 2 cm layer of borax
into container. Place flowers on to borax, keeping them
separate from one another.
Pour more borax around flowers, brushing it into crevices
and folds until flowers are
completely covered and there
are no air pockets. Take care
to retain shape of flowers.

2 Repeat layers until container is full. Replace lid
and seal edges with sticky-
tape. Leave for two weeks
before checking on drying
progress. Flowers may be left
in borax until needed.

3 Remove borax from flowers with paintbrush before
using. You can spray dried
flowers with clear lacquer.

Drying Leaves with Glycerine

MATERIALS
❏ firm leaves on small
branches, such as beech;
camellia; chestnut; haw-
thorn; eucalypts and aspi-
distras
❏ cooled mixture of one-third
glycerine to two-thirds boiling water
❏ tall glass, narrow-necked
containers

METHOD

1 Place approximately 6 cm
of cooled glycerine mix-
ture into each jar. Crush ends
of stems and place stem ends
into jars to rest in mixture.
Leave them in mixture until
small droplets of glycerine
appear on leaf surfaces.

2 Top up glycerine mixture
occasionally if needed.
Some leaves will turn brown,
others take on decorative
streaked effects.

Pressing Flowers

MATERIALS
❏ fresh flowers
❏ blotting paper
❏ heavy book (a telephone
directory is ideal)
❏ scalpel or sharp craft knife

METHOD

1 If flowers have thick stems,
pare away some thickness
with a sharp craft knife or scalpel, allowing the stems to be
pressed flat.

2 Place flowers on to two
layers of blotting paper.
Cover with another two layers
of blotting paper and then place
the flowers and blotting paper
between pages of heavy book.
Add extra weight, perhaps with
a brick, and leave for several
days before checking. Flowers are dry when they are pa-
pery to the touch.

Fireplace Screen

Bring spring into your home all year round! Take motifs from one of your floral furnishing fabrics or a wallpaper and make this lovely 'basket of flowers' to sit in your fireplace when it's not in use. Brighten a dull corner with your lovely creation in spring and summer.

Before You Begin

❏ The size of this screen is entirely up to you. Choose the proportions that best suit your room and fireplace and use our photograph to help you decide.

❏ You will need a power jigsaw or a hand-held fretsaw to cut accurately around the motifs.

MATERIALS
☐ paper or fabric for pictures
☐ piece of ply, particle or craft wood of appropriate size and approximately 1.5 cm thick
☐ two angle irons, at least 10 cm x 20 cm for legs (larger sizes may be needed to support a very large screen)
☐ 2.5 cm thick piece of timber at least 20 cm square for support panel and to attach angle irons
☐ screws for brackets and support panel
☐ PVA adhesive
☐ acrylic paints
☐ power jigsaw or hand-held fretsaw
☐ small sharp scissors
☐ clear gloss lacquer

METHOD
1 Paint both sides of ply, particle or craft wood in same colour as fabric background. Cut out flowers very pre-cisely from paper or fabric and arrange them on the timber to suit size of screen, allowing sufficient space below for basket or urn. Sketch in basket or urn. Paint.

2 Using a paintbrush, coat back of flow-ers and their position on timber with glue. Place each flower into position, coat-ing surface with glue again. Continue do-ing this until picture is built up.

3 When completely dry, cut carefully around outline of flowers and basket, leaving a 1.5 cm margin. Paint edges. Glue and screw square of timber behind basket and screw on angle irons, just a little up from lower edge so that screen tips slightly backwards. You may wish to paint the back of the screen and sign with the date of its making.

4 Seal entire screen with two coats of clear gloss paint.

Below left: Back view of Fireplace Screen
Below: Finished screen

Flower Picture

The six pretty floral motifs have been embroidered separately and then mounted and framed to create this delightful picture. The same embroideries could be used to make six miniature pictures.

Before You Begin

❏ The full-size drawings give the six floral motifs that were used – A wild orchid, B foxglove, C violets, D garlic, E primroses, F cowslip.

❏ The flowers have been worked in a variety of embroidery stitches which are clearly marked on the diagram for that piece.

MATERIALS
☐ Anchor Stranded Cotton, 1 skein each: White 01; Old Rose 075, 076, 077; Parma Violet 0109, 0110; Laurel Green 0208, 0211; Parrot Green 0254, 0256, 0258; Buttercup 0292, 0297; Gorse Yellow 0303
☐ six 25 cm squares of cream, medium-weight embroidery fabric
☐ Milward International Range crewel needles no. 6 and no. 7
☐ tracing paper
☐ dressmaker's carbon paper

METHOD

1 Trace each design and transfer one to centre of each fabric piece.

2 Work each design following stitch diagram and key on pages 200-201. All parts similar to numbered parts are worked in same colour and stitch. Use no. 6 needle for four-strand embroidery and no. 7 needle for three-strand embroidery.

3 When stitching is complete, carefully iron all pieces, before having them professionally framed.

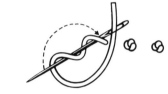

Fig. 1

Fig. 2

FRENCH KNOTS

1 Bring thread out at required position, hold thread down with left thumb and encircle thread twice with needle as shown (Fig. 1).
2 Still holding thread firmly, twist needle back to starting point and insert it close to where thread first emerged. Pull thread through to back and secure it for a single French knot or pass on to position of next stitch as shown (Fig. 2).

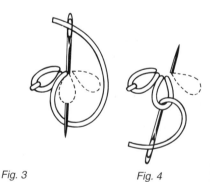

Fig. 3   *Fig. 4*

DAISY STITCH

1 Bring thread through at top and hold it down with left thumb. Insert needle where it last emerged and bring point out a short distance away. Pull thread through, keeping working thread under needle point as shown (Fig. 3).
2 Fasten each loop at foot with a small stitch (Fig. 4).

198

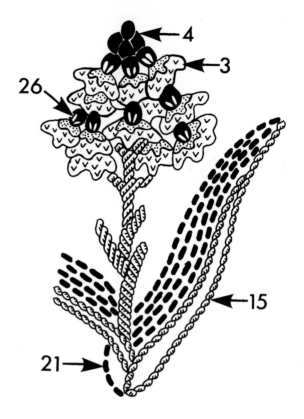

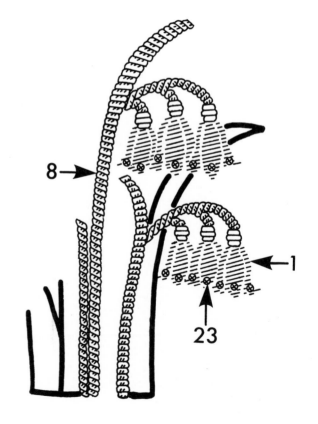

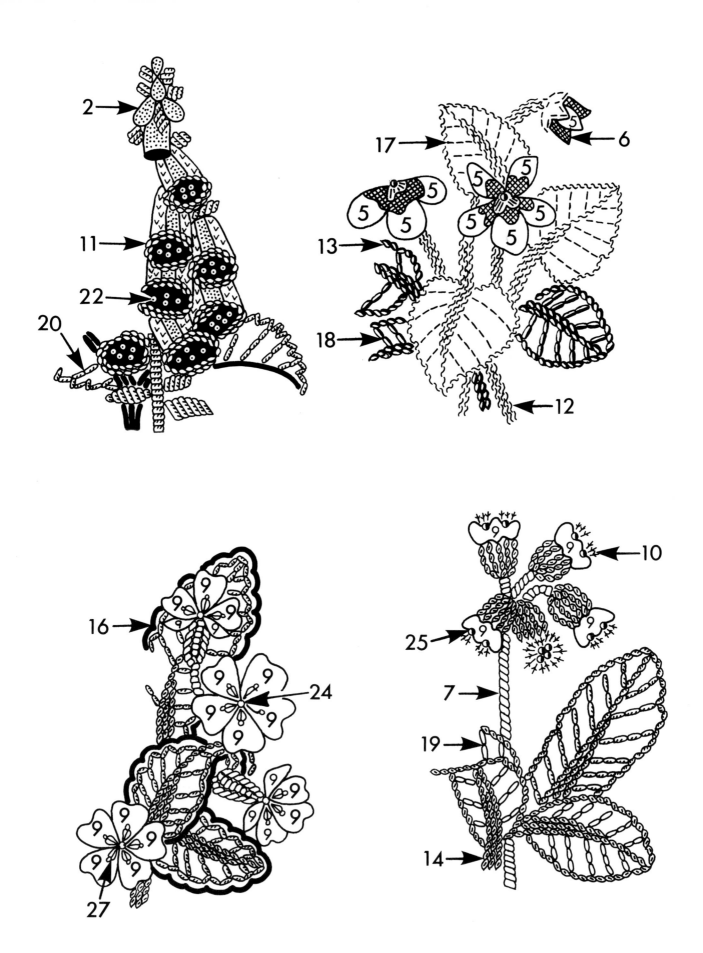

Fabric Flowers

Fabric flowers are an easy, inexpensive accessory. Made from fabric scraps, they will complete a coordinated colour scheme. Make them small or large, and pile them into a lovely cane basket for a welcoming, country look.

Before You Begin

❑ The basis for these flowers is a simple gathered strip of fabric and the finished width of the flowers will depend on the width of the fabric.

MATERIALS
For each one-colour flower:
❑ fabric strip approximately 50 cm x 15 cm pressed over double
❑ bamboo skewer
❑ craft glue or glue gun
For each two-colour flower:
❑ two contrasting fabric strips each 50 cm x 8.5 cm

❑ bamboo skewer
❑ craft glue or glue gun

METHOD

1 Fold one colour strip over double, lengthways, with wrong sides facing. For two-colour flowers, place contrasting strips with right sides facing and stitch along one long side. Turn and press open, then crease and press along seam to fold in half. Curve short ends as shown.

2 Gather along raw edges of each folded strip. Draw up gathers. Beginning at one end, wind or fold fabric strip around end of skewer, gluing to secure as you go.

Above left: Fabric Flowers
Above: Stitched and gathered strips

Continue until all fabric is used, or desired size is achieved. Make flowers full and keep flower base flat.

3 Optional: To stiffen flowers, spray with laundry starch and dry thoroughly with a hair dryer.

Below: Rolling strips around skewer

No-sew Appliqué

If you don't sew, but love the look of appliqué you can create the same effect with bonding fabric or webbing and fabric paints, packaged in nozzled bottles, to fix and outline the motifs.

Before You Begin

❏ Wash all fabrics before using to remove sizing or chemical thickener coating the fibres. If you don't do this first, the sizing will wash out taking the paint and appliqué with it.

MATERIALS

For cushion:
☐ 40 cm square cotton fabric for front and two backs, each 40 cm x 22 cm
☐ 1.70 m piping (optional)
☐ 30 cm zipper
☐ 3.20 m of frill in desired style (see page 174)
☐ 40 cm square cushion insert

For appliqué:
☐ cotton fabric to provide motif for appliqué
☐ 40 cm length of paper-backed bonding fabric or webbing
☐ fabric paint
☐ scrap plain fabric 25 cm x 14 cm for bow appliqué

METHOD

1 Cut out flower motifs with a 2 cm border all around. Cut out bow like the one shown.

2 Place motif on to bonding fabric or webbing with glue side against back of motif. To bond, iron firmly on motif side. Cut around motif precisely. Motif has now absorbed adhesive. Peel away paper backing and position motif (or motifs) on to cushion front.

3 Iron motif on to cushion front, using a pressing cloth, if necessary, to protect fabric. It is sometimes easier to cut out exact shape of the motif in bonding fabric first, such as for bow, then bond as described above. Allow to cool.

4 Outline around all raw edges of motif, using paint and following manufacturer's instructions. Make a line of paint that, when dry, seals edges of appliqué on to fabric. Allow paint to dry for twenty-four hours before making up cushion.

5 Make cushion as Frilled Piped Cushion on page 172.

Above: Squeezing line of paint around bonded motif
Below: No-sew Appliqué Cushion

Down to DETAIL

Appliqué Cushions

If your machine can zigzag, you can appliqué beautiful motifs very easily. Think of appliqué as a way of painting a picture with fabric. Clothes, especially children's clothes, furnishings, table linen and bed clothes can all be made totally original with simple appliqué.

MATERIALS
- [ ] fabric featuring flowers, animals, borders or any motif that will lend itself to being cut out
- [ ] cushion front 40 cm x 40 cm, and two backs, each 40 cm x 22 cm in fabric for cushion that matches perfectly with background of motif
- [ ] 1.70 m contrasting piping (see Down To Detail, page 174)
- [ ] 30 cm zipper
- [ ] 40 cm square cushion insert

METHOD

1 Cut out around motif, leaving 2 cm margin all around.

2 Interface motif as desired, if necessary. Position motif on area to be appliqued. Pin or baste to secure.

3 Zigzag around motif 5 mm in from cut edge. Trim away excess fabric, close to stitching. Stitch again over first zigzag, using a slightly wider satin stitch.

4 When appliqué is complete, place piping around cushion front, with raw edges matching. Attach piping as instructed in Down To Detail on page 174.

5 Insert zipper as instructed in Down To Detail, page 174. Leaving zipper open, place back on front, with right sides facing. Stitch around outside, through all thicknesses, following stitching line for piping. Turn cushion to right side, place insert in cover, close zipper.

Far left: Finished Planter
Left: Inside Planter with base boards removed
Below left: Planter before painting

Versailles Planter

This wonderful timber planter box is in a classic style. It looks equally good on a balcony, patio or garden. If you plan to have it in the open, choose a water-resistant timber and seal it well.

Before You Begin

❏ Make a cardboard template the same size as the end of your support rails and mark accurately, in the middle of it, two drill holes for dowel insertion, 2 cm apart.

MATERIALS

☐ four corner posts, each 75 mm x 75 mm x 600 mm long; eight side rails, each 70 mm x 20 mm x 430 mm long; twenty-four side boards, each 70 mm x 20 mm x 500 mm long; two base supports, each 30 mm x 30 mm x 490 mm long; six base boards, each 70 mm x 20 mm x 440 mm long; thirty-two grooved dowel pieces, each 10 mm in diameter x 50 mm long
☐ jigsaw or fretsaw for shaping
☐ screwdriver
☐ electric drill, 10 mm diameter drill bit
☐ handsaw
☐ hammer
☐ plane or rasp
☐ marking square
☐ sandpaper
☐ wood glue
☐ sixty 32 mm wood screws
☐ approximately 1 m square plastic sheet for lining

METHOD

1 Cut four corner posts to 600 mm long. Sand raw ends. Mark all four posts identically for insertion of dowels that will connect eight side rails to corner posts. Each side rail is held by four dowel pieces, two at each end.

2 Using your template, drill top dowel hole 80 mm down and 30 mm in from top of each corner post, with second 20 mm away. These holes must be no more than 27 mm deep. Drill lower pair of holes with same spacing 80 mm up from bottom. Using template, repeat holes on one other, adjoining side of each corner post.

3 Place six side boards butted together along a side rail to recheck for accurate length. Mark cutting edges and cut side rails. Sand raw ends, then using template, drill two dowel holes in each end of each side rail to align with holes drilled in corner posts. Spread dowel pieces with wood glue and insert into corner posts.

4 Check that remaining side boards are exactly 500 mm long. Mark curved ends, using a cup or small saucer as a template. Cut to shape. Sand all raw edges.

5 Position six side boards over two side rails, with rails approximately 340 mm apart. Note that bottoms of side boards should all be level and that side rails cover bottoms of vertical side boards. Check this distance with your drilled holes, as slight alterations may be necessary. Screw side boards to side rails, from inside.

6 Spread exposed dowel plugs in corner posts with glue. Attach side pieces to corner posts.

7 Mark 1 cm from top all around each corner post and 1 cm in from edges on top of post. With a saw, plane or rasp, cut off top edges at an angle using these lines as a guide. Cut from one line through post to the other, thus creating a 45° angle on each edge. Sand edges neatly.

8 Measure and cut two timber base supports. They should be same length as side rails. Screw each to lower inside edge of bottom side rails at base of opposite side boards. Cut base support boards to fit loosely across base, resting on these supports. The base boards are removable for ease of cleaning, painting or replacing water-damaged timbers etc.

9 To allow planting directly into the box, tack plastic lining inside box. Be sure to have sufficient ease in plastic to allow for soil weight and remove base boards below where drainage holes are cut in plastic lining. Paint planter – if using oil paints, seal and undercoat it first.

Hand Towel

Appliqué this lovely apple blossom motif on to a purchased hand towel. To complete a pretty set, appliqué the same design on to a face washer.

MATERIALS

- ☐ Anchor Stranded Cotton, 1 skein each: Geranium 06; Carnation 023; Rose Pink 049; Grass Green 0240; Gorse Yellow 0302; Cinnamon 0368
- ☐ white hand towel, approximately 56 cm wide
- ☐ one spool white Coats polyester sewing thread
- ☐ one piece each of fine cotton fabric to match thread shades 06, 023 and 049 for flowers, each 20 cm x 10 cm
- ☐ 30 cm x 20 cm fine cotton fabric to match thread shade 0240 for leaves
- ☐ 30 cm x 30 cm iron-on interfacing
- ☐ coloured crayons to match fabrics
- ☐ small piece of thin card for templates
- ☐ Milward International Range crewel needle no. 7

METHOD

1 Following cutting lines, carefully trace flower and leaf shapes and transfer tracings to thin card. Cut out templates.

2 Using templates, draw nine flowers and twelve leaves on iron-on interfacing. Colour in with appropriate crayons. Cut out flowers and leaves.

3 With adhesive side facing downwards, arrange leaf shapes on pale green fabric, spacing them to allow a 6 mm seam allowance all around. Fuse each piece to fabric and cut out with seam allowances.

4 Repeat step 3 for flowers, using three pink fabrics.

5 Clip all around into seam allowances of each piece. Turn seam allowances to wrong side. Baste turned edge in place, beginning and ending stitching on right side of fabric.

6 Arrange leaves and flowers on woven band of hand towel, overlapping leaves and flowers as shown in layout diagram.

7 Using three strands of thread throughout and taking care to keep back of work neat, work back stitch lines of different lengths in 0240, radiating outwards from flower centres. Work a French knot in 0302 at end of each line to represent stamens. Work veins of leaves in back stitch in 0240.

8 Using appropriately coloured Anchor Stranded Cotton, work neat and evenly spaced blanket stitches around edges of all leaves and flowers, stitching through all thicknesses.

9 Using three strands of 0368, work gently curving chain stitches close together, between flowers to represent a thin branch.

10 Carefully remove all basting stitches. Press lightly.

BLANKET STITCH

1 Bring thread out on lower line, insert needle in position on upper line, taking a straight downward stitch with thread under needle point.

2 Pull up stitch to form a loop and repeat. Space stitches evenly (Fig. 1).

BACK STITCH

1 Bring thread through on stitchline, then take a small backward stitch through fabric.

2 Bring needle through again a little in front of the first stitch, take another stitch, inserting needle at point where it first came through (Fig. 2).

CHAIN STITCH

1 Bring needle out at top of line and hold it down with left thumb.

2 Insert needle where it last emerged and bring point out a short distance away. Pull thread through, keeping working thread under needle point (Fig. 3).

FRENCH KNOTS

See page 198 for diagrams and instructions

Flower and leaf patterns

Fig, 1

Fig. 2

Fig. 3

Placement Diagram

For the Children

*T*here are always special things to make for your growing family. This soft activity doll is perfect for little fingers to explore, the doll's house will delight a growing child, and you will remember those all too short childhood years with a clever collage of family photographs.

209

Doll's House

Providing hours of fun, this doll's house is made from cardboard cartons, covered with calico or recycled fabric. You will find that most materials needed are already in your work box or scrap drawer.

MATERIALS
- [ ] one carton in good condition for each storey of the house
- [ ] PVA adhesive
- [ ] spray-on glue or a glue gun
- [ ] masking tape
- [ ] assorted scraps of lace, wallpaper, fabric, plain fabric for exterior walls; paper towel roll for chimney; firm, plain cardboard for stairs
- [ ] florists' cut-edge ribbon or decorative craft ribbon
- [ ] paper cups as bases for table and chairs; empty matchboxes for chest of drawers; notice-board pins for drawer handles; scrap of silver paper for wall mirror; assorted ribbon lengths; small square box for bed; four bamboo skewers for bedposts; scraps of polyester wadding or cotton wool; cardboard or another carton to cut up for roof
- [ ] sharp craft knife
- [ ] peg for doll; pipecleaners (optional)
- [ ] scraps of fabric, lace and wool for doll

METHOD
Instructions are given for a two-storey house. Eliminate stairs if you wish to make a single-storey house.

1 Glue two cartons securely together on top of one another and upside down, so that base of lower carton forms floor of upper level.

2 Cut out fronts of each carton, leaving approximately 10 cm border at sides and top. Cut small opening in one corner of upper floor for stairs. Cut out windows in sides and back, having first decided where you wish to place furniture.

3 Cover entire exterior of house with fabric. This is time consuming, but it is worth taking some trouble to be accurate. Cut out window areas, leaving 2-3 cm of fabric to fold inwards around window edges. If necessary, cover joins in fabric with craft ribbon.

4 Measure for roof, making it slightly longer than house. We used a large piece of cardboard, folded to 90 degrees, open at the ends and with a flat piece of cardboard glued inside to support the angle of the roof and form a base. You may find it easier to secure this piece with masking tape. Cut hole for chimney, remembering that it will be an oval not a circle. Glue chimney into place.

Make some simple furniture from recycled materials

5 Glue fabric carefully over internal walls, using spray-on glue and securing fabric at corners with PVA adhesive.

6 Cut piece for staircase out of cardboard, making sure that it is long enough to reach from upper storey to the floor of the lower one. Crease into steps and cover with fabric, folding edges of

Doll's House staircase

fabric to wrong side. Mark depth of steps then crease cardboard sharply along markings. Cut another piece of cardboard to form side of steps which appears to be an internal wall that extends up to form stair rail. This can be tricky. We used a glue gun because it dries so quickly. Place stairs against outside wall, pin in place. Pin internal wall against steps. Glue steps firmly into place.

7 Gather scraps of lace for curtains and glue to windows. Tie curtains back with narrow ribbons. Glue ribbon around meeting point of floor and walls to form skirting boards and around upper walls to form cornice.

8 To make bed: Fill small square box with polyester wadding or cotton wool, tuck fabric over to cover. Glue to secure. Make a small pillow from same fabric, stuff with wadding or cotton wool. Cut skewers to suitable height and glue into corners of base. Place box top or square of cardboard over skewers to form canopy. Trim canopy with lace, tie bows to corners. Cover edge of bed with gathered lace or fabric to form frill.

9 Group six matchboxes together to form chest of drawers. Cover with fabric to secure. Decorate chest with lace or ribbons. Push notice-board pins through 'drawer' fronts to form handles, and cover

sharp points inside with a glue gun. Cut silver paper into rectangle, cut off corners and glue to wall above chest.

Chairs are circles of fabric tied to cover bases of cut-off plastic cups. Place a little wadding or cotton wool on base, cut out circle of fabric to fit over top of upturned cup and down to floor. Tie ribbon around 'chair' just below wadding. Glue to secure. Tables are made in same way using a clean, upturned food tin. Trim chairs and tables with lace if desired.

Peg Doll

What is a doll's house without a doll? The contents of your scrap drawer are all you need to create these delightful companions. Our doll has no arms but it is easy to use pipe cleaners for arms if you wish. First paint shoes, stockings and face on peg. We wrapped the doll's torso with lace to form bodice and simply gathered a length of lace and fabric for her skirt. Tie a length of ribbon around waist to secure skirt and bodice. Glue on loops of wool for hair. The cap is gathered lace, glued around head from ear to ear.

Add another shawl by trimming a triangle of pretty fabric with lace and securing it over doll's shoulders and at the centre front. Glue if necessary.

A pretty Peg Doll that's easy to make from a clothes peg and scraps of fabric, lace and ribbon

Activity Doll

This activity doll is not just a pyjama bag and cushion, but provides opportunities to practise plaiting, tying shoelaces, doing up buttons and opening and closing Velcro dots. There is even a special little handbag to fill with treasures.

MATERIALS

- ☐ one 40 cm square pillow fabric for front, and two backs, each 40 cm x 22 cm
- ☐ 3.20 m of 20 cm wide frill fabric or wide lace
- ☐ 30 cm zipper
- ☐ wool for hair
- ☐ approximately 50 cm of 115 cm wide pre-quilted cream-coloured fabric for body pieces
- ☐ approximately 1 m of 10 cm wide broderie lace for petticoat or a larger piece of broderie fabric
- ☐ 40 cm coordinating fabric for pinafore
- ☐ 2 m of 2 cm wide braid for pinafore trim

- ☐ 1 m gingham ribbon for hair bows
- ☐ four buttons
- ☐ small quantity of Velcro tape or five sets of Velcro stick-on dots
- ☐ 15 cm x 15 cm scrap plain fabric for shoes
- ☐ 70 cm narrow ribbon or a pair of shoe laces
- ☐ 25 cm x 12 cm scrap of fabric and one button for handbag
- ☐ paints for facial features
- ☐ lace doily or trimmed handkerchief for pocket
- ☐ polyester stuffing for arms and legs
- ☐ 40 cm square cushion insert

METHOD

Pattern Outline: — — — — —

See Pull Out Pattern Sheet at back of book. Use 1 cm seams and neaten any exposed raw edge.

To make body and pillow

1 Cut one body piece, one head piece, four arm pieces and four leg pieces, eight shoe fronts and two shoe backs.

2 Join ends of frill to form a circle. Fold over double with raw edges matching. Gather along raw edges, drawing up gathering to fit around cushion front. With raw edges matching, stitch frill to right side of cushion front. The cushion back pieces are joined after the doll is complete.

3 Place two shoe front pieces together with right sides facing, four times. Stitch across top and down centre front. Turn and press. Make small buttonhole at top inner corner. Place a pair of complete shoe fronts on to the lower ends of front legs. Fold 1 cm on straight top edge of

back shoe pieces to inside. Pin to back leg pieces. With right sides facing, join leg pieces and arm pieces, leaving ends open. Turn. Stuff lightly.

4 Stitch head and body on to pillow front, tucking arms and legs in position underneath body piece. Stitch with zigzag or satin stitch. Tie lengths of ribbon or shoelaces into buttonholes.

To make hair

1 Wind wool around top of a chair until a thickish band is achieved. Slip it off, holding it together securely. Place scrap of ribbon about 6 cm long underneath strands, to run at right angles to wool. Stitch through wool and ribbon to secure. Cut through loops of wool opposite ribbon.

2 Make a smaller band for fringe in same way by winding wool around a piece of cardboard about 8 cm long. Stitch ribbon to wool in same way. Cut through opposite ribbon. Flip wool to one side, forming fringe. Stitch fringe into place across top of forehead. Centre main hair piece on doll's head and stitch in place.

3 Bring wool down to ear level on either side of head, placing some glue underneath to secure. Gather into bunches. Divide wool into three sections. Plait each section and secure by tying length of wool around end of plait. Trim uneven ends. Tie bows.

To make pinafore

1 Cut out one bodice from body shape as directed on pattern. Cut an 8 cm square for pocket. Turn in 5 mm on sides and lower edge. Stitch 1 cm hem at top. Cut a 45 cm x 35 cm rectangle for skirt. Round off lower corners. Gather upper edge of skirt and stitch to lower edge of bodice, matching raw edges.

2 Stitch pocket to skirt, tucking braid under edge as you sew. Trim bodice and skirt edges with braid.

3 Make four buttonholes in bodice top. Sew buttons securely to body, giving them a shank (stem of thread wrapped around with extra thread for strength).

To make petticoat

1 Join together sufficient strips of broderie lace to create a 20 cm x 35 cm rectangle for skirt and a bodice of 10 cm x 14 cm. If using broderie fabric, cut petticoat to same size as pinafore.

2 Gather skirt across 35 cm edge. Stitch to 14 cm edge of bodice. Trim outside edge of petticoat with lace where desired.

3 Attach four Velcro dots to inside bodice, avoiding button positions on pinafore bodice. Attach corresponding Velcro dots to doll's body.

To make handbag

1 Cut a 20 cm x 8 cm rectangle and a strap piece 4 cm x 25 cm. Fold strap double lengthways. Press in raw edges. Topstitch and edgestitch to secure.

2 Fold over 1 cm on one short end of bag and stitch. Cut other short end to a point. With right sides facing, fold up 6 cm on hemmed end and stitch side seams. Fold pointed end edges to wrong side and hem. Turn to right side, press. Make buttonhole. Sew on corresponding button. Attach handle to back of bag.

To complete

1 Experiment on paper first, then decorate doll's face using fabric pencils or paints. Use a little blusher on cheeks.

2 Finish cushion as Frilled Piped Cushion on page 172, omitting the piping.

Pillow Quilt

MATERIALS
☐ work out how many squares of chosen size you will need. This quilt is eight squares by six squares, using 20 cm squares. Each pillow has a front and back so you will need about 4 m of 115 cm wide fabric
☐ polyester fibre for stuffing
☐ lengths of self-fabric rouleaux or contrasting ribbon

METHOD
Use 1 cm seam allowances. As finished quilt will be washable, pre-shrink all fabric before sewing.

1 Cut out required number of squares for your quilt. Place squares in pairs with right sides facing. Stitch around three sides leaving remaining side open for stuffing. Clip corners and turn pillow, making sure to push corners out accurately. Press, turning under 1 cm on open edges.

2 Place pillows in rows as determined by your quilt size, butting edges together accurately. Using a zigzag or similar stitch, sew over butted edges.

3 Stuff squares to make pillows. Take care not to place too much stuffing in each square, as it will be difficult to hold open edges together while sewing. Place open edge of one row butted to stitched edge of next row. Stitch, using zigzag stitch or similar. Continue joining rows until desired quilt size is reached.

4 Knot ends of 25 cm lengths of rouleaux or ribbon and stitch centre of lengths securely to pillow meeting points. Tie rouleaux into bows.

Comic Book Teddy

Don't throw away the children's comics! Store them for a rainy day and the whole family can have fun making these terrific Teddies.

MATERIALS

☐ two round balloons
☐ PVA adhesive
☐ scraps of cardboard
☐ four cardboard toilet roll cylinders
☐ sticky-tape
☐ paper craft ribbon

METHOD

1 Mix equal parts adhesive and water (to make about half a cup) in a bowl to form a milky liquid.

2 Tear comics into strips no more than 3 cm wide – narrower strips are easier to use. Place strips into glue mixture.

3 Blow up two balloons for head and body. Tape over mouths of balloons. Tape them together with sticky-tape. Cut end of each cardboard roll at an angle to allow them to fit snugly against balloons at a good angle. Tape them into position for arms and legs, checking to see that Teddy will sit well.

4 Cut two cardboard ears. Tape them into place.

5 Cover balloons with randomly glued strips. Several layers will be needed. Glue on cut-outs of coloured paper for eyes, feet and nose. Glue on paper waistcoat. Tie bowtie as shown using strips of craft ribbon. Allow Teddy to dry completely then paint with one or two coats of undiluted PVA adhesive to give a shiny, hard surface. PVA adhesive is white on application, but dries crystal clear.

Above: Joining balloons and cardboard rolls

Picture Gallery

What to do with those drawers full of memories?
Make a visual history of your child's life with a collage
of cut-out pictures. When your picture is finished,
frame and hang it on 'permanent exhibition'.

Do It Yourself
projects

*D*oing it yourself is very satisfying, as well as being a great way to save money. As you look around your home, you are sure to see simple jobs that are ideally suited to the home handyperson.

In this section, you will find step-by-step instructions for some very useful projects, such as a wall-mounted kitchen cabinet to give you valuable extra storage space; how to frame and enclose an alcove to create a 'built-in wardrobe'; making a simple picket gate, and even how to hang a mirror to add size and light to your bathroom.

Most of these jobs can be accomplished with the common tools you already own. Check out the DIY Tool Kit on pages 234-237 for all you need to know about choosing the right tools for the job.

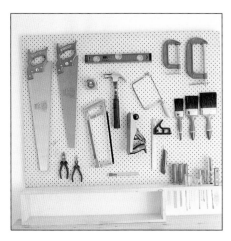

Project 1
Kitchen Cabinet

Keep your good china, glassware and other kitchenware close at hand in this clever wall-mounted kitchen cabinet.

Before You Begin

❏ Except for the gateleg and the dropleaf, this cabinet is made of softwood (pine).
❏ All joints should be drilled, glued and screwed throughout assembly.

MATERIALS

- ☐ two 19 mm thick sides, 1900 mm x 290 mm
- ☐ three 19 mm thick shelves, 3600 mm x 290 mm
- ☐ one 19 mm thick batten (cleat), 1200 mm x 90 mm
- ☐ one 19 mm thick bottom trim, 1200 mm x 40 mm
- ☐ one 19 mm thick support flange, 450 mm x 70 mm
- ☐ one 19 mm thick support, 450 mm x 240 mm
- ☐ one 18 mm thick gateleg, high-density particle (chip) board, 450 mm x 410 mm
- ☐ one 18 mm thick dropleaf, high-density particle (chip) board, 1200 mm x 600 mm
- ☐ 400 mm piano hingeing
- ☐ 1100 mm piano hingeing
- ☐ 35 mm countersunk screws
- ☐ piano hinge screws
- ☐ PVA adhesive
- ☐ paint
- ☐ undercoat
- ☐ oil-based paint
- ☐ paintbrushes

SPECIAL TOOLS NEEDED
- ☐ jigsaw
- ☐ saw

METHOD
Cut out all the components [sides, shelves, batten (cleat), bottom trim, support flange, support, gateleg, dropleaf]. Use a saw to cut the steps on the shelf sides. Using a jigsaw, cut the gateleg and table top to the radii desired.

To make the shelf unit:
1 Start by fastening the batten (cleat) to the underside back edge of the top shelf. Saw 19 mm off the depth of the bottom shelf.

2 Assemble the shelves and sides and complete the assembly with the bottom trim attached flush with the bottom of the sides.

To make the gateleg:
1 Screw through the back of the support flange into the back edge of the support, using four evenly spaced screws. To allow the gateleg to swing freely, saw 12 mm off its top edge for all but the front 100 mm.

2 Using the 400 mm length of piano hingeing, screw the gateleg to the front edge of the support (Fig. 1).

3 Drill through the support flange and screw the whole support structure to the wall with the table top at table height.

To complete:
1 Sit the shelving unit on top of the gateleg and screw through the batten (cleat) to wall-mount the unit.

2 Screw through the bottom shelf into the top of the support. Use the 1100 mm length of piano hingeing to fix the dropleaf to the front trim.

3 Undercoat the cabinet, then paint it with two coats of oil-based paint.

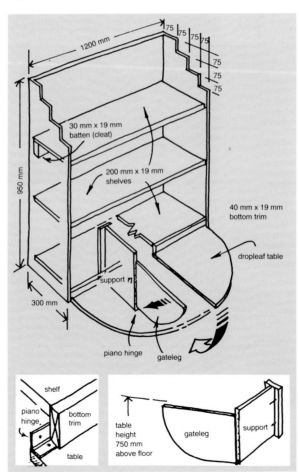

Fig. 1

218

Project 2
Drawer Divider

Are your heirlooms in a clutter? Consider dividing your sideboard drawer into made-to-measure compartments.

❏ Work out how you wish the available space to be divided up to allow for the different sizes of cutlery and the other accessories you wish to store in the drawer. It is best to make a plan on paper with all the measurements marked on it.

MATERIALS
- ☐ paper
- ☐ pencil
- ☐ tape measure
- ☐ plywood strips
- ☐ nails
- ☐ wood glue
- ☐ wood stain or paint
- ☐ paintbrush
- ☐ saw
- ☐ felt or thin wadding

METHOD

1 Measure the depth of the drawer, measuring from a little below the lip of the drawer to allow for adequate clearance.

2 Cut all the plywood pieces you require to the right size, following your plan and the measurements of your drawer.

3 Nail or glue (or both) the sections together. When the glue is dry, you have a neat lift-in/lift-out drawer divider that fits your needs perfectly.

4 Paint or stain the divider to match the sideboard. Before you replace the divider in the drawer, lay a cut-to-size piece of felt or thin wadding in the bottom of the drawer to protect your precious things, then place the divider on top.

Design Idea

Child's Activity Top

Little ones love to help out in the kitchen, but kitchen benches are often too high for them, and standing on stools or chairs is dangerous. Make this special activity top to fit over one of your kitchen drawers at kiddie height. Your child will have a workbench for painting, cutting out or assisting the master chef at work.

Quite simple to make from plywood, following the illustration given here, the top can be removed and stored away when not in use.

board

slat
screw and
glue to board

inside
width of
drawer

219

Project 3
Shelve It!

A number of materials can be used for shelving, depending on where and how the shelves are to be used. The table on page 221 shows the types of shelving materials commonly used, along with a suggested maximum span or bracket spacing for average loading.

There are as many ways of supporting your shelves as there are shelving materials to choose from.

Shelf (Stayed) Brackets

Sometimes called gallows brackets, these are used for supporting heavy loads. Welded steel brackets for supporting shelving up to 300 mm wide can be purchased ready-made, or they can be constructed from timber to suit shelving up to any reasonable width (say 600 mm).

To fix shelf brackets:

1 Select a suitable spacing so as not to exceed the maximum span for the type of shelving to be used (see the table).

2 Strike a level line at the required height of the shelf.

3 For timber-framed structures, the brackets must be fastened to a solid stud using 12- or 14-gauge screws. On brick or masonry walls, drill and plug the wall for a screw fixing or, alternatively, a suitable masonry bolt will provide even more secure fixing for very heavy loads.

Shelf Supports

These are a simple method of providing support for adjustable shelving within a cabinet or wall unit. Supports can be metal, or coloured or clear plastic.

To use shelf supports:

1 Drill a series of holes into the side members of the cabinet or wall unit to fit the pin of the shelf support, usually 5 mm to 6.5 mm in diameter. It is essential that all of the holes are drilled at the same height within the unit or your shelves will not sit straight.

2 On a piece of firm timber, approximately 10 mm x 40 mm, mark out and drill the holes at the required spacing.

3 Clamp this jig to the side members where the holes are required, keeping the bottom even with a fixed line marked on each member.

4 Drill the holes to the depth required, using a depth-stop on the drill bit.

Shelf Brackets

These brackets are useful for shelves holding average loads. They are available in galvanised steel or pressed metal in a variety of sizes to suit shelving up to 300 mm wide of solid timber, plywood or particle (chip) board.

To install shelf brackets:

Strike a level line to indicate the height of the shelf and fix the brackets to this line with 10- or 12-gauge screws.

Timber Battens (Cleats)

Where the end of a shelf butts up to a side wall, a timber batten (cleat) can provide adequate support.

To install a timber batten (cleat):

1 Cut the batten (cleat) from approximately 25 mm x 50 mm DAR (PAR) timber. Mark a level line on the side wall at the height of the shelf.

2 Drill and plug the wall, then secure the batten (cleat) with 10- or 12-gauge screws.

Metal Standards and Brackets

Slotted metal uprights and adjustable brackets provide adjustable shelving for average loads. Shelving is usually of 16 mm melamine-faced particle (chip) board or fibreboard MDF in a variety of colours and widths from 150 mm to 300 mm. The shelves can also be of glass.

To set up the system:

1 Select a suitable spacing for the uprights and locate secure fixing points on the wall.

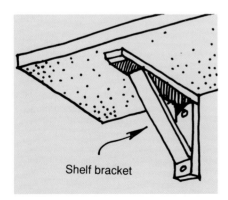

Shelf (stayed) bracket

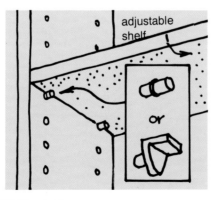

Shelf support

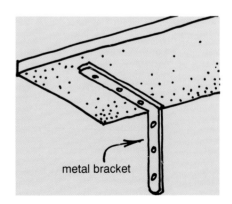

Shelf bracket

2 Strike a vertical line at each upright position and mark the line lightly on the wall. Mark the height to the bottom of the shelf on the first upright and from this point level across and mark a point for the next and any subsequent ones.

3 Using suitable screws (often provided with the system), fix the uprights to the wall at the positions marked.

4 Fix the brackets in the desired positions by means of two lugs which engage into the slots in the uprights.

Ladder Brackets

The ladder bracket is a convenient way of giving support to multiple shelving where fixing points for other types of brackets or battens (cleats) are not available. You can make the brackets to any depth up to 450 mm for linen storage and so on, or 600 mm if part of the space is to be used for hanging clothes.

Brackets can be made from 25 mm x 50 mm DAR (PAR) timber, and consist of uprights and intermediate rails, spaced as required for the shelving. They are preferably dowelled together and need only be nailed to the side walls as a complete unit at, say, four or five fixing points, wherever they can be found.

TYPES OF SHELVING		
Material	**Finished thickness (mm)**	**Maximum span (mm)**
solid dressed (planed) timber	19	900
solid dressed (planed) timber	31	1350
structural plywood	17	900
particle (chip) board	18	700
melamine-faced particle (chip) board sheet glass	16	600

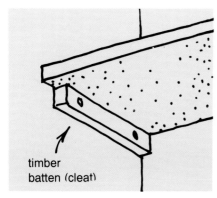

Timber batten (cleat)

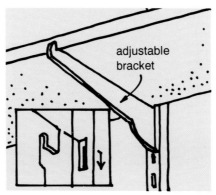

Metal standard and bracket

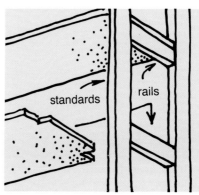

Ladder bracket

Framing an Alcove

Alcoves offer the perfect opportunity to make the most of otherwise small and cramped spaces.

The project shown here is in a bedroom, where a solitary alcove originally made the room appear strangely offset. The space was used as additional hanging space on two levels, as well as shoe and dress jewellery storage. The top hanging level is for seasonal or infrequently used clothes and the lower one provides ready access for more frequently used items. Two standard off-the-shelf doors have been used to enclose the area.

MATERIALS

- ☐ tape measure
- ☐ paper and pencil
- ☐ two 3 m lengths of softwood (pine or similar), 25 mm x 75 mm
- ☐ four 1.50 m lengths of softwood (pine or similar), 25 mm x 75 mm
- ☐ one 1.50 m length of softwood (pine or similar), 25 mm x 50 mm
- ☐ one 19 mm thick length of particle (chip) board, 1500 mm x 240 mm
- ☐ one 15 mm thick length of particle (chip) board, 1500 mm x 650 mm
- ☐ two hollow-core doors, sized to fit
- ☐ four 400 mm long, 16 mm diameter plastic-covered steel rods or similar
- ☐ eight saddle clips
- ☐ three 75 mm butt hinges per door
- ☐ two knobs
- ☐ two roller catches
- ☐ three 600 mm lengths of aluminium strips, 1.50 mm x 25 mm
- ☐ six rubber doorstops
- ☐ nails, screws and wall fixings, as necessary
- ☐ oil-based undercoat
- ☐ oil-based paint
- ☐ paintbrushes

SPECIAL TOOLS NEEDED

- ☐ hammer drill
- ☐ jigsaw
- ☐ spirit level

METHOD

1 Measure up the space accurately so that you can draw a plan of the project. This alcove is 1380 mm wide by a total of 2985 mm high. The total available depth is 440 mm. The alcove has an ornate cornice and an older style, but plain, 170 mm high timber skirting. The floor is carpeted.

2 Cut the two door jambs to size (in this case, standard 25 mm x 75 mm stock without a rebate was used). The thickness of the jamb is the same as the bottom skirting, so it will sit neatly on top. The jambs must be notched to a depth of 25 mm between 1500 mm and 1570 mm, and between 2550 mm and 2620 mm from the base to house the front rail supports.

3 When the jambs are completed, they can be screwed to plugged walls or, if the wall is timber, to the timber frame. To plug the wall, drill holes about 10 mm in diameter with a tungsten-carbide-tipped masonry bit in a hammer drill, set on slow speed and hammer action. They should be in the middle of the jambs so that the plug is covered by the jamb. Smaller plugs can be used for finer work. Drive a soft piece of timber into each hole – then the nails or screws can be driven in. Heavy-duty wall plugs or frame fixings (screws with integral plugs) can also be used and don't require such a large drill.

4 When the jambs are secure, cut the two front rails of 75 mm timber to length and nail them to the housings in the jambs. After marking with a spirit level, nail a similar pair at the same height to the rear wall, once again plugging the wall if necessary. This provides the basic structure for the storage space.

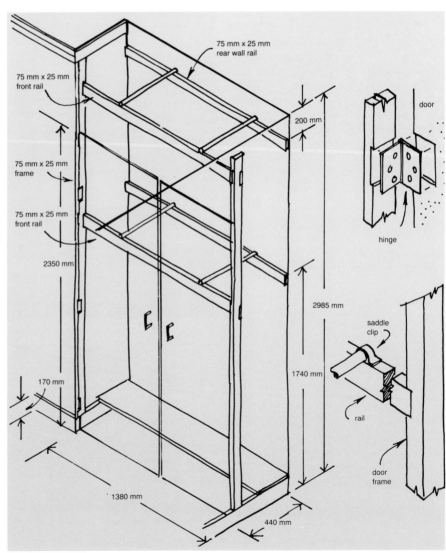

5 Cut the 16 mm plastic-covered steel rods to fit between the front face of the rail support and the rear wall. Hold them in place using simple saddle clips. Purpose-made brass or other rail holders can also be used if you prefer.

6 Lay a 240 mm x 1380 mm piece of 19 mm thick particle (chip) board across the skirtings to act as a shoe shelf. Paint it with an undercoat, then finish with two coats of oil-based paint.

7 Now is the time to fit the doors, one at a time. Butt hinges give the required clearance when the leaves are parallel and the door closed, and therefore need to be let into the door and jamb. To fit the butt hinges to the doors, mark the position of the hinges on each door edge, one 150 mm from the top, one 200 mm from the bottom and one in the middle. Use a sharp chisel to remove a small amount of timber – just enough to allow the hinge flap to sit neat and flush in the door edge – then insert two screws for each hinge. It is best to predrill the screw holes slightly with a smaller diameter drill bit before driving in the screws.

8 Support each door on small wedges to give the correct clearance over the carpeted floor, and mark in the position of the hinges on the jamb. Chisel out enough of the jamb to allow the hinge flap to fit flush, then hold the door in place while you mark and drill the screw holes to get the screws started. Hang the door by inserting a screw in the top and bottom. Before putting in all screws, make sure that the door closes properly and is correctly aligned. If not, make adjustments until it is right, using an adjacent screw hole. Repeat this procedure for the other door.

9 When both doors have been fitted, check that they have sufficient clearance, and that the meeting of the two door edges is parallel and neat. If the fit is close, the meeting stiles may need to be slightly bevelled to the rear to allow the doors to shut. Insert the remaining screws in both doors. Fit the knobs.

10 Fit two catches and keepers to the central rail support and to each door and block them out so that the doors will fit flush across their face.

11 The doors are only 2350 mm high, leaving a gap of about 630 mm above. This is filled using a sheet of 15 mm particle (chip) board. First screw a small batten (cleat) of 25 mm x 50 mm timber to the door jambs above each door, 15 mm in from the front. The particle (chip) board must be cut to suit the cornice profile. A handy tool for this job is a profile gauge. Otherwise, make a cardboard template to suit the cornice and place it on to the two top corners of the particle (chip) board as a cutting guide. Nail or screw the particle (chip) board to the battens (cleats) so that it finishes flush with the jamb.

12 Punch and fill any nail holes, then seal and undercoat using oil-based paints to stop the grain rising. Finish the doors with the undercoat and top coats of paint.

13 Prepare all remaining surfaces for painting by lightly sanding and dusting down before the interior is painted.

Below: The alcove with closed doors
Bottom: Lots of useful storage space

Deskmate

A deskmate is a mobile storage cabinet which is stored out of the way under the desk and rolled out when it is needed.

There are a number of different configurations, ranging from simple storage for paper, envelopes and a few files you may be working on, to a deskmate which can store a printer on the top with the paper feeding from the shelf at the back.

MATERIALS

- [ ] one sheet of 12 mm thick medium-density fibreboard (MDF), 2.40 m x 1.20 m
- [ ] one timber batten (cleat) (DAR/PAR), 25 mm x 25 mm
- [ ] one aluminium angle, 25 mm x 25 mm
- [ ] PVA adhesive
- [ ] particle (chip) board screws
- [ ] 25 mm twisted-shank nails
- [ ] two hinges for particle (chip) board doors
- [ ] four castors
- [ ] all-purpose undercoat
- [ ] oil-based paint
- [ ] paintbrushes
- [ ] fine sandpaper
- [ ] wet and dry sandpaper

SPECIAL TOOLS NEEDED

- [ ] set square or try square
- [ ] handsaw
- [ ] power saw
- [ ] electric drill
- [ ] hammer
- [ ] screwdriver

METHOD

1 Follow the cutting diagram for cutting out the panels. It is best to mark out one panel at a time and cut this out before cutting the next one. This will ensure that you set the panels at the correct size. The side, bottom, middle and back panels should be cut first. Mark out the size of the panel, ensuring the sides are perpendicular to each other by using the set square or try square. When you cut, use a timber batten (cleat) as a guide for the power saw to run along. This will result in a much cleaner job. Measure your saw to find the distance from the guide fence to the side of the blade teeth. Mark this distance from the line you are to cut and temporarily fix the batten (cleat) in position with small nails.

2 Fix the main panels together with PVA adhesive and nails, checking that the panels are square as you go.

3 Once the main panels are fixed in place, fix the screws, placing them approximately 50 mm from the corners and edges. Drill pilot holes smaller than the screw shaft and countersink the hole so that the end of the screw finishes below the face of the panels.

4 At this point, you should check the dimensions for the remaining panels to make sure they are the right size. This is particularly important for the door panel, which should be check-measured and cut after the main panels are fixed together.

5 Fix the door hinges, following the manufacturer's instructions. The hinges allow final adjustment of the door panel by turning grub screws on the face of the hinges.

6 All that remains is to fix the timber battens (cleats), aluminium angle and the castors to the bottom of the unit.

7 When the deskmate is completed, rub down the edges with the fine sandpaper, then apply the undercoat. Leave it to dry, following the instructions on the paint tin. Use the oil-based paint for the final two coats (this will resist abrasions more easily). Sand down with wet and dry sandpaper between coats.

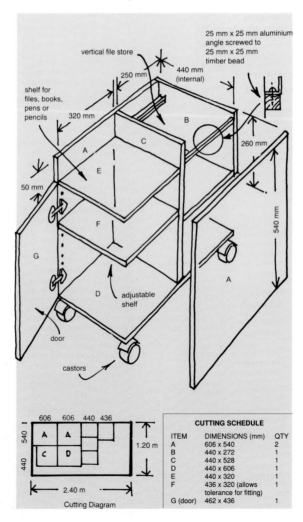

vertical file store

25 mm x 25 mm aluminium angle screwed to 25 mm x 25 mm timber bead

250 mm

440 mm (internal)

shelf for files, books, pens or pencils

320 mm

50 mm

260 mm

540 mm

door

castors

adjustable shelf

Cutting Diagram

606 606 440 436

540

440

1.20 m

2.40 m

CUTTING SCHEDULE

ITEM	DIMENSIONS (mm)	QTY
A	606 x 540	2
B	440 x 272	1
C	440 x 528	1
D	440 x 606	1
E	440 x 320	1
F	436 x 320 (allows tolerance for fitting)	1
G (door)	462 x 436	1

Project 6
Towel Rack

This easy-to-make towel rack is a simple but effective storage solution for your bathroom.

MATERIALS
- ☐ two sheets of 16 mm thick plastic-laminated particle (chip) board, 1000 mm x 200 mm, for the sides
- ☐ four lengths of dowel, 750 mm long x 35 mm diameter
- ☐ 5 m of 16 mm wide iron-on edging strip
- ☐ eight screws
- ☐ eight screw caps
- ☐ waterproof adhesive

SPECIAL TOOLS NEEDED
- ☐ jigsaw
- ☐ electric drill
- ☐ iron
- ☐ centre punch

METHOD
1 Following the diagram given here, mark a semicircular curve with a radius of 100 mm at one end of each side piece. Cut out the curve using the jigsaw.

2 Apply the iron-on edging strip to all the edges of the side pieces, except for the bottom edge, following the manufacturer's instructions.

3 Measure up and mark the position of the drill holes for the dowel rails. Before drilling laminate, you should punch a starting point with a centre punch to ensure a clean drill hole. Drill the holes.

4 Glue, then screw the four lengths of dowel into place, using screw caps to conceal the screw heads.

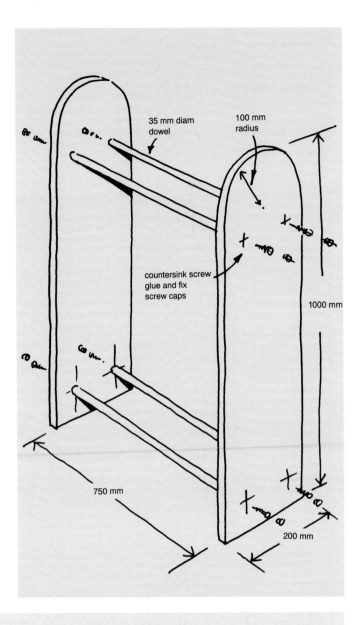

35 mm diam dowel

100 mm radius

countersink screw glue and fix screw caps

1000 mm

750 mm

200 mm

Design Idea

One of the most useful items and one of the hardest things to conceal in any bathroom is the dirty clothes basket (hamper). Clearly, any basket (hamper) is preferable to clothes littering the floor, but a hidden one is even better. In the pretty bathroom pictured here, a simple pull-down bin-type cupboard serves the purpose very well. When the cupboard is closed, it disappears and takes no floor space at all.

Project 7
Bathside Trolley

After a long day, relax in the bath with everything to hand on your own bathside trolley.

MATERIALS

- [ ] two sheets of 16 mm thick plastic-laminated particle (chip) board 460 mm x 460 mm, for the shelves
- [ ] three lengths of 35 mm dowel for the legs
- [ ] three 400 mm lengths of 25 mm dowel for the rails
- [ ] iron-on edging strip
- [ ] 50 mm particle (chip) board screws
- [ ] conical white sleeves
- [ ] screw caps
- [ ] two pairs of castors
- [ ] tape measure
- [ ] pencil

SPECIAL TOOLS NEEDED

- [ ] jigsaw
- [ ] electric drill

METHOD

1 Following the diagram, mark out two curved shapes with a radius of 230 mm at the straight edges on each piece of the particle (chip) board. Cut out the curves, using a jigsaw.

2 Apply the iron-on edging strip to all the curved edges.

3 Measure and mark the height of your bath on the three 35 mm diameter lengths of dowel, taking into account the height of the castors and the height of the two shelves. Cut the lengths of dowel to this measurement.

4 Mark out the positions for the three horizontal rails on two of the 35 mm diameter dowels. Drill and insert horizontally to a depth of 20 mm three 400 mm lengths of 25 mm diameter dowel in these holes to make the back leg structure.

5 Mark out the positions of the ends of the three vertical dowels on the top and bottom shelves. Carefully drill through the shelves into the ends of the dowels. To conceal the heads of the screws in the top shelf, cover them with the white sleeves and screw caps. Fit the conical sleeve over the screw when you are inserting it, then clip the cap in place, after you have driven the screw home. Screw the castors in place.

Design Idea

Don't always rely on colour to add interest to an otherwise dull room. Very interesting effects can be achieved, even in a monochromatic colour scheme, by the use of curved shapes. In this bathroom the front of the vanity has been made to curve in harmony with the glass feature wall behind it.

460 mm

35 mm dowel

35 mm dowel

bath height

230 mm radius

230 mm

castor

Project 8
Wine Bottle Rack

From expensive built-in units to drainage pipes, there are many ways of neatly storing bottles of wine on their sides. Whichever method you choose, it is important to ensure that the arrangement is quite secure. This wine bottle rack can be made in only a few hours, will hold many bottles and has the advantage of being able to 'grow' as required.

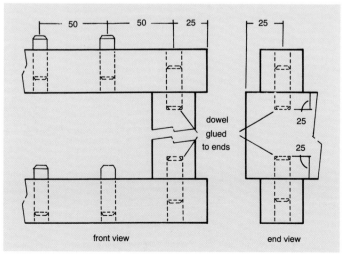

front view   end view

Before You Begin

❏ All the timber for this project is stock size and will be readily available from your local timber supplier.

MATERIALS
❏ six lengths of 100 mm x 38 mm DAR (PAR) softwood (pine) for the end pieces
❏ eight lengths of 38 mm x 38 mm DAR (PAR) softwood (pine) for the rails
❏ one hundred and twenty 38 mm x 8 mm furniture dowels
❏ PVA adhesive
❏ paint or varnish
❏ paintbrush
❏ sandpaper

SPECIAL TOOLS NEEDED
❏ saw
❏ 8 mm drill bit
❏ electric drill
❏ hammer

METHOD

1 Cut the end pieces to be 270 mm long. Drill 8 mm holes in both edges at both ends; four holes in all. The holes should be 25 mm deep, in the centre of the edges and 25 mm from the ends.

2 Cut the rails to be 700 mm long. Drill 8 mm holes that are 50 mm apart, starting 25 mm from the ends. Drill all these holes right through the rails.

3 Glue the dowels into all the holes in the rails with the exception of the end ones. Make sure that all the dowels finish flush on the bottom.

4 Glue four dowels into the ends and make sure they are hammered right down.

5 Sand all the pieces, then paint or varnish them. When the paint or varnish is completely dry, assemble the wine bottle rack.

Project 9
Storage Bed-end

Make this shelf unit for the end of the bed for your bedtime books, bits and pieces or for toy storage in a child's room.

Before You Begin

❏ The size and layout of the shelves and storage recesses can be to any design you choose, as long as there is enough room for the bed and pillow to rest against the bed-end.

❏ Our bed-end is for a bed which is accessible from both sides, that is, not placed lengthways against a wall. The two side shelf units are separate so that you can leave these out or change them to suit your particular needs, such as making a larger shelf unit on one side of the bed only, with perhaps a desk space as well.

❏ Use an oil-based gloss paint for the final coats. This will resist abrasions more easily.

MATERIALS
☐ one sheet of 16 mm thick medium-density fibreboard (MDF), 2.40 m x 1.20 m
☐ one sheet of 16 mm thick medium-density fibreboard (MDF), 1.80 m x 0.90 m
☐ timber batten (cleat)
☐ PVA adhesive
☐ adjustable shelf supports – these come in a variety of types and materials, from brass to plastic
☐ particle (chip) board screws
☐ 25 mm twisted-shank nails
☐ fine sandpaper
☐ wet and dry sandpaper
☐ panel pins
☐ all-purpose undercoat
☐ oil-based gloss paint
☐ paintbrushes
☐ tape measure

SPECIAL TOOLS NEEDED
☐ handsaw
☐ power saw
☐ electric drill
☐ hammer
☐ screwdriver
☐ try square

METHOD
1 Follow the diagram and the cutting schedule given here for cutting out the panels. Use a timber batten (cleat) as a guide for the power saw to run along. This will result in a much cleaner job. Measure your saw to find the distance from the guide fence to the side of the blade teeth. Mark this distance from the line you are to cut and temporarily fix the batten (cleat) in position on this line with panel pins.

2 Start by cutting the main side and top panels (A, B and C), and panel K, which fixes to the end of the bed and acts as a bracing panel. When you have cut each panel, check that the corners are square.

3 Apply adhesive to the edges of the panels, then nail them together, start-ing with panels A and K, followed by B and C. At this point you are able to measure for panels E and D. Cut these panels and nail or screw and glue in position, making sure that they are square.

4 The side shelf units are made as separate units which are screwed to each side of the main bed-end. Cut the side panels (G) together with the bottom and top panels (F and H). Drill blind holes, approximately 50 mm apart, into the side panels for the adjustable shelf supports. Now glue and nail these panels together.

5 Fix the skirting panel (J) in place and make sure the unit is square. It is a good idea to use a piece of offcut timber as a temporary brace at the back until the adhesive is dry and you have finished screwing the panels together. Check-measure, then cut the shelf panels (H), ready to fit into place.

6 When you have completed the nailing and gluing, drill pilot and countersink holes for the screws near each corner. Apply a little adhesive to each screw, before screwing it into place.

7 When the assembly is completed, use fine sandpaper to rub down the edges, then paint with the undercoat.

8 Paint with two coats of the gloss paint, remembering to sand down with wet and dry sandpaper between coats.

CUTTING SCHEDULE		
Item	Dimensions (mm)	Quantity
A	934 x 250	2
B	1093 x 250	1
C	1125 x 250	1
D	625 x 250	1
E	184 x 250	5
F	300 x 250	2
G	734 x 250	4
H	268 x 240	4
J	268 x 100	2
K	dimensions indicated	1

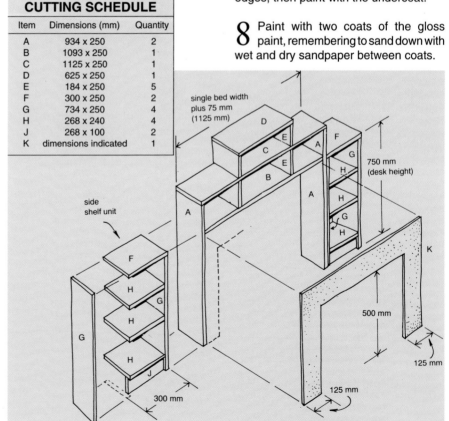

Project 10
Plate Rack

In any kitchen, but especially a small kitchen where space is at a premium, it is important to make good use of the available space.

While it is simple to make, this plate rack will look smart and help to keep your kitchen neat. It is suitable for novices to make and, as all the materials are stock size, they are readily available at your local timber yard.

MATERIALS
- twenty-seven lengths of 25 mm x 25 mm DAR(PAR) softwood at 350 mm long for the legs
- four lengths of 25 mm x 25 mm DAR(PAR) softwood, approximately 500 mm long for the rails
- 54 mm x 32 mm x 8 gauge countersunk screws
- four 520 mm brass, chrome or galvanised steel bolts, threaded full length, with two nuts and washers to suit
- cardboard for spacers
- waterproof adhesive
- clear lacquer

SPECIAL TOOLS NEEDED
- tape measure
- drill
- saw
- screwdriver
- sanding block
- countersinking bit
- paintbrush

METHOD

1 Cut twenty-seven 350 mm long legs from the 25 mm x 25 mm DAR (PAR) softwood. Drill a 4 mm diameter hole for the bolt, 125 mm from one end of each leg. A vertical drill stand is best, but the job can be done carefully by hand with an electric drill.

2 Insert the bolt into the holes and fit the nuts and washers, but do not tighten them. Insert the cardboard spacers (approximately 1 mm thick) between the legs and finger-tighten the bolt (Fig. 1).

3 Lay the assembly flat on a bench, then screw and glue the top rail in place 100 mm below the top of the legs, attaching it only to alternate legs (Fig. 2).

4 Repeat step 3 for the bottom rail, attaching it 97 mm from the bottom of the legs.

5 Turn the assembly over and repeat steps 3 and 4, this time screwing the rails to the legs with no screw on the other side.

6 Cut the rails to an even length where they overhang and sand the ends smooth and flush.

7 Remove the cardboard spacers. Sand the plate rack, then paint with a coat of clear lacquer.

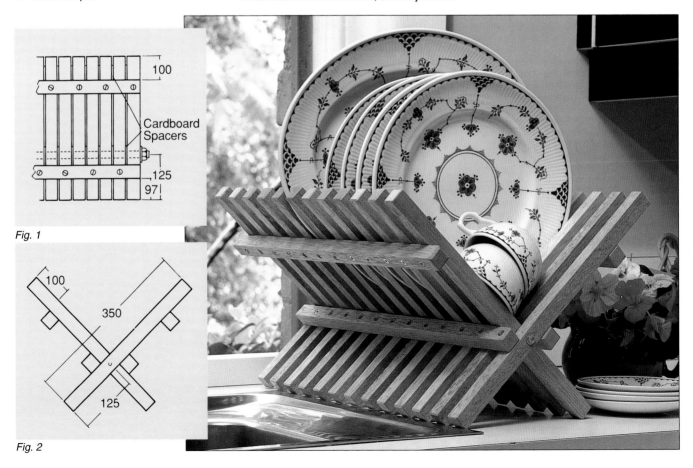

Fig. 1

Cardboard Spacers

100
125
97

Fig. 2

100
350
125

Project 11
Picket Gate

Gates come in many shapes, sizes and materials. However, they all have one thing in common: they deteriorate over time and occasionally need to be maintained, repaired, or completely rebuilt. Building a solid timber picket gate is not difficult, and may be a better alternative to repairing 'old faithful' yet again!

Before You Begin

❏ If the gate posts need replacing, use 100 mm x 100 mm treated timber, set 450 mm into concrete both sides of the gate.

MATERIALS
- ☐ two lengths (the width of the opening) of treated pine, 38 mm (or 50 mm) x 100 mm for the top and bottom rails
- ☐ treated pine, 38 mm (or 50 mm) x 100 mm and 1.5 times longer than the rails, for the brace
- ☐ 25 mm x 100 mm pickets or palings to suit
- ☐ two 100 mm or 150 mm T-hinges
- ☐ gate latch and keeper
- ☐ nails and screws to suit
- ☐ primer or undercoat
- ☐ paint or other finish (timber preservative or stain)
- ☐ paintbrushes
- ☐ tape measure

SPECIAL TOOLS NEEDED
- ☐ saw
- ☐ screwdriver

METHOD

1 Mark and cut the two rails to the correct length. Allow for a clearance of 10 mm at the gate posts.

2 Lay the two rails on a flat surface and place two pickets or palings on them, one at each end. Adjust the distance between the rails so that the bottom rail is about 100 mm up from the bottom of the picket and the top rail down 75 mm to 100 mm from the top of the picket. Nail the two pickets to the rails.

3 Turn the frame over and, measuring the diagonals, square up the frames. Then, hold the brace diagonally across the rails and mark off where it is to be cut. The brace runs from the bottom hinge side to the top latch side. It should be slightly recessed into the top and bottom rails.

4 Dismantle the gate, cut the brace to length and rebate the rails.

5 Prime and undercoat or stain all the timber components, then reassemble the rails and brace, driving a screw into each rail approximately 50 mm from the end of the brace.

6 Turn the frame over and nail all the pickets into place, making sure they are properly aligned.

7 Block up the gate on offcuts of wood to screw the gate to the posts. Screw the long flap of the T-hinge to the gate and the stub side to the post. At first, fix only one screw for each hinge to the post, then check the operation of the hinge, making sure it works and is square. When it is right, fit the rest of the screws.

8 Apply the final coats of paint or stain. When the gate is dry, fix on the latch and keeper.

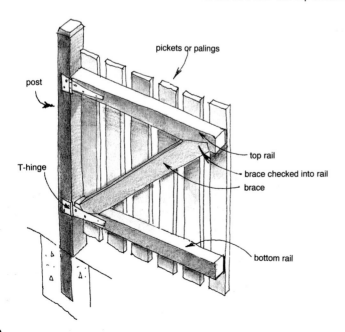

pickets or palings

post

T-hinge

top rail

brace checked into rail

brace

bottom rail

Design Idea

Making your own timber paling fence is not difficult, but will take a little time and effort. Use galvanised steel poles, set into holes and fixed with concrete. Bolt the timber rails to the steel poles, then fix the palings in the same way as for the gate.

Project 12
Hanging a Mirror

Mirror, mirror on the wall . . . If your bathroom is the smallest room in the house, why not create the illusion of extra space with a large wall mirror?

Before You Begin

❏ Don't attempt to drill holes in the mirror yourself – it's a job best left to a glazier.

❏ On solid brick or masonry walls, drill holes and insert wall plugs to hold the fastening screws. On timber-framed walls, screw directly into the studs, if possible. Use hollow-wall fixings, if the studs are not in the right places. If the wall is faced with ceramic tiles, use a masonry drill bit to drill through the tiles and into the wall behind.

❏ If the mirror has predrilled holes near the corners, it will need to be fixed to the wall with mirror screws. Mirrors without holes are attached using either J-clips or corner clips.

❏ Before hanging the mirror, slide a straight board or a spirit level, longer than the mirror is wide, around the wall to see if it wobbles on a high spot. If the wall has irregularities of more than 3 mm, attach a couple of adhesive-backed felt or rubber pads behind the mirror to keep it from coming into contact with the high spots. The mirror must not come into contact with the wall.

MATERIALS
- ❏ mirror
- ❏ mirror screws or clips (J-clips/corner clips)
- ❏ wall plugs (for masonry or hollow walls)

SPECIAL TOOLS NEEDED
- ❏ spirit level
- ❏ electric drill with appropriate bit

METHOD
To fix with mirror screws:

1 You'll need a helper to support the mirror against the wall in the correct position. Use a spirit level to check that the mirror is horizontal, then mark the wall with a pencil through each of the predrilled holes. Remove the mirror, drill holes at the marked points and insert the wall plugs.

2 With your helper supporting the mirror again, secure the screws. At each hole in the mirror, place a spacer washer or rubber electrical grommet behind the mirror, then insert the mirror screw with its cup washer.

3 Tighten the screws only until the cup washers press against the mirror (any tighter and you may crack the glass!). Finally, screw the domehead covers into the threaded heads of the mirror screws (Fig.1).

To fix with J clips:

1 Using the spirit level, mark a horizontal guideline as wide as the mirror for the bottom. Position J-clips about one-third of the width of the mirror in from the edges (Fig. 2). Hold the bottom clips on the guideline and mark the positions for the holes. Drill the holes, insert the wall plugs, then attach the clips with the screws and plastic washers provided.

2 Support the mirror on the bottom clips and draw a line along the top (Fig. 3). Remove the mirror, position the slotted top clips on the guideline, directly above the bottom ones. Attach the top clips in the same way as the bottom ones (Fig. 4).

3 Slide the top clips upwards, replace the mirror in the bottom clips, then push the top clips down to secure the mirror.

Note: If you are using corner clips, position and fix the clips to the wall in much the same way as for J-clips. Secure the bottom clips first, then insert the mirror and attach the top clips.

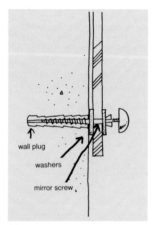

wall plug
washers
mirror screw

Fig. 1

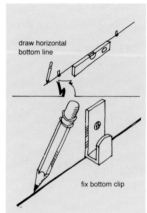

draw horizontal bottom line

fix bottom clip

Fig. 2

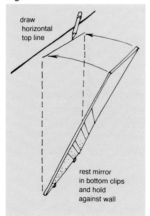

draw horizontal top line

rest mirror in bottom clips and hold against wall

Fig. 3

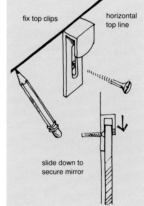

fix top clips

horizontal top line

slide down to secure mirror

Fig 4

The Tool Kit

Before tackling any kind of DIY project, check that you have the right tools. Most of the projects in this book require only basic tools, however an amateur carpenter will find that power tools not only make the job easier and quicker, but also much more accurate.

You can add to your tool kit with every new project – that way all your tools will used. Avoid cheap tools. Good, albeit expensive, tools, should last you a lifetime and will be well worth the money. In most instances, very expensive tools or machinery can be hired or borrowed for one-off jobs.

If you already have an extensive collection of tools, make sure they are sharp and ready for use. Old tools can be just as good as new ones, but they may need to be renovated and resharpened.

Tool Kit

Following is a list of some of the tools you will need.

Hammer

The hammer should be a claw hammer of light-to-medium weight. This type of hammer is used for driving in nails and stubborn objects. It may have a wooden, fibreglass or steel shaft. Before use, slightly roughen the head of the hammer with some emery cloth to ensure it does not skid off the nails. The claw of the hammer is used for extracting nails.

Saw

A panel saw is the most useful wood or wood-panel cutting saw, usually around 450 mm long, with approximately ten teeth to 25 mm and referred to as a 'ten-point'. This saw will cross-cut and rip material of the most commonly used sizes.

Mitre box

This is usually a simple wooden device which enables you to cut timber up to 125 mm wide at the exact angle desired, usually 90° or 45°. More sophisticated types allow for wider cuts.

Chisels

These can be purchased individually, but are best bought in a set of three or more. A good starting set would consist of a 13 mm, 19 mm and 25 mm chisel. Chisels should be of a reasonable quality as they will undergo rough treatment. New chisels generally need to be sharpened before use.

Screwdrivers

Like chisels, these can be bought individually, but a set of five, containing three widths of slotted head and two sizes of Phillips head (crosshead), would be a good starting kit. If you have to drive in or remove many screws, it may be worthwhile investing in a ratchet screwdriver. Electric screwdrivers are also available.

Rule or tape

Most people prefer to use retractable metal tapes, which are available with markings in both metric and imperial units. For some small jobs it may be easier to use a fourfold box rule which folds out to a length of one metre.

Set square (Try square)

Used to mark out and check material for square so that projects can be measured accurately.

Smoothing plane

The most popular is the No. 4 smoothing plane with a cast metal body. This plane is about 200 mm long. A good plane is easy and accurate to use and holds its edge well.

Utility knife

This type of knife is used for cutting a variety of materials and features a fixed, interchangeable or 'snap-off' blade.

Cork block

This inexpensive piece of equipment is most useful when sandpapering. Cover it with a sheet of sandpaper to ensure even sanding without depressions.

Spirit level

Used for checking the vertical and horizontal planes, this is an essential tool if cupboards, doors and worktops are on your job list. A level of between 450 mm and 900 mm will be most useful for home DIY work.

Files

These are available in many shapes, lengths and grades. It is best to start off with a 250 mm general purpose, half-round file.

Pinch bar (crowbar)

A useful item to save your back, it can be used to lift heavy items and pull out large nails.

Pliers

General-purpose pliers will grip both flat and small, round objects and usually incorporate a wire cutter. 200 mm combination pliers will handle most jobs. Those with insulated handles are a good idea.

Adjustable spanner

Buy a size suitable for your project, but 200 mm spanners can handle most general work.

Clamps

Clamps are your second pair of hands, used to hold timber, joints, etc. They come in various sizes and are commonly used in pairs. Two 200 mm G-clamps are the best to start off with. Pipe or sash clamps/cramps are designed to span large pieces.

Vice

Two types of vice are available. The woodworking vice is permanently bolted to the workbench and sits flush with the benchtop. The jaws of the vice are often 'softened' with either plastic or timber blocks. The other type of vice is an engineer's vice – this is bolted to the top of the workbench. This type is designed for metalwork but, with jaw liners, can be adapted for minor woodwork.

Nail punch

Buy one small and one large nail punch for general purpose work.

Hack saw

This is ideal for cutting metal such as bolts, nails, etc. Various tooths are available.

Chalk line

A device that automatically adds chalk to a length of string that can be stretched tight between two points then snapped against the surface where the line is required, leaving a well-defined line.

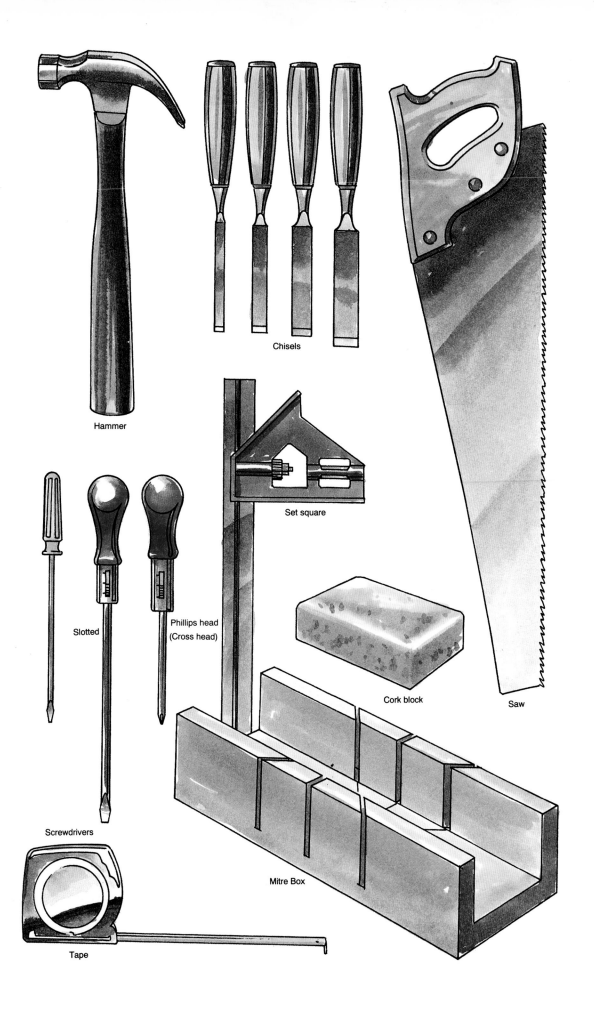

Hammer

Chisels

Saw

Slotted

Phillips head
(Cross head)

Set square

Cork block

Screwdrivers

Mitre Box

Tape

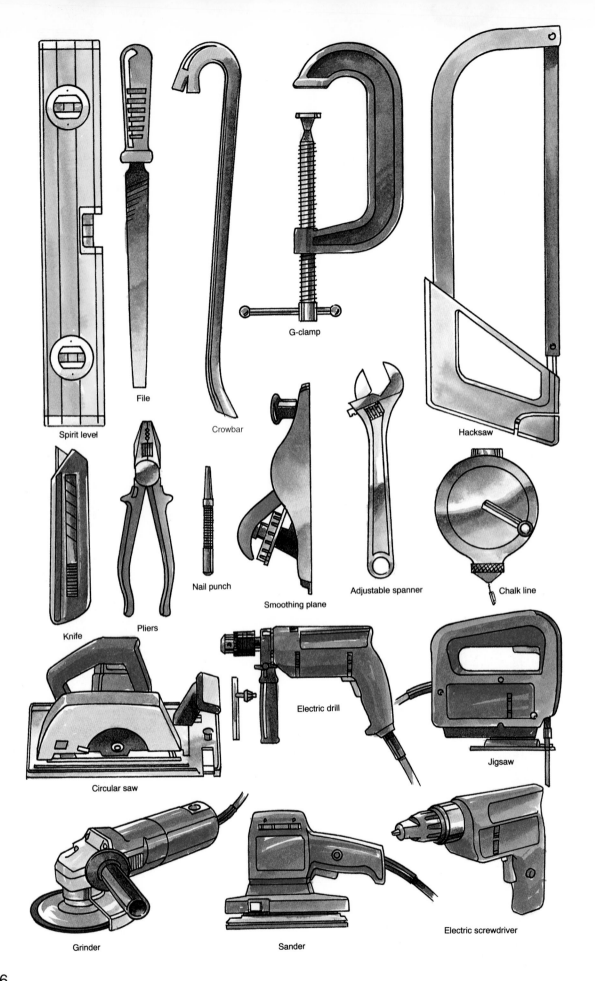

Spirit level

File

Crowbar

G-clamp

Hacksaw

Knife

Pliers

Nail punch

Smoothing plane

Adjustable spanner

Chalk line

Circular saw

Electric drill

Jigsaw

Grinder

Sander

Electric screwdriver

236

Oil stone

The combination of medium and fine stone is best for keeping chisels and planes sharp. You will also need a small can of oil for oiling the stone. Oil stones should never be used dry. It is recommended that you use light machine oil.

Putty knife

A range of different filling knives for applying fillers, plaster or synthetic wood is available.

Brushes

A small selection of brushes for dusting, touching up and broad area painting is most useful.

Protection set

Safety should always be considered: a pair of goggles, a face mask and a set of ear defenders or muffs are a worthwhile investment.

Using a spirit level

A spirit level is used to test the levelness and plumb of any piece of framework. The level has an air bubble inside a sealed glass tube. When the bubble is between two lines at the centre of the tube, the frame is level or plumb, as the case may be. To check the level for accuracy, set it up on a firm base with the bubble at the centre and mark the position of the level on the base. Now reverse the ends of the level and see if the bubble is still centred.

Index